A Lifetime
of Wisdom

A Lifetime
of Wisdom

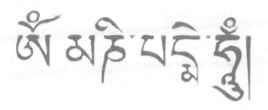

*Essential Writings By and
About the Dalai Lama*

EDITED BY CLINT WILLIS

Marlowe & Company

A LIFETIME OF WISDOM: ESSENTIAL WRITINGS BY AND ABOUT THE DALAI LAMA

Compilation copyright © 2002 by Clint Willis
Introductions copyright © 2002 by Clint Willis

Published by
Marlowe & Company
An Imprint of Avalon Publishing Group Incorporated
161 William Street, 16th Floor
New York, NY 10038

Book Design: Michael Walters

Library of Congress Cataloging-in-Publication Data

Bstan-'dzin-rgya-mtsho, Dalai Lama XIV, 1935-
 A lifetime of wisdom: essential writings by and about the Dalai Lama /
edited by Clint Willis.
  p.: cm
  ISBN 1-56924-573-8
  I. Bstan-'dzin-rgya-mtsho, Dalai Lama XIV, 1935- I. Title: A Life-
time of Wisdom: Essential Writings by and about the Dalai Lama. II.
Willis, Clint. III. Title.

BQ7935.B777 A3 2002
294.3'923'092--dc21   2002018848

9 8 7 6 5 4 3 2 1

Printed in Canada
Distributed by Publishers Group West

For Harper and Abner

Contents

Introduction

We live in the light and shadows cast by other human beings. Parents, children, friends, artists and strangers all become our teachers in the face of our need for instruction. We look to them or their work for comfort and wisdom or simple information. We hope to understand them, in hopes that such knowledge can tell us how to live or how not to live in light of difficulties that include worn out car batteries, broken hearts and our own inevitable deaths.

The Fourteenth Dalai Lama is a teacher who offers skillful solutions to such difficulties. His kindness, his forbearance and above all his happiness—a happiness evident even in photographs—make him a beacon and a blessing to the rest of us.

The Dalai Lama's cheerful aspect is particularly striking in light of his troubles during the past half-century. He was born in 1935—two years after the death of his predecessor, the Thirteenth Dalai Lama—to poor parents in a small farming village in eastern Tibet. His parents named their baby Lhamo Dhondrub, which translates as Wish-Fulfilling Goddess.

Two years later, a series of signs (including images, which appeared in a lake, of a certain monastery and house) led the High Lama Kyetsang Rinpoche to the child. The High Lama identified him as the fourteenth incarnation of the Dalai Lama—a figure who during the course of six centuries had come to serve as the spiritual and political leader of the Tibetan people. The child eventually was taken to Lhasa, where he lived in the thousand-room Potala Palace and received instruction in religious matters.

He assumed political power in 1950 at age sixteen. Tibet faced invasion by Mao's Chinese Communists, who wished to enforce their claims that the country belonged to China. Chinese soldiers tortured and murdered thousands of Tibetans, ravaged hundreds of monasteries and destroyed countless works of art. The Dalai Lama in 1959 fled Tibet, leading some 80,000 followers to India, where he established a Tibetan government-in-exile.

The Dalai Lama during the past four decades has dedicated much of his work to the preservation of Tibetan culture. He has established more than fifty agricultural settlements for exiled Tibetans, created scores of Tibetan schools in India and Nepal, and helped to found more than 200 monasteries.

He also has campaigned for Tibetan independence and for human rights in Tibet, where Chinese authorities continue to attack the country's native religion and culture, exploit its environment and repress its people. The Dalai Lama's nonviolent teachings and his peaceful efforts on behalf of Tibet, which helped earn him the Nobel Peace Prize in 1989, continue to create worldwide sympathy for the Tibetan cause.

The Dalai Lama's career has shown how deeply he takes his people's troubles to heart. His own experience as the leader of an oppressed and exiled people has not been easy. Yet anyone who has seen his smile must acknowledge that his face is the face of a happy man. Faced with our own troubles—and the knowledge that other human beings must endure far greater suffering—it is no wonder that we look to this smiling man for instruction.

What can he teach us? His teachings live in his words, which comfort as well as instruct us. "No world religion," he told an interviewer in 1989. "We have enough religions. Enough religions but not enough real human beings . . . Don't let us talk too much of religion. Let us talk of what is human. Love is human. Kindness is human. Everyone needs love and kindness."

The Dalai Lama's story—as reported by him and by others—also forms part of his teachings. Knowledge of the life is helpful to a right understanding of the words. What comforts and instructs me most about the Dalai Lama is my understanding that he is nothing special—just another person. And I recognize in this human being something deeper than wisdom or even compassion; I see the thing that feeds them: a passion to know the world as it really is. German adventurer Heinrich Harrer met the young Dalai Lama in 1939. Harrer received a cold reception from palace attendants but a warm welcome from the boy, then fourteen years old:

> He beamed all over his face and poured out a
> flood of questions. He seemed to me like a
> person who had for years brooded in solitude

over different problems, and now that he had
at last someone to talk to, wanted to know all
the answers at once.

The Dalai Lama during the difficult years that followed
became no less engaged by the world and all its aspects.
The writer and peformer Spalding Gray in 1991 asked
him how he adjusted to new places as he moved from
hotel room to hotel room during his frequent travels.
The Dalai Lama's response:

I always first inquire to see 'what is there.'
Curiosity. What I can discover that is interesting or new. Then I take a bath . . .

That questing and critical intelligence makes it impossible for the Dalai Lama to overlook the suffering that
goes on all around us—including the famine and violence and oppression that are routine in many parts of
the world. Yet his curiousity springs from and informs
a simple delight in creation.

Some such capacity for clarity and delight is in each
of us. I see it in my two young sons and in their
friends—a wish to know. This wish can encompass bad
as well as good news, is at least partly playful and is not
in any way inimical to mystery.

The cultivation of that kind of desire offers the best
kind of training in patience and other qualities we
need to live happily. The desire is evident in the Dalai
Lama's words and in his story. Attend to both, and you
may come to know better the wish that you carry in
yourself and to live more in accordance with it.

—*Clint Willis*

from Freedom in Exile:

THE AUTOBIOGRAPHY OF THE DALAI LAMA

by *the Dalai Lama*

The Dalai Lama in this excerpt from his 1990 memoir
recalls his childhood and describes the events leading
to his discovery as the new spiritual leader of Tibet.

I fled Tibet on 31 March 1959. Since then I have
lived in exile in India. During the period 1949-
50, the People's Republic of China sent an army
to invade my country. For almost a decade I remained
as political as well as spiritual leader of my people and
tried to re-establish peaceful relations between our two
nations. But the task proved impossible. I came to the
unhappy conclusion that I could serve my people better
from outside.

When I look back to the time when Tibet was still a
free country, I realise that those were the best years of
my life. Today I am definitely happy, but inevitably the

existence I now lead is very different from the one I was brought up to. And although there is clearly no use indulging in feelings of nostalgia, still I cannot help feeling sad whenever I think of the past. It reminds me of the terrible suffering of my people. The old Tibet was not perfect. Yet, it is true to say that our way of life was something quite remarkable. Certainly there was much that was worth preserving that is now lost for ever.

I have said that the words Dalai Lama mean different things to different people, that for me they refer only to the office I hold. Actually, *Dalai* is a Mongolian word meaning 'ocean' and *Lama* is a Tibetan term corresponding to the Indian word *guru*, which denotes a teacher. Together, the words *Dalai* and *Lama* are sometimes loosely translated as 'Ocean of Wisdom'. But this is due to a misunderstanding I feel. Originally, *Dalai* was a partial translation of Sonam Gyatso, the Third Dalai Lama's name: *Gyatso* means ocean in Tibetan. A further, unfortunate misunderstanding is due to the Chinese rendering of the word *lama* as *huo-fou*, which has the connotation of a 'living Buddha'. This is wrong. Tibetan Buddhism recognises no such thing. It only accepts that certain beings, of whom the Dalai Lama is one, can choose the manner of their rebirth. Such people are called *tulkus* (incarnations). Of course, whilst I lived in Tibet, being Dalai Lama meant a great deal. It meant that I lived a life far removed from the toil and discomfort of the vast majority of my people. Everywhere I went, I was accompanied by a retinue of servants. I was surrounded by government ministers and advisors clad in sumptuous silk robes, men drawn from the most exalted and aristocratic families in the land. My daily companions were brilliant scholars and highly realised religious adepts. And every time I left the Potala, the magnificent, 1,000-chambered winter palace of the Dalai Lamas, I was escorted by a procession of hundreds of people.

At the head of the column came a *Ngagpa*, a man carrying a symbolic 'wheel of life'. He was followed by a party of *tatara*, horsemen dressed in colourful, traditional costumes and carrying flags. Behind them were porters carrying my songbirds in cages and my personal belongings all wrapped up in yellow silk. Next came a section of monks from Namgyal, the Dalai Lama's own monastery. Each carried a banner decorated with sacred texts. Behind them followed musicians mounted on horseback. Then followed two groups of monk officials, first a subordinate section who acted as bearers, then monks of the *Tsedrung* order who were members of the Government. Behind these came a posse of horses from the Dalai Lama's own stables, all nicely turned out, caparisoned and led by their grooms.

There followed another troop of horses which carried the seals of state. I myself came next, carried in a yellow palanquin, which was pulled by twenty men, all officers in the army and dressed in green cloaks with red hats. Unlike the most senior officials, who wore their hair up, these had a single, long pigtail running down their backs. The palanquin itself, which was yellow in colour (to denote monasticism), was supported by a further eight men wearing long coats of yellow silk. Alongside it rode the four members of the *Kashag*, the Dalai Lama's inner Cabinet, attended by the *Kusun Depon*, head of the Dalai Lama's bodyguard, and the *Mak-chi*, Commander-in-Chief of Tibet's tiny army. Both of these marched carrying their swords sternly at the salute. They wore a uniform comprised of blue trousers and yellow tunic covered with gold braid. On their heads they wore a tasselled topi. Surrounding this, the main party, there was an escort of *sing gha*, the monastic police. These terrifying-looking men were all at least six feet tall and wore heavy padding, which lent them an even more impressive appearance. In their hands they carried long whips, which they did not hesitate to use.

Behind my palanquin came my two Tutors, Senior and Junior (the former being the Regent of Tibet before I attained my majority). Then came my parents and other members of my family. They were followed by a large party of lay officials, both nobles and commoners, marshalled according to rank.

Invariably almost the entire population of Lhasa, the capital, came to try to catch a glimpse of me whenever I went out. There was an awed silence and often there were tears as people lowered their heads or prostrated themselves on the ground when I passed.

It was a life very different from the one I had known as a small boy. I was born on 6 July 1935 and named Lhamo Thondup. This means, literally, 'Wish-Fulfilling Goddess'. Tibetan names of people, places and things are often picturesque in translation. For example, Tsangpo, the name of one of Tibet's most important rivers—and source of India's mighty Brahmaputra—means 'The Purifier'. The name of our village was Taktser: Roaring Tiger. It was a small and poor settlement which stood on a hill overlooking a broad valley. Its pastures had not been settled or farmed for long, only grazed by nomads. The reason for this was the unpredictability of the weather in that area. During my early childhood, my family was one of twenty or so making a precarious living from the land there.

Taktser is situated in far north-eastern Tibet, in the province of Amdo. Geographically, Tibet can be divided into four principal areas. To the north-west lies the Changtang, an area of frozen desert which runs east-west for over eight hundred miles. It is almost devoid of vegetation and only a few hardy nomads live amidst its desolation. To the south of the Changtang lie the provinces of U and Tsang. This area is bordered to the south and south-west by the mighty Himalayas. To the east of U-Tsang lies the province of Kham, which is the most fertile and hence most populous region in the country. To the north of Kham is situated Amdo. On the eastern borders of both Kham and Amdo lies Tibet's national boundary with China. At the time of my birth, a Muslim warlord, Ma Pu-feng, had recently succeeded in establishing in Amdo a regional government loyal to the Chinese Republic.

My parents were small farmers: not peasants exactly, for they were not tied to any master; but they were by no means nobility. They leased a small amount of land and worked it themselves. The main crops in Tibet are barley and buckwheat and my parents grew both of these, together with potatoes. But quite often their year's work went to ruin due to heavy hailstorms or to drought. They also kept a number of animals, which were a more reliable source of produce. I remember that we had five or six *dzomos* (a cross between a yak and a cow) for milking and a number of footloose chickens for laying. There was a mixed flock of perhaps eighty sheep and goats, and my father nearly always had one or two or even three horses, of which he was very fond. Finally, my family kept a couple of yaks.

The yak is one of Nature's gifts to mankind. It can survive at any altitude above 10,000 feet, so it is ideally suited to Tibet. Below that they tend to die. Both as a beast of burden and as a source of milk (in the case of the female, which is called a *dri*), and meat, the yak is truly a staple of high-altitude farming. The barley which my parents grew is another Tibetan staple. When roasted and ground down into a fine flour, it becomes *tsampa*. There is rarely a meal served in Tibet which does not include *tsampa* and, even in exile, I continue to have it every day. It is not eaten as flour, of course. You must first combine it with liquid, usually tea, but milk (which I prefer) or yoghurt or even *chang* (Tibetan beer) will do. Then, working it with your fingers around your bowl, you roll it into small balls. Otherwise it can be used as a base for porridge. To a Tibetan, it is very tasty though, in my experience, few foreigners like it. The Chinese in particular do not care for it at all.

Most of what my parents grew on the farm was used solely to feed us. But my father would occasionally trade grain or a few sheep either with passing nomads or down at Siling, the nearest town and capital of Amdo, which lay three hours away by horse. Currency was not much in use in these far-flung rural areas and most trade was conducted by barter. Thus my father would exchange the season's surplus for tea, sugar, cotton cloth, a few ornaments perhaps, and maybe some iron utensils. Occasionally he would come back with a new horse, which delighted him. He had a very good feel for them and had quite a reputation locally as a healer of horses.

The house I was born in was typical of our area of

Tibet. It was built of stone and mud with a flat roof along three sides of a square. Its only unusual feature was the guttering, which was made from branches of juniper wood, gouged out to make a channel for rain water. Directly in front of it, between the two 'arms' or wings, there was a small yard in the middle of which was a tall flagpole. From this hung a banner, secured top and bottom, on which were written innumerable prayers.

The animals were kept behind the house. Inside were six rooms: a kitchen, where we spent most of our time when indoors; a prayer-room with a small altar, where we would all gather to make offerings at the beginning of the day; my parents' room; a spare room for any guests we might have; a storeroom for our provisions; and finally a byre for the cattle. There was no bedroom for us children. As a baby, I slept with my mother; then, later, in the kitchen, by the stove. For furniture, we had no chairs or beds as such, but there were raised areas for sleeping in both my parents' room and the spare room. There were also a number of cupboards made of gaily painted wood. The floors were likewise wooden and neatly laid with planks.

My father was a man of medium height with a very quick temper. I remember pulling at his moustache once and being hit hard for my trouble. Yet he was a kind man too and he never bore grudges. An interesting story was told about him at the time of my birth. He had been ill for a number of weeks and was confined to his bed. No one knew what was wrong with him and people started to fear for his life. But on the day I was born, he suddenly began to recover, for no obvious reason. It cannot have been excitement at becoming a father since my mother had already given birth to eight children, although only four had survived. (Of necessity, farming families like ours believed in large families and my mother bore sixteen children in all, of whom seven lived.) At the time of writing, Lobsang Samten, my immediate elder brother, and Tsering Dolma, my eldest sister, are no longer living, but my two other older brothers, my younger sister and my younger brother are still alive and well.

My mother was undoubtedly one of the kindest people I have ever known. She was truly wonderful and was loved, I am quite certain, by all who knew her. She was very compassionate. Once, I remember being told, there was a terrible famine in nearby China. As a result, many poor Chinese people were driven over the border in search of food. One day, a couple appeared at our door, carrying in their arms a dead child. They begged my mother for food, which she readily gave them. Then she pointed at their child and asked whether they wanted help to bury it. When they had caught her meaning, they shook their heads and made clear that they intended to eat it. My mother was horrified and at once invited them in and emptied the entire contents of the larder before regretfully sending them on their way. Even if it meant giving away the family's own food so that we ourselves went hungry, she never let any beggars go empty-handed.

Tsering Dolma was eighteen years older than me. At the time of my birth she helped my mother run the house and acted as my midwife. When she delivered me, she noticed that one of my eyes was not properly open. Without hesitating, she put her thumb on the reluctant lid and forced it wide—fortunately without ill effect. Tsering Dolma was also responsible for giving me my first meal, which, by tradition, was a liquid made from the bark of a particular bush that grew locally. This was believed to ensure a healthy child. It certainly worked in my case. In later years, my sister told me that I was a very dirty baby. No sooner had she taken me in her arms than I made a mess!

I did not have much to do with any of my three elder brothers. Thupten Jigme Norbu, the eldest, had already been recognised as the reincarnation of a high lama, Taktser Rinpoché (Rinpoché is the title given to spiritual masters and means, literally, 'Precious One'), and was installed at Kumbum, a famous monastery several hours away by horse. My next brother, Gyalo Thondup, was eight years older than me and by the time I was born he was away at school in a neighbouring village. Only my immediate elder brother, Lobsang Samten, remained behind. He was three years older than me. But he too was sent to Kumbum to be a monk, so I hardly knew him.

Of course, no one had any idea that I might be anything other than an ordinary baby. It was almost unthinkable that more than one *tulku* could be born into the same family and certainly my parents had no idea that I would be proclaimed Dalai Lama. My father's recovery from illness was auspicious, but it was not taken to be of great significance. I myself likewise had no particular intimation of what lay ahead. My earliest memories are very ordinary. Some people put great emphasis on a person's first recollections, but I do not. Amongst mine I remember, for example, observing a group of children fighting and running to join in with the weaker side. I also remember the first time I saw a camel. These are quite common in parts of Mongolia and occasionally they were brought over the border. It looked huge and majestic and very frightening. I also recall discovering one day that I had worms—a common affliction in the East.

One thing that I remember enjoying particularly as a very young boy was going into the hen coop to collect the eggs with my mother and then staying behind. I liked to sit in the hens' nest and make clucking noises. Another favourite occupation of mine as an infant was to pack things in a bag as if I was about to go on a long journey. 'I'm going to Lhasa, I'm going to Lhasa,' I would say. This, coupled with my insistence that I be allowed always to sit at the head of the table, was later said to be an indication that I must have known that I was destined for greater things. I also had a number of dreams as a small child that were open to a similar interpretation, but I cannot say categorically that I knew of my future all along. Later on, my mother told me several stories which could be taken as signs of high birth. For example, I never allowed anyone but her to handle my bowl. Nor did I ever show fear of strangers.

Before going on to tell about my discovery as Dalai Lama, I must first say something about Buddhism and its history in Tibet. The founder of Buddhism was an historical figure, Siddhartha, who came to be recognized as the Buddha Shakyamuni. He was born more than 2,500 years ago. His teachings, now known as the *Dharma*, or Buddhism, were introduced to Tibet during the fourth century A.D. They took several centuries to supplant the native Bon religion and become fully established, but eventually the country was so thoroughly converted that Buddhist principles governed all society, at every level. And whilst Tibetans are by nature quite aggressive people and quite warlike, their increasing interest in religious practice was a major factor in bringing about the country's isolation. Before then, Tibet possessed a vast empire, which dominated Central Asia with territories covering large parts of northern India, Nepal and Bhutan in the south. It also included much Chinese territory. In 763 A.D., Tibetan forces actually captured the Chinese capital, where they extracted promises of tribute and other concessions. However, as Tibetans' enthusiasm for Buddhism increased, so Tibet's relations with her neighbours became of a spiritual rather than a political nature. This was especially true of China, where a 'priest-patron' relationship developed. The Manchu Emperors, who were Buddhists, referred to the Dalai Lama as 'King of Expounding Buddhism'.

The fundamental precept of Buddhism is Interdependence or the Law of Cause and Effect. This simply states that everything which an individual being experiences is derived through action from motivation. Motivation is thus the root of both action and experience. From this understanding are derived the Buddhist theories of consciousness and rebirth.

The first holds that, because cause gives rise to effect which in turn becomes the cause of further effect, consciousness must be continual. It flows on and on, gathering experiences and impressions from one moment to the next. At the point of physical death, it follows that a being's consciousness contains an imprint of all these past experiences and impressions, and the actions which preceded them. This is known as *karma*, which

means 'action'. It is thus consciousness, with its attendant *karma*, which then becomes 'reborn' in a new
body—animal, human or divine.

So, to give a simple example, a person who has
spent his or her life mistreating animals could quite
easily be reborn in the next life as a dog belonging to
someone who is unkind to animals. Similarly, meritorious conduct in this life will assist in a favourable
rebirth in the next.

Buddhists further believe that because the basic
nature of consciousness is neutral, it is possible to
escape from the unending cycle of birth, suffering,
death and rebirth that life inevitably entails, but only
when all negative *karma* has been eliminated along with
all worldly attachments. When this point is reached,
the consciousness in question is believed to attain first
liberation and then ultimately Buddhahood. However,
according to Buddhism in the Tibetan tradition, a
being that achieves Buddhahood, although freed from
Samsara, the 'wheel of suffering', as the phenomenon of
existence is known, will continue to return to work for
the benefit of all other sentient beings until such time
as each one is similarly liberated.

Now in my own case, I am held to be the reincarnation of each of the previous thirteen Dalai Lamas of
Tibet (the first having been born in 1351 A.D.), who are
in turn considered to be manifestations of Avalokiteshvara, or Chenrezig, Bodhisattva of Compassion, holder
of the White Lotus. Thus I am believed also to be a manifestation of Chenrezig, in fact the seventy-fourth in a
lineage that can be traced back to a Brahmin boy who
lived in the time of Buddha Shakyamuni. I am often
asked whether I truly believe this. The answer is not

simple to give. But as a fifty-six year old, when I consider my experiences during this present life, and given
my Buddhist beliefs, I have no difficulty accepting that
I am spiritually connected both to the thirteen previous
Dalai Lamas, to Chenrezig and to the Buddha himself.

When I was not quite three years old, a search party that
had been sent out by the Government to find the new
incarnation of the Dalai Lama arrived at Kumbum
monastery. It had been led there by a number of signs.
One of these concerned the embalmed body of my
predecessor, Thupten Gyatso, the Thirteenth Dalai
Lama, who had died aged fifty-seven in 1933. During
its period of sitting in state, the head was discovered to
have turned from facing south to north-east. Shortly
after that the Regent, himself a senior lama, had a
vision. Looking into the waters of the sacred lake,
Lhamoi Lhatso, in southern Tibet, he clearly saw the
Tibetan letters *Ah, Ka* and *Ma* float into view. These were
followed by the image of a three-storeyed monastery
with a turquoise and gold roof and a path running from
it to a hill. Finally, he saw a small house with strangely
shaped guttering. He was sure that the letter *Ah* referred
to Amdo, the north-eastern province, so it was there
that the search party was sent.

By the time they reached Kumbum, the members of
the search party felt that they were on the right track. It
seemed likely that if the letter *Ah* referred to Amdo,
then *Ka* must indicate the monastery at Kumbum—
which was indeed three storeyed and turquoise roofed.
They now only needed to locate a hill and a house with
peculiar guttering. So they began to search the neighbouring villages. When they saw the gnarled branches of

juniper wood on the roof of my parents' house, they were certain that the new Dalai Lama would not be far away. Nevertheless, rather than reveal the purpose of their visit, the group asked only to stay the night. The leader of the party, Kewtsang Rinpoché, then pretended to be a servant and spent much of the evening observing and playing with the youngest child in the house.

The child recognised him and called out 'Sera Lama, Sera Lama'. Sera was Kewtsang Rinpoché's monastery. Next day they left—only to return a few days later as a formal deputation. This time they brought with them a number of things that had belonged to my predecessor, together with several similar items that did not. In every case, the infant correctly identified those belonging to the Thirteenth Dalai Lama saying, 'It's mine. It's mine.' This more or less convinced the search party that they had found the new incarnation. However, there was another candidate to be seen before a final decision could be reached. But it was not long before the boy from Taktser was acknowledged to be the new Dalai Lama. I was that child.

Needless to say, I do not remember very much of these events. I was too small. My only real recollection is of a man with piercing eyes. These turned out to belong to a man named Kenrap Tenzin, who became my Master of the Robes and later taught me to write.

As soon as the search party had concluded that the child from Taktser was the true incarnation of the Dalai Lama, word was sent back to Lhasa informing the Regent. It would be several weeks before official confirmation was received. Until then, I was to remain at home. In the meantime, Ma Pu-feng, the local Governor, began to make trouble. But eventually I was taken by my parents to Kumbum monastery, where I was installed in a ceremony that took place at dawn. I remember this fact particularly as I was surprised to be woken and dressed before the sun had risen. I also remember being seated on a throne.

There now began a somewhat unhappy period of my life. My parents did not stay long and soon I was alone amongst these new and unfamiliar surroundings. It is very hard for a small child to be separated from its parents. However, there were two consolations to life at the monastery. First, my immediate elder brother Lobsang Samten was already there. Despite being only three years older than me, he took good care of me and we soon became firm friends. The second consolation was the fact that his teacher was a very kind old monk, who often held me inside his gown. On one occasion I recall that he gave me a peach. Yet for the most part I was quite unhappy. I did not understand what it meant to be Dalai Lama. As far as I knew, I was just one small boy among many. It was not unusual for children to enter the monastery at a very young age and I was treated just the same as all the others.

A more painful memory is of one of my uncles, who was a monk at Kumbum. One evening, whilst he sat reading his prayers, I upset his book of scripture. As they still are today, this book was loose-leafed and the pages went everywhere. My father's brother picked me up and slapped me hard. He was extremely angry and I was terrified. For literally years afterwards I was haunted by his very dark, pock-marked face and fierce moustache. Thereafter, whenever I caught sight of him, I became very frightened.

When it became clear that I would eventually be

reunited with my parents and that together we would
journey to Lhasa, I began to look to the future with
more enthusiasm. As any child would be, I was thrilled
at the prospect of travel. This did not come about for
some eighteen months, however, because Ma Pu-feng
refused to let me be taken to Lhasa without payment of
a large ransom. And having received it, he demanded
more, although he did not get it. It was thus not until
the summer of 1939 that I left for the capital.

When eventually the great day dawned, a week after
my fourth birthday, I remember a tremendous feeling
of optimism. The party was large. Not only did it consist of my parents and my brother Lobsang Samten, but
the members of the search party and a number of pil-
grims came too. There were also several government
officials in attendance, together with a great number of
muleteers and scouts. These men spent their lives
working the caravan routes of Tibet and were indispensable to any long journey. They knew exactly where
to cross each river and how much time it took to climb
the mountain passes.

After a few days' travel, we left the area administered
by Ma Pu-feng and the Tibetan Government formally
announced its acceptance of my candidature. We now
entered some of the most remote and beautiful countryside in the world: gargantuan mountains flanking
immense flat plains which we struggled over like
insects. Occasionally, we came upon the icy rush of
meltwater streams that we splashed noisily across. And
every few days we would come to a tiny settlement hud-
dled amongst a blaze of green pasture, or clinging as if
by its fingers to a hillside. Sometimes we could see in
the far distance a monastery perched impossibly on top

of a cliff. But mostly, it was just arid, empty space with only savage dust-laden winds and angry hailstorms as reminders of Nature's living forces.

The journey to Lhasa took three months. I remember very little detail apart from a great sense of wonder at everything I saw: the vast herds of *drong* (wild yaks) ranging across the plains, the smaller groups of *kyang* (wild asses) and occasionally a shimmer of *gowa* and *nawa*, small deer which were so light and fast they might have been ghosts. I also loved the huge flocks of hooting geese we saw from time to time.

For most of the journey I travelled with Lobsang Samten in a sort of palanquin called a *dreljam* carried by a pair of mules. We spent a great deal of time squabbling and arguing, as small children do, and often came to blows. This put our conveyance in danger of over-balancing. At that point the driver would stop the animals and summon my mother. When she looked inside, she always found the same thing: Lobsang Samten in tears and me sitting there with a look of triumph on my face. For despite his greater age, I was the more forthright. Although we were really best friends, we were incapable of behaving well together. One or other of us would make a remark which led to an argument and finally to blows and tears—but the tears were always his and not mine. Lobsang Samten was so good-natured that he could not bring himself to use his superior strength against me.

At last, our party began to draw near to Lhasa. It was by now autumn. When we were within a few days' journey, a group of senior government officials came out to meet us and escorted our party on to the Doeguthang plain, two miles outside the gates of the capital. There, a huge tented encampment had been erected. In the centre was a blue and white structure called the *Macha Chennio*, the 'great Peacock'. It looked enormous to my eyes and enclosed an intricately carved wooden throne, which was only ever brought out for the purpose of welcoming the infant Dalai Lama back home.

The ceremony that followed, which conferred on me spiritual leadership of my people, lasted one whole day. But my memory of it is vague. I remember only a great sense of homecoming and endless crowds of people: I had never thought there could be so many. By all accounts, I behaved myself well for a few years old, even to one or two extremely senior monks who came to judge for themselves whether I really was the reincarnation of the Thirteenth Dalai Lama. Then, at the end of it all, I was taken off with Lobsang Samten to the Norbulingka (meaning Jewel Park) which lay just to the west of Lhasa itself.

Normally, it was used only as the summer palace of the Dalai Lama. But the Regent had decided to wait until the end of the following year before formally enthroning me at the Potala palace, the seat of the Tibetan Government. In the meantime, there was no need for me to live there. This turned out to be a generous move as the Norbulingka was much the more pleasant of the two places. It was surrounded by gardens and consisted of several smallish buildings which were light and airy inside. By contrast the Potala, which I could see towering magnificently above the city in the distance, was dark, cold and gloomy inside.

I thus enjoyed a whole year free of any responsibility, happily playing with my brother and seeing my parents quite regularly. It was the last temporal liberty I was ever to know.

Inside Out:
THE DALAI LAMA INTERVIEWED BY
SPALDING GRAY

by *Spalding Gray*

Spalding Gray (born 1941) is an actor, a performance artist and a writer. Here he strays from the sociopolitical and religious questions interviewers typically ask the Dalai Lama, and engages him in a more personal conversation during a 1991 interview for *Tricycle: The Buddhist Review.*

*T*enzin Gyatso, the Fourteenth Dalai Lama, is the spiritual and temporal leader of the Tibetan people and the 1989 Nobel Peace Laureate. Born to a peasant family in 1935, in the northeastern province of Amdo, His Holiness was recognized at the age of two, in accordance with Tibetan tradition, as the reincarnation of the Thirteenth Dalai Lama, and a manifestation of *Avalokitesvara*, the Bodhisattva of Compassion. In 1959, he escaped the Chinese invasion of Tibet and lives now in Dharamsala, India.

The Dalai Lama completed 18 years of monastic study with a final examination by 30 scholars of logic in the

morning, by 15 scholars on the subject of the Middle
Path in the afternoon, and in the evening, by 35 scholars
of the canon of monastic discipline and the study of
metaphysics. His Holiness the Dalai Lama then passed
the exacting oral examination with honors and soon
completed the *Geshe Lharampa*—or the highest level of
scholarly achievement in Buddhist philosophy.

Spalding Gray, born in Rhode Island in 1941, calls
himself a writer and performer who has been "circling
my meditation cushion for almost twenty years." His
best known performance is the stage and film version
of his monologue, *Swimming to Cambodia.*

Gray's interest in transcendental philosophy began
with his early exposure to Christian Science. ("My
mother the Christian Scientist was extremely radical
and my father wasn't. My inner dialectic is the pull
between my father, the rather pragmatic doubter, and
my mother. My mother killed herself and my father,
the materialist, survived.")

Around the time that the Dalai Lama prematurely
assumed full political and spiritual leadership of Tibet
in the face of the communist Chinese invasion,
Spalding Gray was banished to boarding school being
branded a "juvenile delinquent" with "very bad, anti-
social behavior."

The paths of the revered Buddhist leader and the
avant-garde performer crossed in a hotel suite at the
Fess Parker Red Lion Inn in Santa Barbara, California,
on April 8, 1991. The Disney-like resort, sprawled
over half a mile of ocean-front property, is the name-
sake of Frontierland's own "Davy, Davy Crockett, King
of the Wild Frontier."

With assistance from translator Thubten Jinpa, and the Dalai Lama's private secretary, Tenzin Geyche, His Holiness and Gray began by comparing the Dalai Lama's own marathon U.S. visit that stretched from Boston to the West Coast and Spalding's cross-country tour of his stage performance of *Monster in a Box*, following its successful run at New York's Lincoln Center.

SPALDING GRAY: *We've both been travelling these last weeks and the most difficult thing that I find on the road is adjusting to each location, each different hotel. And I don't have the centering habits you do. I have a tendency to want to drink the alcohol, which, as you said in an earlier interview, is the other way of coping with despair and confusion. I have a feeling that you have other methods for adjusting. Just what are some of your centering rituals and your habits when you come into a new hotel?*

THE DALAI LAMA: I always first inquire to see "what is there." Curiosity. What I can discover that is interesting or new. Then, I take a bath. And then I usually sit on the bed, crosslegged, and meditate. And sometimes sleep, lie down. One thing I myself noticed is the time-zone change. Although you change your clock time, your biological time still has to follow a certain pattern. But now I find that once I change the clock time, I'm tuned to the new time zone. When my watch says it's eight o'clock in the evening, I feel sort of sleepy and need to retire and when it says four in the morning I wake up.

SPALDING GRAY: *But you have to be looking at your clock all the time.*

THE DALAI LAMA: That's right (*laughs*).

SPALDING GRAY: *Do you dream?*

THE DALAI LAMA: Yes. A few days ago, for three nights in succession, I had some very clear dreams. One night in my dream I met my teacher from when I was a young boy. He was seventy-five years old then. And in my dream he was wearing a Western suit. It was something unexpected (*long laugh*). As usual, he was very kind. Another night my mother was in my dream with my elder brother, my younger brother, and myself, three of us there in Dharamsala where I live now. I was in my room and my mother was there. In my mind, my mother already prepared one *momo* (a Tibetan dumpling). So then I felt, "Oh, my mother will give us those *momos* made in Amdo style, which are especially delicious." Amdo is the province where I was born. So you see, this is a very happy dream.

SPALDING GRAY: *Do you ever try to make your own dreams or control them?*

THE DALAI LAMA: No, that I can't do. Actually you see, occasionally I experience an awareness that I am dreaming in the dream itself, like a lucid dream.

SPALDING GRAY: *Do you try to create that?*

THE DALAI LAMA: No, not deliberately. But sometimes I have these experiences of lucid dreaming where I have the mindfulness that it is a dream state. Sometimes it depends on the physical posture that you adopt.

SPALDING GRAY: *In sleep?*

THE DALAI LAMA: Actually there are some methods for experiencing lucid dreaming. You should not be in a deep sleep. Not quite awake, not deep asleep. Then there is the possibility of having a clear dream. Also it is related to what you eat. As a Buddhist monk, I usually have no solid meal after lunch, no dinner. So that is also a benefit.

SPALDING GRAY: *When I passed your room last night, I saw six empty ice-cream sundae dishes outside your door.*

TRANSLATOR *(after much laughter):* It was members of the entourage.

SPALDING GRAY: *Did you do a meditation this morning?*

THE DALAI LAMA: As usual, from around 4 a.m. until 8.

SPALDING GRAY: *Where did you do it, in this room?*

THE DALAI LAMA: First I take a bath, then I sit on that bed (in the other room) crosslegged.

SPALDING GRAY: *And when you go into the meditation, is it similar every morning?*

THE DALAI LAMA: Similar, yes.

SPALDING GRAY: *And can you tell me a little bit about what it's like?*

THE DALAI LAMA: *(sigh, laugh)* MMMM. If you make

categories—the first portion is the recitation of a mantrum. There are certain mantras aimed at consecrating your speech, so that all your speech throughout the day will be positive. These recitations should be made before speaking. I observe silence until they are finished and if anyone approaches me, I always communicate in sign language. Then I try to develop a certain motivation—shaping my own mind. I try to develop the motivation, or determination, that as a Buddhist monk, until my Buddhahood, until I reach Buddhahood, my life, my lives including future lives, should be correct, and spent according to that basic goal. And that all my activities should be beneficial to others and should not harm others.

SPALDING GRAY: *How long does that take?*

THE DALAI LAMA: Some ten, fifteen minutes. And then I do a deeper meditation where I mentally review the entire stages of the path of Buddhist practice. And then I do some practices aimed at accumulating merits, like prostrations, making offerings to the Buddhas, reflecting on the qualities of the Buddha.

SPALDING GRAY: *Is there a special visualization going on?*

THE DALAI LAMA: Oh, yes. Along with these are some cases of visualization. We call this *guru yoga*. The first part of *guru yoga* means dedicating yourself and your practice to one's own teacher. The second part is deity yoga, transforming oneself into a particular deity. *Deity yoga* refers to a meditative process whereby you dissolve your own ordinary self into a sort of void and emptiness.

From this state your inner "perfected state" potential is visualized or imagined as being generated into a divine form, a meditation deity. You follow a procedure known as the meditation of the three kayas—*dharmakaya*, *sambhogakaya*, and *nirmanakaya*. These correspond to the experience of natural death, the intermediate state, and rebirth as described in the Buddhist literature. With each different deity, there is a different mandala in my daily prayer. All together there are about seven different mandalas involved. These *deity yogas*, they involve visualization of mandalas. That takes two hours.

SPALDING GRAY: *You can see the deity very clearly in your mind with your eyes closed?*

THE DALAI LAMA: Sometimes very clear, sometimes not clear (*laughs*). My physical condition makes a difference, I think. It also depends on the amount of time that I have. If I feel that all my prayers must be completed before eight, then it affects my awareness. If I have a whole morning free, then my concentration increases.

SPALDING GRAY: *Is there a time in your meditation where you are only watching busy things that don't have to do with a mandala? Do you ever just watch chaos?*

THE DALAI LAMA: In my practice, part of it always deals with meditation on emptiness, and *mahamudra* which has a very strong element of that kind of mindfulness meditation. I also undertake a specific meditation on thoughtlessness—nonconceptuality.

SPALDING GRAY: *Do you ever entertain the distractions, invite* *them into your meditation and let all of these women in bikini bathing suits that you must see here out by the pool come into your meditation?*

THE DALAI LAMA: As a monk, I have to avoid that experience, even in my dreams, due to daily practice. Sometimes in my dreams there are women. And in some cases fighting or quarreling with someone. When such dreams happen, immediately I remember, "I am monk." So that is one reason I usually call myself a simple Buddhist monk. That's why I never feel "I am the Dalai Lama." I only feel "I am a monk." I should not indulge, even in dreams, in women with a seductive appearance. Immediately I realize I'm a monk.

Then sometimes in my dreams I see fighting with a gun or a knife, and again I immediately realize "I am a monk, I should not do this." This kind of mindfulness is one of the important practices that I do the whole day long. Then your particular point, about beautiful things or men, women, things that attract: the analytical meditation counters that attachment.

For example, the sexual desire. It is very important to analyze, "what is the real benefit?" The appearance of a beautiful face or a beautiful body—as many scriptures describe—no matter how beautiful, they essentially decompose into a skeleton. When we penetrate to its human flesh and bones, there is no beauty, is there? A couple in a sexual experience is happy for that moment. Then very soon trouble begins.

SPALDING GRAY: *I know that kind of thinking, because I do it all the time. But I consider it neurotic.*

THE DALAI LAMA: What is that?

SPALDING GRAY: *Neurotic, ummm. Mental illness in myself. Because I see it as a dissection rather than looking at the whole. Pulling things apart. I keep thinking what I would like to have is a vision of the whole.*

THE DALAI LAMA: In a way, the Buddhist approach of overcoming attachments and attractions is holistic in the sense that it does not see certain attractive objects existing on their own right but as part of a wider network which is neither undesirable or attractive. Rather it is part of a whole way of existence which is to be transcended. So you don't see any phenomenon alone.

You see, when you contemplate the lack of permanence of another's body or its attractiveness, when you examine being attached to its attractiveness, then you yourself contemplate your own body possessing the same nature. You are aiming toward a goal, so you can transcend all these temptations and attachments. There are meditations that are known as mindfulness on body, mindfulness on feeling, and mindfulness on the mind.

So the procedure is to channel our own energy or our whole mental attitude toward what we call the salvation, or the *moksha* or *nirvana*.

SPALDING GRAY: *Mindfulness on the mind? What mind is being mindful of what mind?*

THE DALAI LAMA: Generally when we say "mind," it gives the impression of one single entity. But within the mind there are many different aspects and factors.

So when you talk of mind examining mind, there could be many different cases. In one case you could reflect on a past experience, which is a memory of the previous mind.

You can also examine your present state of mind. You have different factors within the mind, in some cases you have a sense of recognition that contemplates your own present experience. Mind is not a single entity.

SPALDING GRAY: *How do you experience emptiness? What is that physical experience like? You're having an experience of emptiness yet it is not nothing, it is an experience. So it is something.*

THE DALAI LAMA: When we talk of the Buddhist concept of emptiness, it should be understood in terms of "empty of independent identity." Emptiness of intrinsic reality. As you progress in your meditation, you get to a point where you loosen your grip. Your attitude becomes more flexible and you realize the absence of an intrinsic independent reality of phenomena.

SPALDING GRAY: *Is that happening in your body as well as your mind? Is it integrated within you physically? How does your feeling of your heart and stomach and eyes change, physically, when you get closer to that? Do you begin to feel as though you are disappearing or getting closer to being here?*

THE DALAI LAMA: Not disappearing, but of course, this is on the personal level. When I was in my thirties, for a time I really concentrated my studies on the nature of emptiness. We call it *shi-ne.* One day I was doing analytical meditation while I was reading. Then a certain strange experience occurred and afterwards I had a new outlook. I had an intensive experience of emptiness. After that, things and objects appeared as normal, just as they appeared before, but there was this strong underlying awareness that they did not possess intrinsic reality.

SPALDING GRAY: *Are you always in touch with your body and your breath when you're having this experience?*

THE DALAI LAMA: Not in this kind of meditation. In other kinds of meditations you concentrate on certain nerve centers or on specific energy points within the body. This type of meditation requires a kind of solitary retreat that needs to be undertaken for a longer period of time. It is difficult for me to find time now.

SPALDING GRAY: *Recently I read a book written by a Westerner, Stephen Butchelor, called* The Faith to Doubt. *He questioned a lot of things about Tibetan Buddhism. I bought the book because of its title. And when I talk to you now, I have a sense that your most solid identity is as a simple Tibetan Buddhist monk. And I have no identity, although I told you I tell stories, that's my job. But I don't feel like anything, and it's very disconcerting at times, but I am always doubting. And I'm trying to have the faith to doubt and look at doubt as being something positive as well, not just existential angst. Don't you ever doubt?*

THE DALAI LAMA: There may be a variety of doubts, but no explicit doubt. If you accept that the whole mind is just the product of brain, of this body, then there are many new questions there, many doubts. Even if you accept the big bang theory, you say "why did this happen?" "Why did so many galaxies happen?"

And with each changing moment, "why are these things happening?" A lot of questions arise.

If you accept that the big bang happened without any cause, that also is very uncomfortable, and still more doubts arise. With the Buddhist explanation, there are sentient beings who utilize these galaxies and these worlds. This is the foundation that leads to the Buddhist concept of rebirth or the continuity of consciousness.

SPALDING GRAY: *So doubt becomes a mystery. Death in the Western sense, the concept of death, can be finally mysterious. One Western writer called Ernest Becker, who wrote* The Denial of Death, *said "We don't know anything beyond it. We must bow down to that mystery because there is no way of knowing what is coming next," and the thing that has always confused me and interested me about Tibetan Buddhism is the extremely complex system of knowledge about after-death states and reincarnation.*

THE DALAI LAMA: The most subtle consciousness is like a seed and it is a different variety of consciousness than the consciousness developed by a physical being. A plant cannot produce cognitive power. But in every human being, or sentient beings with certain conditions, cognitive power develops. We consider the continuity of the consciousness to be the ultimate seed. Then once you understand this explanation, subtle consciousness departs from this body—or we say subtle consciousness departs from grosser consciousness. Or we say the grosser dissolves into the most subtle mind.

There are some cases, very authentic, very clear, where people recall their past lives, especially with very young people. Some children can recall their past experience. I do not have any sort of strong or explicit doubts as to this possibility. But since phenomena such as after-death experiences, intermediate states and so forth, are things that are beyond our direct experience, it does leave some slight room for hesitation. For many years in my daily practice, I have prepared for a natural death. So there is a kind of excitement at the idea that real death is coming to me and I can live the actual experiences. A lot of my meditations are rehearsals for this experience.

SPALDING GRAY: *Do you have one predominant fear that you often struggle with, the thing you fear the most?*

THE DALAI LAMA: No, nothing in particular.

SPALDING GRAY: *You are feeling not fearful?*

THE DALAI LAMA: Because of the political situation, sometimes I have fears of being caught in a kind of terrorist experience. Although, as far as my motivation is concerned, I feel I have no enemy. From my own viewpoint, we are all human beings, brothers and sisters. But I am involved in a national struggle. Some people consider me the key troublemaker. So that is also a reality (*pause*). Otherwise, comparatively, my mental state is quite calm, quite stable.

SPALDING GRAY: *How do you avoid accidents?*

THE DALAI LAMA: (*laughs*) Just as ordinary people do, I try to be more cautious. One thing I can be certain of is that I won't have an accident because of being drunk or being stoned by drugs.

SPALDING GRAY: *But you are flying a lot and the pilots are drinking. That's what I'm always afraid of. I've always said I would never fly on a plane where the pilot believes in reincarnation. When you get on a plane to fly, do you have to work with your fears?*

THE DALAI LAMA: Oh, yes. Yes.

SPALDING GRAY: *And do you meditate on the flights or do you feel that you can help keep the plane up? Do you have more power than the average person flying on the plane? I believe that about myself some-times, that if I concentrate on a particular image that I have in my mind that the flight will go better.*

THE DALAI LAMA: I used to have a lot of fear when flying. Now I am getting used to it. But when I get very afraid or anxious, then yes, as you mentioned, I recite some prayers or some mantra and also, you see, the final conclusion is the belief in karma. If I created some karma to have a certain kind of death, I cannot avoid that. Although I try my best, if something hap-pens, I have to accept it. It is possible that I have no such karmic force, then even if the plane crashes, I may survive.

SPALDING GRAY: *You walk out.*

THE DALAI LAMA: Yes. So that belief, also you see, is very helpful. Very effective.

SPALDING GRAY: *I first read about Tibet in John Blofeld's book,* The People Flew. *Did you ever see anyone flying in Tibet?*

THE DALAI LAMA: No, but one thing surprised even me. One elderly nun who lives now in Dharamsala told me that when she was young, she spent a few months at a mountain place quite near Lhasa. She met there an elderly practitioner, around eighty years old, living in a very isolated area. She discovered he was the teacher for around ten disciples, and two monks among them were flying through the air off one side of the mountain. Now you see, they would fly using this part (*holding up the sides of his robe*).

SPALDING GRAY: *Like a hang glider.*

THE DALAI LAMA: Yes, you see, she said they could fly one kilometer, with their arms out like this. She told me last year that she actually saw it. I was surprised, very surprised (*laughter*). Have you ever been to India?

SPALDING GRAY: *Yes, for five months in 1972, I toured all around India, performing in* Mother Courage, *a play by the German playwright Brecht. I'm sorry that we have to stop now. I appreciate your time, thank you.*

THE DALAI LAMA: Very good questions. I enjoyed your questions. Thank you very much.

from Kindness, Clarity, and Insight

by *the Dalai Lama, translated by Jeffrey Hopkins*

Each day the Dalai Lama recites the verses of the *Eight Stanzas for Training the Mind*, which remind him of the importance of altruistic behavior. He discussed the verses at the Tibetan Buddhist Learning Center in Washington, New Jersey in 1979, during his first visit to America.

I am very happy to be visiting one of the oldest Tibetan Buddhist centers in America, and I would like to extend my warm greetings to all who have come here, particularly to the Kalmuck-Americans, who are, in comparison to us Tibetans, elder refugees. For many centuries there has been a strong relationship between the Mongolian and Tibetan peoples, by means of which Tibetan Buddhism became the Buddhism of Mongolia. Right through to the present Mongolians have mainly studied the Buddhist religion in the Tibetan language and prayed in Tibetan as well, and my own name "Dalai" was given by a Mongol chieftain. Thus the Dalai Lama has a special connection with the Mongolian people.

Under the bright sun in this fine park are gathered many who speak a variety of languages, wear different styles of dress, and are different perhaps also in religious faith. However, we are all the same in being human. We all innately have the thought "I," and we all want happiness and do not want suffering. Those who have cameras and are taking pictures, the monks sitting before me, all those standing and sitting in the audience share the thought, "May I have happiness, and may I avoid suffering." We spend our lives within such a thought appearing innately in our minds.

Further, we all equally have the right to achieve happiness and avoid suffering. From among the many different techniques for doing so, each of us has our own estimation of what the best is and leads his or her life accordingly. When we investigate to determine the nature of the happiness we seek and the suffering we wish to avoid, we find that there are many different forms of these; however, in brief, there are two types: physical pleasure and suffering, and mental pleasure and suffering.

Material progress is for the sake of achieving that happiness and relieving that suffering which depends upon the body. But it is indeed difficult to remove all suffering by these external means and thereby achieve complete satisfaction. Hence there comes to be a great difference between seeking happiness in dependence upon external things and seeking it in dependence upon one's own internal spiritual development. Furthermore, even if the basic suffering is the same, there is a great difference in the way we experience it and in the mental discomfort that it creates, depending upon our attitude towards it. Hence our mental attitude is very important in how we spend our lives.

There are many religions that set forth precepts and advice on how to adjust one's mental attitude, and all, without exception, are concerned with making the mind more peaceful, disciplined, moral, and ethical. In this way the essence of all religions is the same, even though in terms of philosophy there are many differ ences. Indeed, there would be no end to argument if we concentrated just on the philosophical differences, but this would create unnecessary work for us. Far more useful and meaningful is to try to implement in daily life the precepts for goodness that we have heard in any religion.

In a sense, a religious practitioner is actually a soldier engaged in combat. With what enemies does he or she fight? Internal ones. Ignorance, anger, attachment, and pride are the ultimate enemies; they are not outside, but within, and must be fought with the weapons of wisdom and concentration. Wisdom is the bullet, the ammunition; concentration—the calm abiding of the mind—is the weapon for firing it. Just as when we fight an external enemy, there is injury and suffering, so also when we fight internally, there is internal pain and hardship. Thus, religion is an internal matter, and religious precepts have to do with inner development.

To approach this from another viewpoint: We are going deep into outer space based on modern science and technology developed through human thought; yet, there are many things left to be examined and thought about with respect to the nature of the mind—

whether it is caused or not, and if it is caused, what its substantial cause is, what its cooperative conditions are, what its effects are, and so forth. For developing the mind, there are many precepts, and from among these, the main are love and compassion. The Buddhist doctrine has many finely developed and powerful techniques capable of advancing the mind with respect to love and compassion. A good mind, a good heart, warm feeling are most important. If you have such a good mind, you yourself will be comfortable, and your family, mate, children, parents, neighbors, and so forth will be happy as well. If you do not have such a good mind, just the opposite occurs. The reason why from nation to nation, continent to continent, people are unhappy is just this. Thus, in human society good will and kindness are the most important things. They are very precious and necessary in one's life, and it is worthwhile to make effort to develop a good heart.

From every viewpoint we are all the same in wanting happiness and not wanting suffering. However, oneself is only one whereas others are infinite in number. Therefore, based on the great difference between the amount of satisfaction there is in just oneself being happy and the amount of satisfaction there is in an infinite number of people being happy, others are more important than oneself. If oneself, one person, cannot stand suffering, how can any sentient being stand it? Therefore, it is right to use oneself for others' welfare and a mistake to use others for one's own purposes.

To use whatever capacities of body, speech, and mind one has for the benefit of others, it is necessary to generate mind of altruism wishing to remove others' suffering and to achieve others' happiness. Whether one believes in a religion or not, whether one asserts that there are former and future lifetimes or not, there is no one who does not appreciate compassion. Right from the time of birth, we are under the care and kindness of our parents. Then, later at the end of our lives when we are pressed by the suffering of aging, we are again very much reliant on the good heart and compassion of others. Since it is the case that at the beginning and end of our lives we are dependent on others' kindness, it would be only appropriate if between those two periods we cultivated a sense of kindness towards others.

No matter whom I meet and where I go, I always give the advice to be altruistic, to have a good heart. I am now forty-four years old, and from the time when I began to think until now I have been cultivating this attitude of altruism. This is the essence of religion; this is the essence of the Buddhist teaching.

We should take this good heart, this altruism, as the very basis and internal structure of our practice, and should direct whatever virtuous activities we do towards its increase higher and higher. We should suffuse our minds with it thoroughly, and should also use words, or writings, as means of reminding ourselves of the practice. Such words are the *Eight Stanzas for Training the Mind* written by the Ga-dam-ba Ge-shay Lang-ri-tang-ba (*gLang-ri-thang-pa*, 1054-1123); they are very powerful even when practiced only at the level of enthusiastic interest.

> 1 *With a determination to accomplish*
>   *The highest welfare for all sentient beings*

Who surpass even a wish-granting jewel
I will learn to hold them supremely dear.

Never mind *neglecting* other sentient beings, you should take them as a treasure through which temporary and final aims can be achieved and should cherish them one-pointedly. Others should be considered more dear, more important than yourself. Initially, it is in dependence upon sentient beings—others—that you generate the altruistic aspiration to highest enlightenment. In the middle, it is in relation to sentient beings that you increase this good mind higher and higher and practice the deeds of the path in order to achieve enlightenment. Finally, in the end, it is for the sake of sentient beings that you achieve Buddhahood. Since sentient beings are the aim and basis of all of this marvellous development, they are more important than even a wish-granting jewel, and should always be treated with respect, kindness, and love.

You might think, "My mind is so full of the afflictive emotions. How could I possibly do this?" However, the mind does what it is used to. What we are not used to, we find difficult, but with familiarity, things which were once difficult become easy. Thus Shāntideva's *Engaging in the Bodhisattva Deeds* says, "There is nothing which, with time, you cannot get used to."

  2 *Whenever I associate with others I will learn*
    To think of myself as the lowest among all
    And respectfully hold others to be supreme
    From the very depths of my heart.

If you cultivate love, compassion, and so forth for your

own welfare, seeking happiness for yourself, you are bound within a selfish viewpoint which will not lead to good results. Rather, you should have an attitude of altruism, seeking the welfare of others from the very depths of your heart.

Pride in which, cherishing yourself, you view yourself as superior and others as inferior is a major obstacle to the development of an altruistic attitude respecting and cherishing others. Therefore, it is important to rely on the antidote to pride and, no matter who you are with, to consider yourself lower than others. If you assume a humble attitude, your own good qualities will increase, whereas when you are full of pride, there is no way to be happy. You will become jealous of others, angry with them, and look down on them, due to which an unpleasant atmosphere will be created and unhappiness in society will increase.

It is on the basis of false reasons that we take pride in ourselves and feel superior to others, and, conversely, we can counter pride by reflecting on others' good qualities and our own bad qualities. Consider, for instance, this fly buzzing around me. From one viewpoint, I am a human being, a monk, and of course am much more important than this very small fly. However, viewed another way, it is no surprise that this weak lowly fly who is continually overcome by obscuration is not engaged in religious practice; further, this fly is not engaged in bad actions accomplished through sophisticated techniques. I, on the other hand, as a human being with full human potential and a sophisticated mind, might misuse my capacities. Should I—a supposed practitioner, a supposed monk, a supposed human being, a supposed cultivator of the altruistic aspiration—use my capacities in a wrong way, then I am far worse than a fly. Thinking this way automatically helps.

However, maintaining a humble view of oneself in order to counter pride does not mean that you should come under the influence of those who are engaged in wrong practice. It is necessary to stop and make answer to such persons; however, although it may be necessary to give a strong reaction to someone, it should be done within an attitude of respect.

> 3 In all actions I will learn to search into my mind
>   And as soon as an afflictive emotion arises
>   Endangering myself and others
>   Will firmly face and avert it.

If when practicing such a good altruistic attitude, you leave your afflictive emotions just as they are, they will create trouble, for anger, pride, and so forth are obstacles to the development of altruism. Thus, you should not let these go on and on but, relying on their antidotes, immediately stop them. As I said before, anger, pride, competitiveness, and so forth are our real enemies. Our battleground is not external but within.

Since there is no one who has not gotten angry at some time, we can understand on the basis of our own experience that anger does not yield happiness. Who could be happy within an attitude of anger? What doctor prescribes anger as a treatment? Who says that by getting angry you can make yourself happier? Therefore, we should not allow any opportunity for these afflictive emotions to be generated. Even though there is no one who does not value his or her own life, if we come under the influence of anger, we can even be brought to the point of wishing to commit suicide.

Having identified the various types of afflictive emotions, when even the slightest form of one begins to be generated you should not think, "This much is probably okay," because it will only become stronger and stronger, like a small fire that has started in a house. There is a Tibetan saying, "Don't make friends with 'It's-probably-okay'," for to do so is dangerous.

As soon as you start to generate an afflictive emotion you should think of the opposite type of quality, using reason to generate an opposite attitude. For instance, if you start to generate desire, reflect on ugliness or establish your mind in mindfulness of the body or mindfulness of feeling. When you get angry, cultivate love; when you generate pride, think about the twelve links of dependent-arising or the divisions of the various constituents. The basic antidote to all these faulty states is the wisdom realizing emptiness, which will be discussed in the final verse.

Most important upon generating an afflictive emotion is to rely at once on the appropriate antidote and stop it entirely before it can develop more. However, if you cannot do that, at least seek to distract your mind from the afflictive emotion—go out for a walk, or contemplate the inhalation and exhalation of the breath.

What is the fault of generating the afflictive emotions? When the mind comes under the influence of an afflictive emotion, not only do you become uncomfortable right then and there, but also this induces bad physical and verbal deeds which cause suffering in the future. For instance, anger can lead to violent words and eventually to violent physical acts in which others are hurt. These actions establish predispositions in the mind that bring about suffering in the future.

Thus it is said, "If you want to know what you were doing in the past, look at your body now; if you want to know what will happen to you in the future, look at what your mind is doing now." The Buddhist theory of actions and their effects means that our present body and general situation have been formed by our past actions and that our future happiness and suffering are in our own hands right now. Since we want happiness and do not want suffering, and since virtuous actions lead to happiness and non-virtuous ones lead to suffering, we should give up the non-virtuous and engage in virtue. Although it is not possible in a few days to take upon yourself the complete practice of abandoning the non-virtuous and assuming virtue, you can gradually get used to these and develop your practice to higher and higher levels.

> 4 I will learn to cherish beings of bad nature
> And those pressed by strong sins and sufferings
> As if I had found a precious
> Treasure very difficult to find.

When you meet with persons of bad character or those who have some particularly strong sickness or other problems, you should neither neglect them nor create a distance between yourself and them, feeling them to be alien, but rather generate an especially strong attitude of cherishing them and holding them dear. In the past in Tibet, those who were engaged in this type of training of the mind took on themselves the burden of serving persons who had leprosy much as the Christian monks and so forth do nowadays. Since it is in relation to such persons that you can cultivate the altruistic intention to become enlightened as well as patience and the voluntary assumption of suffering, coming in contact with them is to be viewed as like finding a precious treasure.

> 5 When others out of jealousy treat me badly
>   With abuse, slander, and so on,
>   I will learn to take all loss
>   And offer the victory to them.

Even though in the worldly way it is proper to respond strongly to someone who has unjustifiably and without reason accused you, it does not fit in with the practice of the altruistic aspiration to enlightenment. It is incorrect to respond strongly unless there is a special purpose. If someone out of jealousy or out of dislike treats you badly with abuse or even strikes you physically, rather than responding in kind, you should suffer the defeat yourself and allow the other to have the victory. Does this seem unrealistic? This type of practice is very difficult indeed but must be done by those who seek one-pointedly to develop an altruistic mind.

This does not mean that in the Buddhist religion you only take the loss all the time and purposely seek out a bad state of life. The purpose of this practice is to achieve a great result though undertaking small losses. If circumstances are such that there is no great fruit to be gained through taking a small loss, then you can, without any hatred but with a motivation of compassion, respond in a strong manner.

For instance, one from among the forty-six secondary precepts of the Bodhisattva vow is to answer appropriately and halt someone who is engaged in a wrong activity. It is necessary to stop an evil action that is being done by someone else. In one of his previous births, Shākyamuni Buddha was born as the captain, the Compassionate One. On his ship were 500 traders, and among them was one who thought to kill the other 499 and take all of their goods. The captain tried many times to advise the man not to do such evil, but he held to his plan. The captain had compassion for the 499 persons who were in danger of being killed and wanted to save their lives; he also had compassion for the man who was planning to kill them and who by doing so would accumulate tremendous bad karma. Thus he decided that, having no other means to stop him, it would be better to take upon himself the karmic burden of killing one person in order to spare that person the karma of killing 499, and he killed the would-be murderer. Because of his compassionate motivation, the captain accumulated great merit, even through a deed of killing. This is an example of the type of activity that a Bodhisattva must do in order to undertake the appropriate action to stop someone else's doing an evil deed.

> 6 When one whom I have benefitted with great hope
> Unreasonably hurts me very badly,
> I will learn to view that person
> As an excellent spiritual guide.

When you have been very kind and helped another a great deal, that person should indeed repay you with kindness.

If, instead of showing kindness, the person is ungrateful and shows a bad manner and so forth to you, it is a very sad circumstance, but within the context of the practice of altruism, you should have a sense of even greater kindness toward that person. Shāntideva's *Engaging in the Bodhisattva Deeds* says that someone who acts like an enemy towards you is the best of teachers. In dependence on a spiritual teacher you can form an understanding of patience but cannot gain an opportunity to practice patience; the actual practice of implementing patience comes when you encounter an enemy.

In order to develop true and unbiased love and compassion, you must develop patience, and this requires practice. Therefore, one training in altruism should think of an enemy as the best of spiritual teachers and, considering him in this sense to be kind, view him with respect.

It is not necessary that someone or something have a good motivation towards you for you to have a sense of respect and cherishing. For instance, the doctrines that we are seeking to achieve, the true cessations of suffering and so forth, do not have any motivation at all, and yet we cherish, value, and respect them highly Thus, the presence or absence of motivation makes no difference in terms of whether something can be helpful for increasing good qualities and accumulating merit.

Still, motivation—a wish to harm—is the basis for determining whether someone is an enemy or not. A doctor, for instance, may cause us pain performing an operation, but since he has done it from a motivation to help we do not consider him an enemy. It is only in relation to those wishing us harm—enemies—that we can truly cultivate patience, and thus an enemy is absolutely necessary; it cannot be cultivated in relation to your lama.

There is a Tibetan story of a fellow who, while circumambulating a temple, saw someone sitting in meditative posture. He asked the meditator what he was doing, and the meditator answered, "I am cultivating patience." Then that person said something very harsh to the meditator and the meditator at once answered back angrily. This response came because although he had been cultivating patience, he had not encountered anyone who was harming him or speaking badly to him; he had had no chance to *practice* patience. Thus, the best of all situations for the practice of patience is an enemy, and for this reason someone engaged in the Bodhisattva practices should treat an enemy with tremendous respect.

Without tolerance, without patience, you cannot develop true compassion. In the ordinary way, compassion is usually mixed with attachment, and because of that it is very difficult to feel compassion for one's enemies. You have to work to develop true love and compassion which extend even to enemies—those whose motivation is to harm you—and for this you need the experience of dealing with enemies. The most difficult period in one's life is the best chance to gain real experience and inner strength. If your life goes very easily, you become soft; when passing through the most tragic circumstances you can develop inner strength, the courage to face them, without emotional feeling. Who teaches this? Not your friend, not your guru, but your enemy.

> 7. *In short, I will learn to offer to everyone without*
>   *exception*
>   *All help and happiness directly and indirectly*
>   *And respectfully take upon myself*
>   *All harm and suffering of my mothers.*

This stanza sets forth the practice of giving and taking—out of love giving your happiness and causes of happiness to others and out of compassion taking from others their suffering and the causes that would make them suffer. These are the two main attitudes of a Bodhisattva: compassion which is to care about others' suffering and love which wishes for others to have happiness. When, training in these two, you come upon people who are manifestly undergoing suffering, you should practice giving and taking, thinking:

> This person is suffering very badly and, though wanting to gain happiness and alleviate suffering, does not know how to give up non-virtues and adopt virtuous practices; hence he/she is bereft of happiness. I will take this person's suffering and give this person all of my happiness.

Although there may be exceptional persons who actually can physically do this, it is very difficult; most of us can only imagine doing it. However, mentally doing this practice of removing suffering from others and taking it upon yourself is very helpful internally and has the effect of increasing the determination to do so in actuality. This practice is done in conjunction with the inhalation and exhalation of the breath—inhaling others' pain and exhaling your happiness to them.

> *8 I will learn to keep all these practices*
> *Undefiled by the stains of the eight worldly conceptions*
> *And by understanding all phenomena as like illusions*
> *Be released from the bondage of attachment.*

In terms of method, these practices should be done one-pointedly within altruistically seeking the benefit of others; you should not come under the influence of the eight worldly styles of behavior—like and dislike, gaining and losing, praise and blame, fame and disgrace. If these practices are done with a motivation to inflate yourself, to cause others to think that you are a religious person, to gain renown, and so forth, then the practice is not pure but has become defiled by worldly concerns. Instead, virtue should be totally for the sake of others.

The latter part of the stanza refers to the factor of wisdom: You should engage in this practice from the viewpoint of knowing that compassion itself, the practitioner of compassion, and the objects of compassion are like a magician's illusions in that they appear to exist inherently but do not. In order to understand these three factors as like illusions, it is necessary to know that even though these factors appear to be inherently existent, they are empty of such inherent existence.

For instance, if someone who is working at the altruistic intention to become enlightened were to view himself or herself as existing in his or her own right, or were to view the persons for whose sake enlightenment is being sought as inherently existent, or were to view enlightenment itself as inherently existent, this viewing of inherent existence would in fact prevent that meditator from achieving enlightenment. Instead, it is necessary to view yourself—the cultivator of the altruistic intention—the enlightenment you are seeking, and all other sentient beings—those for whom you are seeking enlightenment—as not inherently existent, but rather as like illusions, existing one way but appearing in another. By means of viewing these as like illusions their inherent existence is refuted.

This refutation of inherent existence is not a case of removing something that formerly existed. Rather, you are identifying that something which never did exist does not exist. Due to our own ignorance, phenomena appear to exist inherently even though they do not; due to this appearance of inherent existence, we conceive that things exist the way they appear; due to that, we are drawn into afflictive emotions and thereby are ruined. For instance, you look at me and think, "There is the Dalai Lama," and suddenly, without any fabrication, it seems to your mind that there is a Dalai Lama that is separate from his body and independent even of his mind. Or, consider yourself. If your name is David, for instance, we say, "David's body, David's mind," and it seems to you that there is a David who owns his mind and body and a mind and body that this David owns, does it not? We say that the Dalai Lama is a monk, a human, a Tibetan. Does it not seem that you are saying this not with respect to his body or his mind, but that there is something independent?

Persons do exist, but they do so only nominally, through designation. Yet, when they appear to our minds, they appear not as existing through the force of being posited by names and terminology but as if they exist in their own right, able to set themselves up, self-instituting. Although it is a fact that phenomena do not exist in and of themselves, that they depend on something else for their very existence, they appear to us to be independent.

If things did in fact exist the way they appear—if things did exist so concretely—then when one looked into and investigated them, this inherent existence should become even clearer, more obvious. However, when you seek for the object designated, you cannot find it under analysis. For instance, conventionally there is an I undergoing pleasure and pain, accumulating karma, and so forth, but when we analytically search for this I we cannot find it. No matter what the phenomenon is, internal or external, whether it be one's own body or any other type of phenomenon, when we search to discover what this phenomenon is that is designated, we cannot find anything that is it.

This which gives rise to the appearance of I is mind and body, but when you divide this into mind and body and look for the I, you cannot find it. Also the whole, body, is designated in dependence upon the collection of the parts of the body; if you divide this into its parts and look for the body, you cannot find it either.

Even the most subtle particles in the body have sides and hence parts. Were there something partless, it might be independent, but there is nothing that is partless. Rather, everything exists in dependence on its parts, is only designated in dependence on its parts—

its basis of designation—through the force of conceptuality; there is nothing which is analytically findable. There is no whole which is separate from its parts.

However, these things appear to us as if they do exist objectively and in their own right, and thus there is a difference between the way things appear to our minds and the way they actually exist, or the way we see them to exist when we analyze. If they did exist in accordance with how they appear to be established in their own right, this mode of existence should become clearer and clearer as we investigate. Yet, we can come to a decision through our own experience that when we search for these things, analytically we cannot find them. Thus they are said to be like illusions.

Since phenomena appear to us in a way that is different from what we discover when analyzing, this proves that their concrete appearance is due to a fault of our minds. After you understand that these phenomena which appear to exist in their own right are empty of existing in the way that they appear, you have realization of phenomena as like illusions in that there is a composite of knowing the appearance of phenomena and understanding that they are empty of existing in the way they appear.

What is the benefit of understanding this? Our afflictive emotions of desire, hatred, and so forth arise because we superimpose upon phenomena a goodness and badness beyond that which they actually have. For instance, when we get very angry or desirous, we have during that time a strong sense of the goodness or badness of that object, but later when these emotions calm down and we look at those same objects, we ourselves will even find our earlier perception laughable. The benefit or assistance of wisdom is that it prevents us from superimposing on objects a goodness or badness beyond what is actually there, whereby we are able to stop desire and hatred.

Thus, the two parts of this unified practice are method and wisdom—method being the cultivation of the altruistic attitudes of love and compassion and wisdom being the view understanding the non-inherent existence of all phenomena. These two must be in union.

I recite these verses every day and, when I meet with difficult circumstances, reflect on their meaning. It helps me. Thinking that they might help others as well, I have explained them here. If this helps your mind, practice it. If it does not help, there is no debate; just leave it. The dharma, or doctrine, is not for the sake of debate. These teachings were spoken by the great masters in order to help, not for people to quarrel with each other. Were I as a Buddhist to quarrel with a person of some other religion, then, I think, if Buddha were here today, he would scold me. The doctrine is to be brought into our own mental continuum for the sake of taming it.

In conclusion, my request, my appeal, is that you try as much as you can to develop compassion, love, and respect for others, to share others' suffering, to have more concern for others' welfare, and to become less selfish. Whether you believe in God or not, in Buddha or not, does not matter. The important thing is to have a good heart, a warm heart, in daily life. This is the principle of life.

from Awakening the Mind, Lightening the Heart

by *the Dalai Lama*

The Dalai Lama often reminds us that you don't have to be a monk to practice the Dharma.

L ife as a free and fortunate human being is referred to here as something precious. Such a human life is found rarely, but individuals who possess it can achieve great things because of it. Yet it is not enduring but fragile and extremely transient. It is important that we are aware of these characteristics of our lives and then prepare ourselves for making the best use of them. It is easy to see that human potential far exceeds the abilities of other living creatures in the world. The human mind has far-reaching vision. Its knowledge is boundless. Because of the power of the human mind, new discoveries and inventions abound on our planet. But the crucial thing is that all these innovations should promote happiness and peace in the world. In many instances this is not the case. Unfortunately, too often human ingenuity is used in a misguided way to create disturbances, disunity, and even war.

The achievements of human intelligence are obvious. The ideas and activities of even a single individual can have far-reaching benefits for millions of people and other living creatures. When our human skills are channeled in the right direction, motivated by a proper attitude, wonderful things happen. Therefore, the value of human life is inestimable. From a more strictly spiritual perspective, it is on the basis of a human life that we can develop different types of insight and realization. Only the human mind can generate infinite love and compassion. Being more concerned about other sentient beings than ourselves and working tirelessly in their interest are among the noble attributes of human nature.

Life as a human being is extremely valuable in terms of achieving both our temporary and ultimate goals. In this context, the temporary goal refers to attaining higher rebirth, and the ultimate goal refers to nirvana and full enlightenment. These goals are precious and difficult to attain. To do so, individuals must be in a position to practice and to accumulate the necessary causes. Only human beings are endowed with the opportunity and intelligence to achieve these goals. If we are to be reborn in the higher realms, we need to refrain from unwholesome actions and practice virtues like generosity and patience. When we engage in right practices, we have the potential to achieve nirvana and Buddhahood.

Once we have gained some conviction that life as a free and fortunate human being is rare and precious, we should reflect that it is not permanent. Although life as a human being has such potential, it is short-lived and does not last. According to the textual instruction, we should meditate here on three fundamental topics: the certainty of death, the uncertainty of when it will occur, and that when death does take place, only the individual's spiritual realization will be of any help. These points can be easily understood and present no intellectual challenge. However, we must meditate on them over and over again until we are deeply convinced. Everyone agrees that sooner or later we all have to die. So the certainty of death is not in question. Rich or poor, young or old, all must die one day. Death is uniform and universal, and no one can either deny or defy this fact of life.

What fools us is the uncertainty of the time of death. Even though we know very well we have to die, we assume that it will be after some time. We all think that we are not going to die soon, and we cling to a false belief that death will not occur for years and years. This notion of a long and indefinite future stretching out ahead of us deters us from serious spiritual endeavor. The whole purpose of meditation on impermanence and death is to move us to engage actively in spiritual practices.

Let me lay out some general guidelines that can help to make our spiritual practice productive and fruitful. Our spiritual pursuit consists, as I have already explained, of meditation sessions and the postmeditation period. People often have the impression that spiritual practices are done only during meditation sessions; they ignore the need for practice during the postmeditation period. It is important to realize that this approach is mistaken. Practice during the postmeditation period is equally important. Therefore, we need to understand how the two kinds of practice complement each other. Spiritual understanding gained in meditation should enhance our understanding during the postmeditation period and vice versa. As a result of the inspiration gained during the meditation sessions, we can develop many virtues like compassion, benevolence, respecting others' good qualities, and so forth. During the session, it is much easier to assume a certain degree of piety. But the real test is when we are faced with the outside world. Therefore, we must be diligent in our practices during the postmeditation period.

When we sit and do our prayers and meditation, we certainly find some peace of mind. We are able to generate compassion toward the poor and needy and feel more tolerant toward our rivals. The mind is more relaxed and less aggressive. But it is really difficult to maintain this momentum when we are confronted with the circumstances of real life. Meditation is like training ourselves for the real world. Unless we engage in a harmonious blend of our experiences of the meditation and postmeditational periods, our spiritual endeavor will lose its much-needed effect. We can be kind and compassionate during our meditation, but if someone harasses us on the road or insults us in public, it is very possible we will become angry and aggressive. We might even retaliate on the spot. If that happens, all the kindness, patience, and understanding we developed in our meditation instantly vanish. Of course, it is very easy to be compassionate and altruistic when we are sitting comfortably on our seats, but the test of the practice is when we encounter a problem. For example, when we have the opportunity to fight and we refrain from fighting, that is Dharma practice. When we have the power to bully someone and we refrain from doing so, that is Dharma practice. So, the real Dharma practice is to control ourselves in such circumstances.

To make our spiritual practice stable and enduring, we must train consistently. A fair-weather practitioner has little hope of achieving his or her goal. It is extremely important to practice the teachings day after day, month after month, and year after year. Anyone who practices consistently can develop spiritual realizations. Since every impermanent phenomenon changes, one day our wild and rough minds will become disciplined and wise, fully relaxed and peaceful. Such wonderful mental qualities can be developed simply by seeing the advantage of virtuous thought and action and the drawbacks of delusion. Nevertheless, it is vital that the practitioner learns the proper technique and method. In the quest for spiritual realization, we do not have to use brute force.

When I was receiving teachings from Khun-nu Lama, he told me a story of someone in Lhasa doing circumambulations. Someone else was meditating there, and the one circumambulating asked, "What are you doing?" The other replied, "I am meditating on patience." The first retorted, "Eat shit!" and the meditator jumped up, shouting in anger. This clearly shows that the real test of practice is whether we can apply it when we encounter disturbing situations. I feel that practice after the session is probably more important than the practice we do during the session. During the session we are actually refueling or recharging our energy to be able to do the practice after the session. Therefore, the more we are able to mold the mind during the session, the better we will be able to face difficulties afterward.

The text explains the nature of the special kind of human life that has the freedom to practice the Dharma. Individuals who have the freedom and opportunity to do Dharma practice are not encumbered by wrong views. They are free from the constraints of birth as an animal, a hungry spirit, or a hell being. They have avoided being born in a place where the Buddha's teaching does not prevail or in a remote barbaric land. Nor have they been born dumb or stupid.

Imagine being born as a bird, concerned only with finding food. We would have no opportunity to practice the Dharma. Fortunately, we have not been born as birds or animals but as human beings. But, even as human beings, we could have been born in a remote land where the Buddha's teaching was unheard of. Wealth and intelligence would make no difference; we would not be able to practice the Dharma. My Western friends come from places where there used to be no practice of Buddhism. But, because of their positive instincts and the changing times, we have been able to meet and share the teachings. At one time, Western lands would have been called remote lands where people were not free to practice. We should appreciate not only that we have been born as human beings, but also that we all now have the conditions necessary for putting the Dharma into practice.

Life as a human being is the most suitable basis for attaining nirvana and Buddhahood. Since we have found such a great opportunity, nothing could be worse than failing to put it to good use. We have found this precious human birth as a result of accumulating great virtue in the past. We must put it to good effect now by continuing to practice the Dharma. Otherwise we will be like the merchants of old who went to great lengths to cross the ocean in search of jewels, only to return empty-handed. This human body is likened to a ship in which we can cross the ocean of suffering of the cycle of existence. Having found it, we have no time to sleep and not do the practice.

Life as a free and fortunate human being is very difficult to find because its cause is difficult to create. Most human beings are involved in unvirtuous activities, and therefore most of us will take inferior rebirths. On the basis of present conduct and behavior, it will be difficult for most of us to be born as human beings in our next lives. And if we do not obtain human life, we will engage only in negative activities, with no opportunity to practice Dharma.

Life as a free and fortunate human being is also rare simply in terms of numbers. If you compare the number of sentient beings in the human realm and those in the realms of animals and so forth, you will find that animals and birds far outnumber human beings. Even when they have obtained life as human beings, very few turn their minds toward Dharma practice. Therefore, we have to generate a wish deliberately to extract meaning from our lives as human beings.

It is clear from what we have discussed here that life as a free and fortunate human being is extremely rare.

Those of us who are endowed with all these special features must realize that we have the ability to achieve great goals. Here, where I am teaching the holy Dharma, we are surrounded by countless birds and insects. But, far from understanding these teachings, they have not the slightest thought of virtue. They only think about food. So it is not sufficient that the Dharma be available. Individuals require a working basis that enables them to understand and put the teachings into practice.

Because of the long tradition of Great Vehicle Buddhism in Tibet, Tibetans have acquired certain innate positive qualities. They are given to saying kind and sympathetic words. Even in remote nomadic areas, illiterate Tibetans pray for the sake of all sentient beings, thinking of them all as having been their mothers in past lives. I have met many people from these places, who ask me to come back to Tibet soon for the benefit of all mother sentient beings. It sometimes makes me laugh that they think of motherly sentient beings only in Tibet and nowhere else. Anyway, the important thing is that, because of their compassion, they have strong positive instincts to care for sentient beings.

Buddhism flourished in China in the old days, and Tibetans believed the emperors to be emanations of Manjushri, the Bodhisattva of Wisdom. In retrospect, I think we were naive in our sincerity and failed to gain a reciprocal response. Consequently, we Tibetans have had to suffer. There have been great political upheavals since the Communists took power. They seem to hate Buddhism as if it were poison. Because of indoctrination, the Chinese react to each other with hostility, suspicion, jealousy, and other negative thoughts. During campaigns to eliminate birds and insects for ideological reasons, even children were recruited. Under such circumstances, their natural instincts to be kind and virtuous are suppressed. On the other hand, in Tibetan families every effort is made to instill virtuous imprints in the minds of the young.

Life as a free and fortunate human being can be viewed in various ways. We are not qualified merely by being born as human beings. Imagine being born during what is known as a dark age, when a Buddha has not manifested in the human world. You may possess wealth, power, and influence, but spiritually you will be in the dark. At such times there is no Dharma in the world.

It is important to understand what is meant by practice of the teachings. Different modes and procedures are aimed directly or indirectly at molding the unruly mind and disciplining it, subduing negative aspects. For example, we recite prayers and do meditation. Such practices should promote goodness of heart and foster virtues like kindness and patience. They should subdue and eliminate negative aspects of the mind like animosity, anger, and jealousy, because these are a source of disturbance and unhappiness for ourselves and others. This is why practice of the Dharma is beneficial.

This automatically leads to the question, Is it possible to practice the teachings? The answer is an emphatic yes. At this juncture we have obtained this human life. We have the fortune to have met appropriate spiritual masters who are compassionate and capable in guiding us on the proper path. We also have freedom and opportunity to engage in spiritual practice.

We should not think of postponing our practice of Dharma until the next life. This is a mistake, because it will be difficult to be born as a human being in the future. Nor should we think that we will put off our practice until next year or even next month. That we will die is inevitable, but we do not know when it will be. Of the many practices open to us, generating the awakening mind is the most important.

It is important to remember that everyone innately possesses Buddha nature and that disturbing emotions are only temporary afflictions of the mind. By properly practicing the Dharma, these disturbing emotions can be completely removed, and our Buddha nature will be revealed in all its potential.

All our spiritual practices should be directed toward developing the altruistic thought of the awakening mind. In order for this sublime thought to arise, it is essential to understand sentient beings' plight. This helps us to generate kindness and compassion for others. Unless we have some experience of suffering, our compassion for others will not amount to very much. Therefore, the wish to free ourselves from suffering precedes any sense of compassion for others. The goal of all our spiritual practices should be the awakening mind. This is the supreme and most precious of all the Buddha's teachings. In order that our sense of the awakening mind be effective and powerful, meditate on death and the law of cause and effect. Meditate, in addition, on the vicious nature of the cycle of existence and the benefits of nirvana. All these practices are complementary because they each serve to provoke us into developing the awakening mind.

The second step in developing the awakening mind

is to think about death and the impermanent nature of things as well as the disadvantages of not doing so. Thinking about death and impermanence opens the door to achieving excellent qualities in this life and the next. Meditation on death and miseries of the lower realms of existence is of primary concern to those practitioners who are trying to ensure the welfare of their own future lives. They aim to achieve their goals by taking refuge in the Three Jewels and observing the law of cause and effect. Such practitioners principally abstain from the ten unvirtuous actions.

Through the process of meditation, individuals seeking a happy rebirth come to realize that the body is impermanent and subject to decay. It is under the sway of disturbing emotions and past actions, both of which ultimately stem from the ignorant conception of true existence. Whatever arises because of ignorance is miserable by nature. Practitioners who merely seek a happy rebirth chiefly meditate on coarse impermanence, observing that we all die, flowers wither, and houses collapse. Those who seek the peace of nirvana meditate on subtle impermanence, observing that all phenomena are subject to momentary change.

On the other hand, if you do not think about death and simply try to forget it, you will involve yourself only in activities concerned with this life. Even if you pretend to practice the Dharma, you will do it mainly for the benefits of this life. So not remembering death leads to a very limited kind of existence. But thinking about death reminds us of the next life, which reduces our emphasis on the things of this life. Of course, we have to work to maintain our livelihood, but we will not forget the next life. We need to think about death and impermanence because we are too attached to the goods of this life: our possessions, relatives, and so forth. Fear of death, to one who practices the Dharma, does not mean fear of becoming separated from relatives, wealth, or one's own body. From that point of view, fear is pointless because sooner or later we have to die. A more useful fear is the fear of dying too soon, without having been able to do what is necessary to ensure a better future life.

It is common knowledge that death is certain and that no one can avoid it. Instead of disregarding it, it is better to prepare beforehand. Numerous scriptures explain the advantages of remembering death and disadvantages of ignoring it. If we prepare for the eventuality through meditation, when it strikes it will not come as such a shock or be so hard to cope with. If we anticipate trouble in the future, we take precautions. When we are mentally prepared for what might happen, we are not caught unawares when calamity actually befalls us. Thus we meditate on death, not in order to create terror or unhappiness for ourselves, but to equip ourselves to face it when it comes. As long as we remain in the cycle of existence, we will not be free from sickness, old age, or death. Therefore, it is wise to prepare ourselves for what is inevitable. We need to make ourselves familiar with the process by which death occurs and the intermediate state between lives that follows it. If we do so, when we encounter these different events we will be able to face them with determination and courage.

As I said above, in reflecting on death there are three major points to remember. These are that death is certain, that the time of death is unpredictable, and that at the time of death nothing will help except our understanding of the Dharma. The inevitability of death is obvious and goes without saying. Nevertheless, we should reflect on how death occurs in relation to time and place. Not a single individual will avoid death. Death is a universal condition. This has been true in the past, remains so at present, and will continue to be true in the future. Whatever physical existence we adopt will not be immune to death. Even Buddhas have left their bodies behind, so what can be said of ordinary beings?

In terms of place, there is nowhere that can be regarded as a death-free zone. Wherever we stay we cannot avoid death. We cannot hide in the mountains, we cannot remain in space beyond death's reach. Death comes upon us like the falling of a huge mountain from which there is no escape. We may be brave, cunning, and clever, but whatever tactics we use, there is nowhere to escape from death, not high in the mountains, deep in the sea, in the densest forest, or in the crowded city. There is not a single person in history who has not had to die. Even the most spiritually evolved have passed away, not to mention the most powerful kings and the bravest warriors. Everyone, rich and poor, great and small, man and woman, has to die.

When meditating on death, we should pay closest attention to its unpredictability. The uncertainty about when death will strike actually impedes our spiritual endeavors. We accept that death will definitely come one day, but since its time of arrival is not fixed, we tend to think of it always as being some way off. This is an illusory notion. As a matter of fact, we are constantly racing toward our death without stopping even for a moment.

We may be alive today, but sometimes death overtakes

us without our finding the time to practice the Dharma. We cannot add something to lengthen our lives. Life continuously and uninterruptedly declines. Years are consumed by months, months are consumed by days, and the day is consumed by hours. Our lives are destroyed as quickly as a drawing on the surface of water. Just as the shepherd drives his flock to the fold, old age and sickness drive us toward death. Because of our physical structure, we are unlikely to live longer than a hundred years. Our life span is defined by our karma. It is not easily extended. Of course, prayers for long life, longevity empowerments, and so forth might enhance one's life to some extent, but it is very difficult to prolong or add to it. Things we did just a few days ago now exist only in our memories. We cannot have these experiences back. This is true even of the experiences we had this morning. Since then, a few hours have passed, which means that our lives are a few hours shorter. Life is ebbing away with every tick of the clock.

As each week follows another, we fail to notice time passing. Sometimes, when I have a vivid recollection of my life in Lhasa, it seems I experienced it only a few days ago. We have been in exile over thirty years, but it is only when we meet old friends from Lhasa or their children that we realize what a long time it has been. We have a tendency to think of the past as something that happened quickly and the future as stretching out into the distance. Consequently, we always tend to think that we still have a lot of time to practice. We think of it as a future project. We are deceived by this negative tendency.

Even while we are alive, we do not have much time to

practice the Dharma. Half our lives we spend asleep. The first ten years we are merely children, and after twenty we begin to grow old. Meanwhile, our time is taken up with suffering, anxiety, fighting, sickness, and so forth, all of which limit our ability to practice.

One hundred years from today, not one of us, except the one or two born in the last few days, will still be alive. We have a strange habit of talking about someone dying in a certain place, without thinking that the same death will overpower us. It never occurs to us that we too will die. The television reports people being killed, but we always remain the viewers, not the ones who are going to die. Therefore, thinking about the inevitability of death, we should determine to practice the Dharma, to cease procrastinating by starting today. Of the many levels of practice, meditation on the awakening mind is the most important, so we should resolve to do that now.

In Buddhist cosmology, our planet is referred to as the Southern World. Since we inhabit this world, our life span is extremely uncertain, whereas the life span of beings in the Northern world is said to be definite. It is difficult to take the scriptural description of these worlds literally. What is important about the Buddha's teaching is his explanation of the Four Noble Truths and his instructions on how to transform the mind. Sometimes I lightheartedly tell people that the Buddha did not come to India to draw the maps of the world. When there is a contradiction between the scientific account and the Buddhist scriptural description of the universe, we should accept what can be observed to be true. There is no need to be dogmatic or narrow-minded about it. This is not to disparage the Buddha's fundamental teachings. Reflecting on these, we can appreciate the vast profundity of the Dharma. What the scriptures do say is that the life span of the beings of our world is extremely unpredictable. Sometimes people die when they are still very young, and sometimes they live into ripe old age.

In our meditation on death we should consider the factors that bring it about. The conditions that sustain life are limited. Ironically, sometimes even these cause death. Food and shelter are among our basic needs, but occasionally bad food or overeating can be fatal. Our bodies are composed of elements, which are by nature opposed to each other. When we talk about good health, we mean that these opposing elements are in proper balance. When that balance is disturbed, we suffer from different ailments. On the outside our bodies seem to be solid and strong, but the human metabolism is so subtle and complex that if something happens to one part of the body it can disrupt the functions of the other organs. The body is like a machine with many delicate components. The heart, for instance, has to beat twenty-four hours a day. It could stop at any time. Then what would we do?

Even at the best of times there is no guarantee that we will not die tomorrow. We may believe that because someone is in perfect health, she will not die for a long time. We may think that because someone else is weak and ill, he will die soon. But these are mere assumptions. There are so many causes and conditions for dying that we do not know when death will strike. You may think that, in the event of an earthquake, you have a very solid house. You may think that, if a fire breaks out, your feet are swift and you will be able to run away.

Still, we do not have any guarantee that we can protect ourselves against every eventuality. Therefore, we should take every precaution and prepare to face this unknown situation. We can be sure that our deaths will come; we are only unsure when.

Finally, at the time of death, nothing can help except your Dharma practice. When you die, you have to go alone, leaving everything behind. You may have many wonderful friends and relatives, but at that time none of them can help you. Whoever is dearest to you is absolutely helpless. You may be rich, but wealth cannot help you at the time of death. You cannot take a single penny with you. Instead, it is more likely to be a cause of worry. Your best friend cannot accompany you to your next life. Even a spiritual master cannot take his or her most devoted disciples to the next world. Every one of us has to go alone, propelled by the force of our karma.

I often reflect on my own situation as the Dalai Lama. I am sure there are people who are prepared to sacrifice their lives for me. But when my death comes, I have to face it alone. They cannot help me at all. Even my own body has to be left behind. I will travel to the next life under the power of my own actions. So what is it that will help us? Only the imprints of positive actions left on our minds.

Both positive and negative karmic imprints are deposited on the subtle consciousness. This subtle consciousness is known as the primordial consciousness or clear light, which has no beginning or end. This is the consciousness that came from previous lives and goes on to the next. It is the karmic imprints upon it that give rise to experiences of pain and happiness. When you come to die, only the imprints of your positive deeds will help you. Therefore, while you are alive, and especially when you are young, your mind is fresh, and you are able to do a systematic practice, it is important that you prepare yourself for death. Then you will be able to face it properly when the time comes.

The process of death takes place through the gradual dissolution of your internal elements. If you have made your mind familiar with this process, at the time of death when it actually takes place you will be able to handle it. Similarly, if you have become familiar with meditation on love and compassion and ex-changing your happiness for the suffering of other sentient beings, these practices will help you. If you have been a real Dharma practitioner, you will face death contentedly.

Of course, if you believe we have only this present life, then at death everything comes to an end. But if you accept the possibility of future lives, then death is just like changing your clothes. The continuity of the mind goes on. However, as we have no idea what the future holds, it is necessary to engage now in practices that will help us then. Even in this world we need friends and support in times of difficulty. When we have to face the unknown alone we will have only our previous practice to support us.

Now when we talk about Dharma practice, people sometimes misunderstand what it means. So let me put it in perspective. Practicing the Dharma does not mean you have to give up your profession or do away with your possessions. There are various levels of practice according to individual ability and mental disposition. Everyone cannot renounce this world and meditate in the mountains. This is not practical. How long could we survive? We would soon starve. We need farmers to grow food, and we need as well the support of the business community. These people also can practice the teachings and integrate their lives within the bounds of the Dharma. Business people must make profit to earn their living, but the profit should be moderate. Similarly, people in other trades and professions can work honestly and conscientiously without contradicting Dharma. In this way they can serve the community and help the overall economy.

I usually advise people to devote half their time to the affairs of life and half their time to the practice of the teachings. This, I think, is a balanced approach for most people. Of course, we need the real renunciates who dedicate their whole lives to practice. They are worthy of our respect and veneration. We can find them among all traditions of Tibetan Buddhism. There are many meditating in the Himalayas.

After our deaths we do not disappear; we take rebirth. But we cannot be confident that our rebirths will not be in miserable circumstances. We do not take birth voluntarily; we are compelled to do so through the force of our actions. Our actions are of two kinds, positive and negative. If we are to ensure our future well-being, it is important to cultivate wholesome actions. Because existence as an animal, hungry spirit, or inhabitant of hell is extremely miserable, practitioners aspire to attain a more fortunate rebirth. The principal way to fulfill this wish is to abstain from the ten unvirtuous actions. These ten misdeeds include three physical activities—taking life, taking what is not given, and abusive sexual

behavior; four verbal activities—lying, slander, harsh
words, and idle gossip; and three mental activities
covetousness, malice, and wrong view. Abandoning
these ten is crucial if we want to achieve a fortunate
rebirth.

The practice of this kind of morality should be
understood within the context of the law of karma or
action. Every action is bound to produce results. This
means that whatever positive or negative activities you
do, you will experience similarly positive and negative
results. Whatever actions you do will follow you just
like the shadow of a bird flying in the sky. Actions also
have the potential to increase and multiply. Even if you
do a small positive or negative action, the eventual
result can be tremendous. You should not think that a
particular misdeed is insignificant and will not harm
you in the future. Just as a large vessel is filled by drops
of water, even minor negativities will harm you later. If
you have not performed an action, you will not have to
face its result, yet once an action has been done, its
effects will never merely disappear. This means that
you will have to face its results.

Reflecting on this, you should cease all negative activities and make an effort to accumulate wholesome
deeds. Of these, the most important is training in the
precious awakening mind, aspiring to attain enlightenment for the benefit of all sentient beings. At the same
time, we must appreciate that the workings of karma
are subtle and difficult to understand. The subtle play
of action and result is extremely difficult to understand, and we may not be able to use our reason at all.
Thus our only recourse is to depend on the explanation of someone with experience. If we are to rely on

that, we first have to verify that that person is authentic and trustworthy. We can do this by observing his or her conduct and examining those of his or her teachings that we can understand. Satisfying ourselves of their validity is grounds for regarding the teacher as trustworthy.

In our daily lives we see many things directly and can understand them immediately. We can say that this is a peach tree or that is a banana tree without having to use reason or rely on a trustworthy authority. However, when something is behind me, I do not see it directly with my eyes. But if I hear the mewing of a cat, because of my familiarity with cats I can reason that there is a cat behind my seat. There are also partially obscure phenomena that we cannot perceive directly through our senses but that we can infer on the basis of certain marks or indications. For example, my birthday falls on the fifth day of the fifth month of the Tibetan calendar. This is not something I can discover for myself. I simply have to rely on what my parents have told me. I know that they have no reason to lie about it and were of sound mind. I can safely trust their word, even though I cannot see the matter directly or reason about it.

Now, the subtlest workings of actions and their results or karma are extremely difficult for the human mind to understand. Ordinary people like us cannot comprehend such extremely obscure phenomena either by direct perception or by way of reasoning. No amount of analysis and examination can help us here. We have to depend on someone who has knowledge and experience of these phenomena, such as Buddha Shakyamuni. We do not do so merely by saying that he is great or he is precious. We depend on his words. This is justified because a Buddha does not lie; he possesses great compassion and the omniscient mind, which is the result of eradicating all mental defilements and obstructions. The Buddha's loving-kindness is unconditional and universal. His sole mission is to help sentient beings in whatever way is useful. In addition to his universal compassion, the Buddha is endowed with the wisdom directly apprehending emptiness. These attributes of compassion and wisdom qualify the Buddha as an authentic teacher. He is someone on whom we can rely when our own reason fails.

The ethical discipline of abstaining from the ten unwholesome actions is the actual refuge that protects us from falling into unfortunate states of existence. This practice is sustained by faith in karma or the law of cause and effect. Such faith is acquired by trusting in the words of the Buddha. This is why we have to establish that he is reliable and trustworthy, which we do by examining his teachings. The Buddha's doctrine is vast and profound. His fundamental teachings of the Four Noble Truths are impeccable. Their relevance and validity are beyond question. His explanation of self-lessness as a method for achieving nirvana and Buddhahood is lucid and rational. Analyzing these teachings through logical reasoning will cause our faith and respect to grow.

We can classify human beings into three major categories: those who believe in religion, those who are against it, and those who are uncommitted. The majority fall into the third category. Such attitudes reflect people's different ways of achieving their own well-being. There are those who rely on material comfort and those who rely primarily on spiritual satisfaction.

The Communist Chinese are against religion in general and Buddhism in particular. They denounce religion as a poison, claiming that it harms economic growth and is a tool of exploitation. They even say that religion is an empty and meaningless pursuit. Tibetans, on the other hand, believe in the Buddha's teaching and see it as a source of peace and happiness. Broadly speaking, Tibetans are indeed happy, peaceful, and resilient in the face of difficulties. Those who oppose religion tend to be more anxious and narrow-minded. It is also noticeable that Tibetans do well without having to work so hard, while the Chinese struggle much harder to survive.

Positive, meritorious activity results in happiness and success. The forces involved in the law of cause and effect are not physical entities, but if we observe them carefully we can learn how they operate. When we Tibetans became refugees, our lives were initially very hard. We possessed not an inch of land and had to depend on others for support. In the course of time, our situation improved. This is our good karma coming to fruition. Similarly, in ordinary life some people are more successful than others for no obvious reason. We just say that he or she is lucky, but these are instances of the working of positive karma.

We should stop not only all negative activities, but also the motivation that gives rise to them. It is important to refrain from the ten unwholesome deeds both from a spiritual point of view and because they are contrary to acceptable human behavior. Wanton slaughter of animals, killing human beings, and abusive sexual behavior like rape are against the law everywhere. Nowadays we see many new laws being made, but whatever punishments are prescribed, people always seem to find ways of escaping them. Unless there is a sense of propriety and restraint on the part of individuals, it will be difficult to maintain peace and tranquillity in society. A sense of shame and conscience is more effective than the threat of falling foul of the police and risking punishment. If we have a spiritual practice that provokes a real transformation within the mind, we will not have to depend on external forces. If there is control within individuals' minds, there will be discipline and peace throughout society.

Therefore, we should all try to avoid the ten unwholesome deeds throughout our lives and at least try to avoid engaging in them frequently. We should be especially careful about killing. If you kill even a small insect with great anger, attachment, or ignorance, it can serve to propel you into an unhappy rebirth. Even if you manage to be reborn as a human being, you will tend to have a short life and to be inclined to kill again. In this way you will constantly accumulate negative activities and so will have negative experiences for many lives to come. You can see evidence of this in small children who, even when they are only two or three years, are very fond of killing insects. They have strong imprints left on their minds, resulting in this tendency to kill.

When we are young we are more susceptible to recalling our actions and experiences from previous lives, before they are overlaid by present experience. As we grow up these vivid experiences, whether they are positive or negative, begin to decrease. Later, even though we may not have a vivid memory of it, the force of our actions still lingers in the mind. Likewise, even though we may not later remember certain actions we performed in the early part of our lives, they still retain their potential. A single negative act is not negative only at the time it is done; later it can propel us into a miserable state of existence, where we encounter unceasing suffering.

If you think about this you will take more care. When you appreciate the drawbacks of killing, you will try to avoid doing it. Even when you are bothered by a mosquito and you feel you have a reason to kill it, try to refrain from doing so. You may not be able to donate blood, but at least refrain from shedding it. Of course, it is not that easy, as I know from my own experience. When the mosquito bites you for the first time you may be patient with it. But the second time you become a little more agitated, and when it does it a third time you start to think of killing it.

It is important to think about the faults of killing. Then if you have the opportunity to kill someone but refrain from doing so, you will really be practicing the virtue of not killing. If you say you are avoiding killing when you are not actually in a position to kill, it does not mean very much. A result of not killing is that in the future you will take a better rebirth, such as that of a human being. Your life will be long and you will have a natural dislike of killing and will avoid taking other beings' lives. Actions not only give rise to positive or negative experiences in this life but have a similar effect in future lives.

If we examine our present behavior and mental disposition, we can easily conclude that we have engaged in negative activities in the past. We can also easily see what kind of activities we are more familiar with on the basis of our present experience. Some people who must have become quite accustomed to saying their morning prayers have no difficulty in doing so now. But for those of us without such habituation, it is very difficult to sit and do our prayers daily. Even those among us who are ordained and have been practitioners for years are still easily carried away by disturbing emotions. This shows that we have performed negative activities in the past.

The way to purify these negativities is to call to mind whatever negative activities you have done and openly admit them. To do this you can take refuge in the Three Jewels and generate the awakening mind. Then, with a sense of regret for whatever unwholesome deeds you have done, promise never to repeat them in the future and to engage persistently in spiritual practice. You should continue doing this until you receive a clear indication, for example in your dreams, that your unwholesome deeds have been purified.

Unless you make an attempt to think about the sufferings of the cycle of existence, you will not generate an aspiration for liberation. And unless you think about how you fall into the cycle of existence, you will not understand the method for putting an end to it. You should meditate on the sufferings of the cycle of existence in general as well as those of specific realms of existence. There is no certainty in the cycle of existence. Sometimes, because of the changes of rebirth, your friend becomes your enemy and your enemy becomes your friend, your father becomes your son and your mother becomes your spouse, and so forth. Nothing is certain, so you do not know who is your real enemy and who is your real friend. Even in this life there is no certainty. We call someone who makes us happy a friend. We regard wealth and friends as trustworthy sources of happiness, but if we think more deeply, they are unreliable because they are subject to change.

Lack of satisfaction is one of our greatest sufferings. We enjoy a certain level of wealth or experience in the hope that it will give us some satisfaction, but satisfaction eludes us. The more we enjoy something, the more we desire something else. We see many people surrounded by wealth and attention who still have no contentment. And when they feel deprived of satisfaction and contentment, they think they are the most miserable people in the world. Until we really experience the cycle of existence as just a series of ups and downs, our spiritual practice will not be successful.

We also have to give up our bodies again and again, being born again and again, undergoing the highs and lows of our changing lives. At one point we may be born as kings of a celestial realm, but in our next lives we might fall to a state of unbearable suffering. Whatever wealth we accumulate we must finally leave behind. However respected our names, however widespread our fame, and however great our wealth, we will eventually have to give them up. Whatever has come together must finally part. We wish to enjoy life with our friends and relatives, but in the end we all have to part.

When you die you go alone, and the only light to accompany you derives from the spiritual practice or positive acts you have done. Thus the cycle of existence is unreliable. It is unreliable because you have to give up your body again and again, you cannot rely on receiving help or harm from others, you cannot rely on finding prosperity, and you cannot rely on your companions. No matter how much you enjoy life's pleasures, there is no contentment. Because you have entered the womb over and over again, your series of births is untraceable, which indicates that you have been wandering in the cycle of existence for a beginningless time.

Now let us think about the drawbacks of the human world that we actually experience. It is characterized by the sufferings of birth, sickness, old age, and death. There is no one who can escape these miseries. We have no memory of how we suffered at birth, and the sufferings of our own old age are equally elusive. The Kadampa masters used to say that it is good that old age only comes upon us gradually. If it were to occur all at once—if we were to wake up one morning suddenly wrinkled, bent, and white haired—the shock would be unbearable.

All these sufferings originate from our sense of desire, aversion, and other disturbing emotions. Ignorance is the root of them all. People are born due to the force of karma and disturbing emotions. Therefore, far from being a good beginning, birth is just the beginning of a long stream of suffering. From this point of view, it is ironic that we celebrate birth as something special and continue to observe the birthday every year. Because we are born under the sway of karma and disturbing emotions, we are controlled by many negative forces. How then can we expect to find joy and happiness? We are all like the Tibetans who are under the control of the Communist Chinese. Under such oppressive authority, which shows no respect for the law of cause and effect and which has no mercy, no sense of shame or decency, how can they enjoy peace and happiness?

The suffering of old age creeps up on us, so we hardly notice it. In fact, aging starts from the very moment we are born. It attacks us gently, and although old age is not pleasant, its gradual onset makes it bearable. At the age of twenty we enter adulthood. When we reach about forty, some of our hair turns white and some more of it falls out. Curiously, these are regarded as signs of maturity and dignity. Because aging is not very obvious, we do not see where it is leading. One important thing to remember is that aging is part of our physical makeup. It is not something imposed from outside. So long as we have this contaminated body, we will be subject to the sufferings of birth, old age, sickness, and death. The most intelligent and effective means of overcoming such misery is to eliminate its cause.

These days advanced medical science ascribes many of the causes of sickness to external agents such as bacteria and viruses. But the fundamental cause lies with our physical makeup. Our bodies are susceptible to sickness. All our physical and mental components, including our bodies, are the products of contaminated actions and disturbing emotions. Therefore, our ailments have both physical and mental aspects. We suffer because that is the nature of our bodies. But there is no point in developing a dislike for our bodies. The wisest strategy is to find the causes of suffering and eliminate them. So long as we are under the control of disturbing emotions, real happiness will be hard to find.

The purpose of meditating on suffering is not to

cause more anxiety but to inspire us into eradicating its causes. Practice of meditation on the true path leads to the cessation of sufferings and their causes. From this point of view, an intelligent person can see the unfathomable wisdom of the Buddha's beginning his teachings with the Four Noble Truths. Appreciating the merits of nirvana and the drawbacks of the cycle of existence naturally stimulates an individual to engage in practices like the three trainings in ethics, concentration, and wisdom. This is the path that can deliver us to the state of liberation.

The altruistic thought of the awakening mind is the gateway to the Great Vehicle. It literally refers to expanding or extending the mind. By and large, we are usually preoccupied with our own interests and welfare. However, those interests concern only one individual, no matter how important. Other beings are infinite in number, and therefore their interests and welfare are far more important than those of a single individual. When you generate the awakening mind, you extend your care and concern to the well-being of everyone else. The aspiration to attain the fully awakened state of a Buddha for the sake of all sentient beings is a pure and powerful intention. As a result, both others and ourselves will enjoy lasting peace and happiness.

It is important to be aware that disturbing emotions and the obstructions to complete knowledge are but adventitious stains on the mind. They are not intrinsic to the nature of the mind and therefore can be completely removed. The import of this is that omniscience is something we can achieve. Naturally, if we have achieved omniscience, we are in the best position to help others. In trying to be helpful, mere sincerity and dedication are not enough. It is essential to understand each individual's interest and capacity and mental disposition. Then our efforts to fulfill sentient beings' welfare will be effective, and we will able to gradually lead them to Buddhahood.

The awakening mind is the most supremely positive thought. It is worth employing every means and method to generate it. Even in our ordinary everyday life, kindness and good-heartedness are highly valued. This is obvious even in relation to animals like dogs and cats. Kinder, more peaceful dogs attract a better response than those that are aggressive. The same applies in human society. We all like to be around kind people. Their peaceful and relaxed nature is soothing and joyful.

When the head of the family is kind and broad-minded, the rest of the family enjoys peace of mind. Disputes and arguments naturally occur, but when dealt with on the principle of forgiving and forgetting, they cease to be so disruptive. Under the circumstances, such a family is bound to enjoy peace and prosperity. When an aggressive, narrow-minded, and selfish person is head of the family, the reverse is true. Even on an individual level we all appreciate those who are kind and openhearted. If we hold grudges against our fellow beings, we naturally become suspicious of them. This leads to a vicious circle of hatred. Can we expect to enjoy peace and happiness under such circumstances?

Human beings are not intrinsically selfish, because selfishness is a form of isolation. We are essentially social animals depending on others to meet our needs.

We achieve happiness, prosperity, and progress through social interaction. Therefore, a kind and helpful attitude is the source of happiness. And the awakening mind is supreme among all such beneficial thoughts. This is what motivates an individual to seek the inconceivable qualities of a fully awakened Buddha in order to benefit infinite sentient beings. This precious thought underpins the noble deeds of the bodhisattvas, the awakening champions embarked on the path to enlightenment. Therefore, realizing the value of the awakening mind, we should make it the central theme of our practice.

Meditations on the Ways of Impermanence

by *the Seventh Dalai Lama, translated by Glenn H. Mullin*

The Seventh Dalai Lama, Gyal-wa Kal-zang Gya-tso
(1708-1757), was a prolific writer. He was best known for
his spiritual poetry, prayers and hymns.

To the Lama-lha, my Refuge, my father,
The recollection of whom dispells all sadness,
I turn for spiritual guidance;
Bless my mind with your transforming
    powers,
That the thought of death may never
    evade me,
That I may practice the holy Dharma
    perfectly.

On the golden mountains far in the distance,
Rings of mist hang like belts on the meadows.
Now seemingly solid, so soon they dissolve.
My mind turns to thoughts of my death.

In spring, the season of warmth and growth,
The stalks of the crops were turquoise green.
Now, autumn's end, the fields lie naked and
   parched.
My mind turns to thoughts of my death.

On each branch of the trees in my
   garden
Hang clusters of fruit, swelling and ripe.
In the end, not one piece will remain.
My mind turns to thoughts of my death.

From behind the peaks of Mount Potala
The sun rose like an umbrella in the sky.
Now it has gone, fallen behind the western
   ranges.
My mind turns to thoughts of my death.

They die old, they die young, day upon day.
I am asked to throw their souls to a pure land
Or to prophesy their conditions of rebirth.
My mind turns to thoughts of my death.

Gray clouds cover the sky, obscuring it;
The first drops of rain are about to fall,
To be scattered everywhere by the dark,
   red wind.
My mind turns to thoughts of my death.

In the belly of the vast plateau below me,
The campfires of visiting traders glow like
   stars;

But tomorrow they depart, leaving only
    refuse.
My mind turns to thoughts of my death.

Warm summer days, the earth thronging with
    life;
The minds of the people are lost in gaiety.
Suddenly the cold winter wind crashes them
    down.
My mind turns to thoughts of my death.

High above, turquoise dragons roared in
    harmony;
Around me, cuckoo birds chattered
    sweetly.
But times have changed; where are they now?
My mind turns to thoughts of my death.

Dharma, the precious teachings of the
    Awakened Ones,
Is a medicine supreme, curing all the mind's
    ills.
These days many saints of old look down
    from Pure Lands.
My mind turns to thoughts of my death.

Hard it is to leave the mother who carried us,
And hard to part from relatives and friends;
Yet as the years pass, our links with them
    corrode.
My mind turns to thoughts of my death.

A young man, with teeth for the future,
With plans for months and years ahead, died,
Leaving but scant traces. Where is he now?
    Gone!
My mind turns to thoughts of my death.

Buddha attained the glorious, immortal
    vajrabody,
Yet he still enacted a death scene.
This body of flesh, blood and bone, covered
    in skin,
Like a bubble of water, is bound to perish.

From very birth a child sees his parents age,
Sees them each day come closer to the
    grave.
How can you say to me, "But I am still
    young"?'
I warn you there is no hope of hiding from
    death.

Spirits were high with expectations this
    morning
As the men discussed subduing enemies and
    protecting the land.
Now, with night's coming, birds and dogs
    chew their corpses.
Who believed that they themselves would die
    today?

Look and ask among the people of your land
For anyone even a hundred years old.
You will be lucky to find even one!

Do you not think your own death certain?
If you look closely at and contemplate deeply
The people and things that appear around you,
You can see that all are in constant flux.
Everything becomes the teacher of
    impermanence.

I remember this body when it was a child's,
And as it gradually took the form of a
    youth.
Now its every limb is twisted and worn.
It is my own body, yet it delights not even my
    own eyes.

The mind itself is impermanent, constantly
    oscillating
Between feelings of pleasure, pain and
    indifference,
The fruits of positive,
Negative and neutral karmas.

Look where you will, at yourself or others,
Life passes like a flash of lightning.
When Yama's agents surround you, intent on
    murder,
What do you think will happen to you?

Relatives, friends, wealth and property
Shine with splendor in the eyes of worldly
    people;
Thus they bind themselves in shackles of
    attachment.
This pathos; how will it end?

Body lying flat on a last bed;
Voice whispering a few last words;
Mind watching a final memory glide past:
When will that drama come for you?

If you create nothing but negative karma,
You will stand naked of instincts to benefit
    the hereafter.
Where will you go after death?
The mere thought of it makes you flinch.

Therefore I myself and beings like me
Should leave behind meaningless ways
And entrust ourselves to the gurus, Yidams
    and Dakinis,
Begging them to prepare us for death's road.

In order to die well, with the joy and
    confidence
Of being within the white rays of spiritual
    awareness,
It is essential to begin readying yourself now.
Familiarize yourself with the profundities of
    the sutras and tantras.

By this song may those like me,
Irreligious people little better than savages,
Be caught in the flames of renunciation.
May they evolve in spirit
And may they attain to liberation.

from Stages of Meditation

by *the Dalai Lama*

A great Indian Buddhist scholar named Kamalashila in the eighth century wrote a text called *The Middle Volume of the Stages of Meditation*. The Dalai Lama comments on that text in this discussion about bringing compassion to meditation.

C ompassion is one of the major causes for realizing the state of omniscience. It is important at the beginning of the practice, during the practice, and even after realizing the results of our spiritual endeavor. Now the question is: How should we meditate on it?

The way to meditate on compassion will be taught from the outset. Begin the practice by meditating on equanimity. Try to actualize impartiality toward all sentient beings by eliminating attachment and hatred.

Compassion is a mind that focuses on the sentient beings that are miserable and wishes them to be free from suffering. Compassion can be of three types, depending on the aspect of wisdom that accompanies it. These three are: compassion focused on sentient beings, compassion focused on phenomena, and compassion focused on the unapprehendable. All three are the same in being minds that earnestly desire sentient beings to be free from their misery. They are distinguished not in terms of their aspect, but in terms of their object of focus, because all three have the same aspect of wishing sentient beings to be separated from suffering. Compassion focused on sentient beings is so-called because it focuses merely on sentient beings without specifying their characteristics of being impermanent or empty of inherent existence. Compassion focused on phenomena refers to that compassion which not only focuses on sentient beings, but also focuses on sentient beings characterized by impermanence. Likewise, compassion focused on the unapprehendable refers to that compassion which focuses on sentient beings characterized by the unapprehendable, or their lack of inherent existence.

When we look at it from another angle, the merit of generating a kind thought is obvious. This is true whether you believe in a particular religion or not. A person's general goodness is in direct correlation to the force, or quality, of the kind thoughts he or she generates. A kind person finds a lot of admirers, and they feel close to such a person. We can observe this phenomenon even among animals. Animals exhibit great joy and delight when they see people who are kind to them. And they enjoy being around such persons. Conversely, people who are aggressive and hold evil designs are regarded with suspicion even by animals and birds. Animals and birds run away when they hear their voices or even their footsteps. Therefore, a kind motivation or a kind heart is an extremely valuable quality.

People who possess compassion are amiable to all and their pleasing nature attracts friends everywhere. It is easy to observe the attraction of their compassionate motivation when we notice even strangers taking delight in their company. Let us take some simple examples that clearly illustrate the meaning of kindness. For instance, when someone smiles, it creates joy in other people's hearts without costing anything. Unless we are peaceful and joyful at heart, we will have no guarantee of winning friends, even if we possess great wealth. When we are competitive and aggressive, it is hard to gain much substantial benefit even if we lavish wealth on others. On the other hand those who are sincerely interested in helping others have peace and joy at heart. They create an atmosphere of harmony around them. Thus it should be clear that a kind heart and a helpful attitude are the very foundation of happiness, both for others and ourselves for now and forever.

The positive qualities produced by helpful intentions are widely recognized as worthwhile and desirable. All the major religions of the world teach their followers to become good people, to practice patience, and to develop an interest in helping others. There is unanimity concerning the positive value attached to these fundamental principles. In Buddhism particularly, since its doctrine is based on compassion, a great deal of emphasis is placed on this practice.

So, what is the Buddhist technique for meditating on compassion? On the one hand we need to develop loving-kindness toward suffering beings, and secondly we must identify the nature of suffering. Maintaining awareness of these two points, and focusing your mind on the infinite number of beings, you will be able to generate a strong wish that all of them gain freedom from suffering and its causes. You should begin the process by attempting to develop loving-kindness toward beings who are in misery. For this purpose, meditation on equanimity is taught.

If we examine the state of our ordinary minds, we may see how they segregate sentient beings into three groups—those to whom we feel close, those for whom we feel aversion, and those toward whom we are indifferent. We regard certain beings as close friends and relatives. We hold others at a distance, with the thought that they have harmed us, our friends, relatives, and possessions in the past, that they do it now, and will do the same thing in the future. With thoughts like these, we generate aversion toward those beings. Under such circumstances, even if we talk about cultivating compassion for all beings, in reality, as far as our own purposes are concerned, our compassion toward others is one sided and superficial. Therefore, in order to generate true compassion for all beings, we must first develop an attitude of equanimity, an impartial thought that views all sentient beings equally.

It is also important to recognize that, although we feel close to our friends and relatives and are generally kind to them, this particular kindness springs from attachment and grasping. A selfish motive is behind our apparent kindness. We are biased, thinking that this person has benefited me in this way or that person related to me in that way. So when we use the term "kindness" in everyday terms, we refer to something that would more accurately be called attachment.

What do we mean when we speak of a truly compassionate kindness? Compassion is essentially concern for others' welfare—their happiness and their suffering. Others wish to avoid misery as much as we do. So a compassionate person feels concerned when others are miserable and develops a positive intention to free them from it. As ordinary beings, our feeling of closeness to our friends and relatives is little more than an expression of clinging desire. It needs to be tempered, not enhanced. It is important not to confuse attachment and compassion. In some texts, the term "attachment" is used to denote compassion. Though attachment shares some similarity with compassion, it is produced in dependence on the misconception of true existence. Compassion, on the other hand, does not necessarily depend on the misconception of true existence. A compassionate thought is motivated by a wish to help release beings from their misery.

Broadly there are two major techniques for developing equanimity. According to the first, we think about the uncertainty of relationships, and about impermanence, and suffering, and come to see the futility of clinging to some people and hating others. According to the second technique, seeing that all beings are the same in terms of wishing to gain happiness and to be free of suffering, we try to develop an impartial attitude toward all beings. The root text briefly summarizes this second method for developing equanimity:

> All sentient beings desire happiness and do not desire misery. Think deeply about how, in this beginningless cycle of existence, there is not one sentient being who has not been my friend and relative hundreds of times. Therefore, since there is no ground for being attached to some and hating others, I shall develop a mind of equanimity toward all sentient beings. Begin the meditation on equanimity by thinking of a neutral person, and then consider people who are friends and foes.

All sentient beings are exactly the same in that every one desires happiness and seeks to avoid misery. We are not isolated entities disconnected from each other. The happiness and suffering of other beings affect us. This mutual relation is obvious. Sentient beings have been kind and have benefited us directly and indirectly throughout beginningless time. These beings are intrinsically the same as us in their pursuit of happiness and effort to avoid suffering. Thus, it is essentially logical for us to train in cultivating an impartial attitude wishing for the happiness of all beings.

In order to actualize a state of mind that regards everyone equally, at times it can be more effective to meditate on particular individuals. Visualize three individuals: one who has done us harm in this life, our enemy; one who has benefited us directly, our friend; and one who has neither harmed nor benefited us, a stranger.

When we examine the mind's usual automatic response, we note that regarding the enemy, the mind thinks, "This is my foe." It becomes irritated and resentful or hateful. Thinking about the friend, the mind feels relaxed and comfortable. Toward the stranger, there is neither irritation nor feelings of delight. The next step is to look for the reasons for these types of responses. The reasons are in fact superficial and based on narrow, self-serving attitudes. We are attached to friends and relatives because of the temporary benefit they have brought us in this life. We hate our enemies because of some harm they have inflicted on us. People are not our friends from birth, but become so due to circumstances. Neither were our enemies born hostile. Such relationships are not at all reliable. In the course of our lives, our best friend today can turn out to be our worst enemy tomorrow. And a much-hated enemy can change into our most trusted friend. Moreover, if we talk about our many lives in the past, the unreliability of this relationship is all the more apparent. For these reasons, our animosity toward enemies and attachment toward friends merely exhibits a narrow-minded attitude that can only see some temporary and fleeting advantage. On the contrary, when we view things from a broader perspective with more far-sightedness, equanimity will dawn in our minds, enabling us to see the futility of hostility and clinging desire.

When, through prolonged meditation, we are able to equalize our feelings toward those three individuals—the friend, foe, and stranger—we gradually extend the scope of the meditation to our neighbors, our fellow citizens, and our compatriots. Eventually, we extend the meditation to include all the beings in the world. Starting with specific individuals is an effective way to develop perfect equanimity. If we initially meditate on a vast number of beings, our practice of equanimity may appear to be fairly sound, but when we are confronted by specific individuals we will realize how little ground we have gained. For this reason the technique of gradually expanding the scope of our meditation is praised and recommended by many masters of the past.

Let us consider the concept of the beginningless cycle of existence. It may be described on one level as a continual cyclic process from one instant to the next under the influence of disturbing emotions and karma. This situation has its causes, but the causes are not permanent. If the causes were permanent, the result would have to be permanent. Neither is the cycle of existence a product of the intention of Ishvara, whom some believe to be the creator. So what is the cycle of existence? It comes into existence sharing the essential nature of its causes. The two root causes for being born in the cycle of existence are karma and disturbing emotions, with the latter dominating. The ignorance that is a misconception of true existence is the most serious among the three principal disturbing emotions. Ignorance that is a misconception of true existence is not something imported from elsewhere, but is a creation of consciousness.

The natural thing to do is to investigate whether consciousness exists or not. It may be difficult to come to any definite conclusions, and we may have to limit ourselves to saying it exists in the nature of things. However, the ignorance which is at the root of all the other disturbing emotions and which is a cause for birth in the cycle of existence comes into existence at the same instant as consciousness. And consciousness has no beginning. If we were to assert that consciousness does have a beginning, numerous fallacies would ensue. If, for example, we accept an inanimate physical entity as consciousness's starting point, by implication we are accepting results from inappropriate causes.

In normal cause and effect relations, both cause and effect are of the same category. When we observe the cause and effect relations of physical objects, the result maintains intrinsically the same nature as its cause. Consciousness too follows a similar pattern. Every moment of consciousness produces a subsequent result of the same category, that is, another moment of consciousness. For these reasons, Buddhist scriptural texts expound the notion of beginningless mind and the beginningless existence of sentient beings. Thus, the cycle of existence is said to have no beginning.

The text mentions that in the course of being born in this beginningless cycle of existence, sentient beings have been our relatives countless times. Here we need to recall and reflect on the kindness of sentient beings. Every one of them has benefited us directly or indirectly. The kindness and benefit rendered by our friends and relatives of this life are quite obvious. Even strangers are of immense value as a basis for accumulating merit. Loving-kindness and compassion are cultivated in relation to the infinite number of sentient beings by remembering their kindness to us.

As an outcome of these practices, the awakening mind of bodhichitta is generated. Thus, the training to accumulate merit and wisdom is done in relation to sentient beings and we are enormously benefited. Therefore, we depend on the kindness of sentient beings to achieve the final unsurpassed goal. It is from this perspective that the *Guide to the Bodhisattva's Way of Life* by Shantideva explains that sentient beings and Buddhas are equal in terms of their helping individuals attain the state of Buddhahood. Sentient beings are of immense value and help, regardless of their intentions. On a mundane conventional level, enemies are those who cause us harm, and we are hostile to them for doing so. But, viewed in another light, we can gain great experience and training from our relationships with our enemies. It is in relation to enemies that we can primarily practice patience and tolerance and thus reduce the burden of anger and hatred. We should take maximum advantage of this opportunity to enrich and enhance our practice of patience. It is for reasons like these that some treatises describe our enemies as our best teachers. In short, all sentient beings, including our enemies, give us great help in various ways and directly or indirectly render us much-needed service.

> After the mind has developed equanimity toward all sentient beings, meditate on loving-kindness. Moisten the mental continuum with the water of loving-kindness and prepare it as you would a piece of fertile ground. When the seed of compassion is planted in such a mind, germination will be swift, proper, and complete. Once you have irrigated the mindstream with loving-kindness, meditate on compassion.

To illustrate the way to generate benevolence and compassion, Kamalashila draws an analogy with the cultivation of crops. Just as a seed will grow if you plant it in ground moistened with water, you can cultivate compassion when you have prepared the mind with thoughts of loving-kindness as the basis. Having cultivated equanimity toward all sentient beings, we should see all sentient beings as similar in having been our close friends and relatives in many lives, and as similar to us in desiring happiness and disliking suffering. Having trained your mind in this way, you will feel very close to all beings and develop great empathy for them. The more an individual finds sentient beings attractive and dear to his or her heart, the more he or she will be concerned about their misery and pain. Therefore, having meditated on equanimity, we should meditate on loving-kindness. Having moistened our mind with the water of loving-kindness, if we plant the seed of compassion in it, its growth will be swift and smooth.

from The Joy of Living and Dying in Peace

by *the Dalai Lama*

The Dalai Lama often stresses the importance of patience. In this teaching he discusses patience as a means of managing anger.

*A*mong all the factors that can help sustain the awakening mind and safeguard this wholesome thought from degeneration, the practice of patience is the most effective. This is because when people attempt to hurt us or inflict harm upon us, there is a great danger of our losing our kind and compassionate attitude. Only the observance of patience can help us.

The first step in this process is to think about the benefits of patience and the dire consequences of anger and hatred. Practicing patience is the most effective way to maintain our peace of mind. Whether we are confronted by adverse circumstances or hostile forces, we will remain undisturbed and our minds will still be clear. In the long term, we will be able to develop courage and strong determination. On the other hand, anger and hostility can cause great damage in this life as well as in future lives. No matter how polite and amiable we normally are, when anger erupts, all our good qualities vanish in seconds. For instance, someone may have been a close friend, but because of something we say or do in anger, we can lose that friendship. Anger disturbs our own peace of mind as well as that of everyone around us. It creates conflict and unhappiness. Anger has the potential to hamper our progress in life. It gives rise to coarse physical and verbal behavior that we would otherwise be too embarrassed to engage in. When we are overcome by anger, we might even go to the extreme of taking someone's life. Such negative actions leave strong imprints on the mind that can result in our taking birth in miserable forms of existence. Whatever virtuous qualities you have accumulated over countless eons by practicing generosity and making offerings to the Buddhas can be destroyed in one instant of anger. This refers particularly to occasions when a person becomes angry with a bodhisattva. No other negative deed compares with anger as an obstacle and hindrance to cultivating the spiritual path. Similarly, there is no penance equal to patience. Therefore, reinforce patience in as many ways as you can.

Anger can have several causes, unhappiness and anxiety among them. We tend to respond to events and circumstances in our lives irrationally. When something is troubling us, we tend to blame other people for the problem. Instead of reacting instantly, we should examine the problem with a cooler head. The first step is to see if there is a solution. If the problem can be solved, there is no need to worry about it. But if the problem cannot be overcome, worrying about it will do no good. By adopting a more rational approach we can prevent events from disturbing our minds. Let us take an example. If someone strikes us with a stick, our usual impulsive reaction is to be angry with that person and want revenge. What the Dharma teaches us is that we should calm down and look for the real cause. Now the question is, which is the real cause—the person, his or her deluded mind, or the stick that actually struck us? When we follow this line of reasoning it becomes clear that we should be angry with the disturbing emotion that prompted the person to act violently. This is an example of how we should be more rational in the way we respond to negative events in our lives.

So long as our mind is filled with the pain of anger, we will never experience peace and happiness. As we all know, as soon as anger arises within us it becomes difficult for us to breathe. We feel suffocated. Under such circumstances how can we sleep or enjoy the taste of our food? We will have no mental or physical peace, and without sleep our minds will become unstable. The scriptures explain that the result of generating anger in this life is to be born as an ugly person in the future. Of course there are some cunning people, and I count some of the Tibetan aristocrats among them, who, the angrier they feel inside, the more they outwardly smile. Apart from them, most of us show anger immediately. For example, in Amdo, the region of northeastern

Tibet that I come from, the moment the people there become angry their faces turn red. We have a Tibetan saying: "Do not behave like the people from Amdo." Central Tibet is known as the land of the Dharma. Although the people who live there might not have been able to discipline and transform their minds, some have learned to control the expression on their faces, so that they can still smile even when they are angry.

When anger flares up within us we immediately look ugly. Our faces become wrinkled and red. Even animals, like cats, express anger in very ugly ways. When you are aware of the negativity of disturbing emotions and you watch someone get angry, you are able to see the evidence clearly before you. Anger not only makes us ugly to look at, it also makes us stupid and clumsy. It robs us of our sense of discrimination. If someone harms you and you become angry in return, does that compensate for the harm you have undergone? In the short term anger is of no use, and its effect on our future lives will just be to induce further suffering. The alternative, since you have already been harmed, is simply to bear it and meditate on patience. This course is much better, because it will at least stave off some future suffering. If you get angry, then besides the harm you have already suffered, you will experience further suffering in the future. Anger is a factor that is of no use at all. Just put it behind you.

Although the tantric texts speak of "using hatred in the path," the connotation of the word "anger" in this case is different. We cannot use ordinary hatred on the spiritual path, because such hatred eliminates our compassion and makes our mind rough and wild.

Because of anger, we might take the lives even of those who have given us material help, who have shown us kindness and respect. Because of anger we disappoint our friends and turn down gifts. In short, anger never brings peace and happiness. No one is peaceful and happy when they are angry. Anger is an enemy that brings forth negative results.

After you have thought about the advantages of patience and the disadvantages of anger, you should try to understand the causes that give rise to anger. Then you can begin to overcome anger by eliminating its causes. What fuels anger is frustration when we do not achieve what we want or when we experience what we do not want. Anger arises with all its destructive ramifications. The fuel that feeds anger is mental distress, and this is what we must try to prevent. Ordinary enemies may do us harm, but they do other things as well. Even our enemy has to sleep, eat, and look after his family and friends. Ordinary enemies cannot make a continuous and concerted effort to disturb and destroy other people's minds. Anger, however, only and always disturbs the mind. Its only function is to do us harm. Therefore, whatever the cost, we should prevent anger from ever arising by not fueling it with mental distress.

Remaining upset does not fulfill our wishes or bring us happiness and peace. It is disturbing and disruptive. If you feel something unpleasant is about to happen to you, but it is possible to avert it, there is no need to be upset about it; simply do what must be done to avert it. But if nothing can be done, again there is no point in getting upset. Feeling upset will not help. Anxiety and worry solve no problems. If the causes and conditions have come together, we cannot stop them coming to fruition. This is the law of nature. When your predicament cannot be changed, you will only make it worse if you give in to fear, anxiety, and worry. When two people are afflicted by the same kind of sickness, but one is also subject to great anxiety while the other is not, it is quite clear which of them is worse off.

If you compare Tibetan refugees with those from other countries, you will find that the Tibetan attitude is generally courageous. Tibetans do not get too excited or too depressed; despite the depth of suffering they have had to face, they have been able to bear it. Some have encountered intolerable suffering. They have spent up to twenty years in prison, and yet some of them have told me that it was the best time of their lives, because they were able to do intense prayer, meditation, and virtuous practice. Here is the difference in mental attitude. Most people faced with such suffering day and night would lack the fortitude to bear it. But if you can accept the opportunity and use it for transforming the mind, some good can come of it. Therefore, if something can be changed or transformed, there is no need to worry. And if it cannot be changed, there is also no need to worry, because worrying will not solve the problem.

As spiritual practitioners our attitude should be that we will voluntarily undergo hardship in our pursuit of a higher purpose. Faced with minor worldly problems and sufferings, we should be able to adopt a broad-minded attitude so that they will not bother us. If we are able to transform our attitude toward different levels of suffering, it will change our lives. Reflecting on suffering actually has positive results; without it we are unable to generate a determination to be free of this cycle of existence. Therefore, with a firm mind we should reflect on the nature of suffering. There are people who mortify and mutilate themselves under the guise of religion. If people are prepared to undergo hardship for such meaningless purposes, why can't we undergo certain hardships to attain the state of liberation, an enduring state of peace and happiness? Why do we flinch from hardship for the sake of liberation?

It is the nature of the mind that the better acquainted it becomes with doing something, the easier that thing is to do. If we are able to view suffering from a transformed perspective, we will be able to tolerate even greater levels of suffering. There is nothing that does not become easier with familiarity. If we get used to putting up with minor hurts, we will gradually develop tolerance for greater pain. We see many people who put up with being attacked by insects, with the discomfort of hunger and thirst, with being pricked and scratched by thorns as they go about their way of life. People face all such meaningless sufferings easily once they get used to them. Therefore, when we encounter minor problems due to heat and cold, wind and rain, sickness and injury, to fret will only make the problem worse. Some people, instead of being frightened at the sight of their own blood, become even more courageous. Others, at the sight of any blood, let alone their own, fall down in a faint. The difference arises because people have different degrees of mental stability. Some are resolute, others quire cowardly. If you learn voluntarily to face minor problems, you will gradually become invincible to the different levels of suffering. It is the way of the wise that, faced with suffering, they never allow their minds to become disturbed.

When you wage war on the disturbing emotions, there is no doubt that you will have hardship and problems. In ordinary life no one goes to war expecting to experience peace and happiness. Some will be killed, many will suffer. When we wage war on the disturbing emotions, positive forces are quite weak, while the disturbing emotions are very powerful. There is no question that we will have to undergo hardship in this conflict. We must accept it without becoming discouraged. Voluntarily accept minor sufferings in order to gain victory over the real enemy like hatred that resides within. The person who wages such a war and gains victory is a real hero.

When we think of someone as an enemy, we normally tend to think of him or her as having independent existence. We also think of the harm done by that enemy as having independent existence. But if your enemy shoots and wounds you, it is actually the bullet that strikes your body, not the enemy. Just as a weapon is wielded by a person, so the person is controlled by the disturbing emotions residing within him or her. Normally we get angry with the person. Why do we never get angry with the basic cause of harm, the disturbing emotion? Why do we not get angry with the bullet that actually strikes us? Why do we hate only the person who stands between these two? You might answer that the person contributed to what happened. In that case, you should be angry with yourself, because you also contributed to what happened. If you had not been there, no one could shoot or otherwise harm you. The suffering you experience is not just a result of the weapon with which you were hurt; your own body is also responsible. The enemy provided the weapon, but you provided the target with your body. If someone hurts you, remember also that in the past you have similarly harmed other sentient beings and that as a result you are being harmed today. It is just the ripening of your own past misdeeds. Although you are being harmed by other sentient beings it is your own fault; you are responsible for it.

Whether someone is a friend or enemy, if you find them doing something inappropriate, you should remember that they do so as the result of many causes and conditions. Thus, there is no need for you to feel unhappy. If everything happened through the force of our own will without depending on anything else, then everyone would create happiness, because happiness is what everyone wants. But because of inattention and ignorance we engage in negative activities and inflict harm on ourselves. Under the influence of strong, disturbing emotions people will even kill themselves, despite their strong instinct for self-preservation.

Consequently, it is not surprising that sentient beings harm each other. When we see such things happen, instead of feeling anger we should generate compassion. Even if you cannot do that, what is the use of getting angry? If you say that people are harmful by nature, it is still not worth getting angry with them. It is the nature of fire to burn. If you get burned, there is no point in being angry with the fire. The best thing is to avoid getting burned. Since sentient beings are basically good by nature, and their bouts of anger and hatred are temporary, there is no point in getting angry with them. If the sky is suddenly filled with smoke, there is no reason to get angry at the sky. So why blame other people and get angry with them?

Your enemy harms you out of confusion and

ignorance. If you too get angry out of confusion, both of you are at fault. How can you say one is correct and the other is not? The harm you experience today is provoked by your past misdeeds. If you do not like it, why did you commit those mistakes? Since everything is dependent on your actions, why get angry with someone else? As long as you do not purify your misdeeds, negative consequences are bound to occur.

By focusing on so-called enemies and meditating on love, compassion, and patience, we can purify many of our earlier misdeeds. Enemies give us the opportunity to accumulate virtuous qualities through our practice of patience, but by harming us they fall into unfavorable states of existence and remain there for a long time. Our own past negative deeds cause us to be harmed by the enemy. But as a result of harming us, the enemy accumulates negative deeds and suffers in the future. In this sense, it is actually we who are responsible for the accumulation of our enemy's negative deeds and we who send the enemy into unfavorable rebirths. This is how we indirectly destroy other sentient beings. The enemy provides us an opportunity to practice patience and thereby achieve Buddhahood, and in response we send him to hell. By providing us with the opportunity to cultivate patience, enemies actually benefit us. So, if we want to get angry with anyone, we should get angry with ourselves. And if we want to be pleased with anyone, it should be with our enemy.

The mind is not physical. No one can touch it, no one can harm it directly, and therefore no one can destroy it. If someone says something threatening, harsh, or unpleasant to you, it does you no actual harm, so there is no need to get angry. It is important that you just relax and stay calm and peaceful, paying no attention to what other people say. There is no need for you to feel unhappy or afraid. If you say that others' insults will hinder your prosperity, the response is that material goods have to be given up sooner or later anyway. If you say that it is proper to get angry in order to obtain certain goods, the response is that however good something may be you will not keep it longer than this life. But the fruit of the anger that you have expressed to obtain it will stay with you for many lives.

Life can be compared to two dreams. In one dream you experience happiness for one hundred years and then wake up; in another dream you experience happiness for only a moment and then wake up. The point is that after you have awakened you cannot enjoy the happiness of your dreams again. Whether you live a long life or a short life, you will have to die. Whether or not you had many possessions and whether or not you enjoyed them for a long time, at the time of death you leave everything behind as if you had been robbed by a thief. You have to travel to the next world empty-handed.

The Communists in Tibet denigrate the Buddha, Dharma, and Sangha. They destroy stupas and temples out of disrespect. You should not be angry with such destruction, because even if someone damages images of the Buddha, the scriptures and stupas, they cannot do any harm to the actual Buddha, Dharma, and Sangha. If your friends and relatives are harmed by others, it is because of their past actions and many other causes and conditions. There is no place for anger. When embodied beings are harmed both by animate and inanimate phenomena, why should you be especially bent on retaliating against those who possess a mind?

When there is a lack of social harmony, remember that sentient beings have different dispositions, different ways of thinking, different ways of seeing things. This is natural. If some agitation, confusion, or disturbance arises, you should be able to see it as a result of your own action and so avoid resentment. Cultivate love and compassion instead. This is how to make yourself alert to accumulating virtuous deeds. For example, someone loses his or her house in a fire and moves elsewhere. Because of this experience, he or she will dispose of everything flammable. Likewise, when the fire of hatred arises in connection with something you are attached to, there is a danger of your merit being burned up. You should get rid of the object of attachment.

Sometimes we have to sacrifice minor pleasures for the sake of peace and happiness. For example, it would be better to pay a fine by way of punishment than to have your hand chopped off. If we are unable to tolerate even the minor sufferings of this life, why do we not refrain from anger, which gives rise to the torments of hell? For the sake of fulfilling our desires we risk suffering in hell for thousands of years. Such sufferings fulfill neither our own purpose nor the purposes of other sentient beings. On the other hand, if you appreciate the advantages of patience and the disadvantages of anger, undergoing hardship in order to overcome anger becomes tolerable. Putting up with such hardship is a source of great achievement. You will finally be able to remove the temporary and ultimate sufferings of sentient beings. Therefore, it is worth voluntarily accepting minor hardships and sufferings in order to accumulate immeasurable merit and achieve lasting peace and happiness.

If it makes someone happy to praise your own qualities, you welcome it. But you feel jealous to hear praise of the qualities of other people. This is inappropriate. If that is how you feel, what is the use of the prayer "May all sentient beings be happy"? It becomes just wishful thinking. If you really want all beings to be happy, and that is why you have cultivated the awakening mind, how can you be put out when they find some happiness through their own efforts? If you want sentient beings to be delivered to the exalted state of Buddhahood, why do you feel distressed when they obtain possessions and respect? If it is your responsibility to look after someone, but that person turns out to be able to look after himself, does it not make you happy? We say, "May all sentient beings have happiness and may they be separated from suffering." If sentient beings find happiness and reduce their suffering of their own accord, it is worth rejoicing about. But if you do not like sentient beings attaining peace and happiness, why talk about their attaining enlightenment?

People who are angry when others prosper have no awakening mind within them. Whether someone else is given something or not does not affect you. The gift does not belong to you and you will not obtain it, so why do you feel unhappy? Why do you abandon your merit, reputation, and good qualities by getting angry? Why do you give up the very qualities that allow you to achieve wealth and respect? Because of your own negative deeds, not only will you fail to strive for liberation, but you prefer to compete with those who have accumulated merit and receive gifts as a result. Is this appropriate?

Why do you feel happy when your enemy is miserable? Your simple wish for him to be unhappy cannot harm him. And even if he experiences suffering according to your wish, why should you feel happy? If it gives you satisfaction, such a negative attitude will only be a cause of your downfall. Once you are caught on the hook of the disturbing emotions, you will encounter great suffering. You will be impelled to live in hell. Neither praise nor reputation will turn into merit, nor will they prolong your life. They will give you neither strength nor good health. If you are able to decide what is useful and what is not, you will discover the benefit of respect and esteem. You may admit that there is no physical advantage but that you derive mental relief. If mental satisfaction is what you seek, why not take to your bed and get drunk? If all you want is temporary relief, you might as well take drugs.

Foolish people give up everything for the sake of fame. To be called heroes they let themselves be killed in battle. What is the use of sacrificing life and wealth for a mere name? People who worry about a decline in their name and fame are like those small children who work hard to construct a sand castle and cry the moment it collapses. Therefore, when someone praises you, do not feel too happy. Name has no essence; fame has no meaning. Attraction to name, fame, and respect will distract you from virtuous activities. For example, monks and nuns study the scriptures. Initially when they join a monastery they are humble. Gradually as they become more educated, they become scholars or

earn the title of *geshe*. They acquire students and followers and completely change. Nowadays, I find that
some teachers who have Western students get very
puffed up. Businesspeople are similar. When they are
successful in business they show it off by wearing
expensive rings and watches. In Tibet, they would wear
expensive earrings. In the long run, of course, earrings
will only tear their ears and are of no other use.

When people who are supposed to be staying high
in the mountains meditating gain a little reputation,
they tend to leave their retreat and come down to the
plains. Initially they may give advice to people about
the need to meditate on impermanence and suffering.
But gradually they themselves forget about these qualities and become inflated with negative qualities like
jealousy and competitiveness. Weak and humble
people, generally speaking, do not deceive and bully
others. It is only in those people who have something
to show off that jealousy and competitiveness arise.
This is why praising ourselves and garnering respect
are very dangerous. They stimulate the arising of
negative qualities. Therefore, it is better to view those
people who always find fault with us as actually protecting us. They prevent us from falling into unfavorable states of existence.

While we labor under the burden of disturbing
emotions and negative actions, why do we need the
additional burden of respect and reputation? Rather
than getting angry with those people who would free us
from the bondage of respect and reputation, we should
value them. We are always bent on entering the path
leading to suffering; then, as if we were blessed by the
Buddha, our enemy comes and closes the door to hell

by damaging the reputation we are so attached to. No fruit can arise without cause, and if the cause exists the fruit will follow. Here the fruitlike result is the practice of patience, while the cause is being harmed by other people. Therefore, patience arises because of the harm inflicted by your enemy. How can you say that such harm represents an obstruction of merit? Patience is possible only because of your enemy. For example, the presence of a beggar provides an opportunity for us to give. How could we call a beggar an obstruction to the practice of generosity?

There are many beggars in the world, so it is easy to practice generosity. But enemies and people who do us harm are generally rare, because if we do not harm other people, they will not normally harm us. This makes the circumstances for practicing patience quite rare. Our enemy provides us with the opportunity to practice patience without our having to harm anyone else, so we can rejoice in the opportunity and appreciate the value of our enemy. The enemy enhances our practice of the path of the bodhisattva because he contributes to the practice of patience.

Patience is extremely important for a bodhisattva, and patience can be developed only because of the presence of the enemy. Since our practice of patience is the result of both our own effort and the presence of the enemy, the resultant merit should first be dedicated to our enemy's happiness. You might say that even though the enemy provokes the practice of patience, it was not his or her intention to do so. He or she did not think, "I will give this person the chance to develop patience." But then why do we express respect for nirvana? Nirvana, the true cessation of suffering, has no intention or motive to benefit the person who achieves it. Why do we regard it as something precious? The enemy becomes your enemy because he or she has an intention to harm you. How could you practice patience if everyone, like a doctor, always tried to help you? It is your enemy who has enabled you to practice patience.

There are two objects in relation to whom we can collect merit. One is sentient beings, and the other is the Buddha. By pleasing the countless sentient beings, we can achieve the purposes of ourselves and others. We can achieve the perfection of positive qualities. Since sentient beings and the Buddhas have contributed equally to the attainment of Buddhahood, why do we show so much respect for the Buddha but ignore and bully sentient beings? The Buddhas, who are our ultimate objects of refuge, bring immeasurable benefit to countless sentient beings. The way to please them is to please sentient beings. There is no other way for us to repay their kindness. For the sake of helpless sentient beings, the Buddhas have given up even their bodies and have even entered into the unceasing suffering of hell. Likewise, bodhisattvas have generated the awakening mind and entered into spiritual practice only for the sake of sentient beings. We will be able to repay their kindness by helping sentient beings ourselves. Therefore, however much harm certain sentient beings may bring us, we should always react positively, trying to do only what will benefit.

In order to carry out those activities that will please the Buddhas, we should regard ourselves as servants to other sentient beings. Even if sentient beings trample on our heads and kill us, we will not retaliate. The Buddhas and bodhisattvas possess great compassion, so there is no doubt that they will look after sentient beings. They have practiced for countless eons for the welfare of sentient beings. Since we are followers of the Buddha, why do we not become the protectors of sentient beings, why do we not pay them respect? This is the best practice to please the Buddhas and bodhisattvas and at the same time fulfill our own temporary and ultimate purposes. In this way all sentient beings, right down to the smallest insects, will become our friends. Wherever we live, the environment will be peaceful and calm. From life to life we will travel from one state of peace to another. Therefore, keeping a low profile, free from pride, and benefiting sentient beings is the best way of fulfilling our own purpose as well.

Normally, we take refuge in the Buddha, Dharma, and Sangha. With great purity of mind we pay our respects before images of the Buddhas and bodhisattvas. But when we see sentient beings, particularly those we think of as enemies, we generate jealousy and competitiveness. There is a great contradiction here. If we know someone we regard as a close friend, someone we love very much, we always try to avoid doing what would displease him or her. For example, you might like hot, spicy food but have a close friend who does not. If you really have regard for your friend when you invite him or her to dinner, you would prepare the food according to his or her taste. On the other hand, if you invite him or her to eat and prepare very hot, spicy food, full of chilis, it is clear that you do not really regard that person as a genuine friend. So it seems that we do not really see the Buddha even as a close friend. His only thought and concern is for the welfare of sentient beings. What do we do? On the one hand we pay respect to the Buddha, but at the same time we completely neglect sentient beings. It is for the sake of sentient beings that the Buddha accumulated merit. It is for the sake of sentient beings that the Buddha generated the awakening mind. It is for the sake of sentient beings that the Buddha became enlightened, while we completely neglect sentient beings. It is unfortunate that in doing so we do not pay the Buddhas even the regard we would show a close friend.

Anger is the force that destroys your virtuous qualities; therefore, you should challenge anger and try to eliminate it. Instead of feeling unhappy and hostile toward your enemy, view him or her as your most cherished spiritual teacher, who teaches you the practice of patience. Normally we regard retaliating against our enemy as something worthy. Even from a legal point of view, you have a right to defend yourself. However, if you are trying to cultivate the awakening mind from the depth of your heart, you try to cultivate a strong positive mental attitude wishing to benefit sentient beings. Consequently, if you are able to cultivate a strong sense of compassion and loving-kindness toward your enemy, you will be able to generate similar loving-kindness and compassion toward all sentient beings.

It is like removing a huge stone that has been blocking the flow of water in a canal. Once you remove the stone, the water immediately starts to flow. Similarly, once you are able to cultivate loving-kindness and compassion toward your enemy, you will easily be able to cultivate loving-kindness and compassion toward all sentient beings. Therefore, if you are able to see the enemy as the supreme basis of the practice of patience, and if you are able to generate a stronger kind of compassion in relation to your enemy, this indicates success in your practice. By pleasing sentient beings we will not only be able ultimately to attain Buddhahood; even in this life we will earn a good reputation and find peace and happiness. We will make more friends. We will have no enemies. Life will be relaxed. While we remain wandering in the cycle of existence, as a result of practicing patience over many lives, we will have an attractive physical form. We will live a long life free from sickness, and we will attain the peace of the ruler of the universe.

We have found this precious human life and have met with the teaching of the Buddha. We have understood the advantages of the practice of patience and the disadvantages of anger. Whether or not we have the capacity to practice it now, at least we have understood that what has been explained is reasonable. Therefore, let us always follow this path, which guarantees peace, both now and in the future.

from Four Essential Buddhist Commentaries

by *the Dalai Lama*

Thirty-Seven Bodhisattva Practices was written by a 14th-century Tibetan monk and is one of the most widely taught texts in the Tibetan Buddhist tradition. Here the Dalai Lama offers his teaching on the work.

S o now set a Bodhichitta motivation to listen to these teachings. It is "Thirty-seven Bodhisattva Practices" by Thogmey zangpo and is divided into three parts, the beginning, the actual discussion and the end. The actual discussion is divided into the three levels of motivation, as explained in the "Lam-rim", the "Graded Path".

(1) "At this time when we have obtained a fully endowed human rebirth of liberties and endowments difficult to find, a Bodhisattvas' practice is to listen, think and

meditate unwaveringly day and night in order to free ourselves and others from the ocean of cyclic existence."

Dharma is a system of methods to make an
unpeaceful and an untamed one tamed. All of us are
equal in wanting happiness and not any suffering, and
Dharma is what brings this about. But people do not
know how to practise it. If we look at our human body,
although we might think of it merely in terms of its
being in the category or lineage of our parents, if we
look more profoundly we see that it is in the category
of having liberty and endowments. Liberty means
freedom to practise Dharma, and look at us here. We
do have the freedom to come here and to practise
Dharma, don't we? We are not deaf, we are not missing
various faculties that would prevent us from hearing
the teachings and so on. We have all the conducive
conditions for practice and whatever is nonconducive
is not here. We have, in fact, eight liberties and ten
endowments.

Many people in the world have a human birth but
few have the independence and freedom to practise the
Dharma. We are very fortunate therefore to have such a
rare opportunity. Also there are spiritual teachers
available and present in the world, following the
example of the Buddha and carrying on his deeds.
These are good effects we are experiencing now which
have resulted from causes similar to them in the past.
In other words, our good fortune now must be from
virtuous causes we have previously enacted and therefore to obtain such opportunities and such a working
basis once more in the future, we must accumulate the
virtuous causes for this now. If we act without attachment, aversion or closed-minded ignorance, it will not

be difficult to accumulate virtuous causes for a precious human rebirth in the future. But in fact as we
rarely act this way, we must take as much advantage of
the present opportunity as we can. Never be discouraged or feel inadequate. We must practise as much
virtue as we can.

A virtuous or a tamed mind is not something we can
buy in a store, plant in a field or obtain from a bank.
It comes from the actual practice of taming our mind.
We must practise in order to receive glimpses of
insight, lasting realisations and various experiences.
Thus we must follow the examples of the great teachers
of the past. In Tibet there were first the great Nyingma
Lamas, then after there were Atisha and the Kadam
lineage, the Sakya Lamas, Marpa, Milarepa and Gam-
popa of the Kagyu lineage and so on. All of them
underwent great difficulties and by exerting tremendous efforts became enlightened. It is just up to us to
follow their example. We should examine ourselves and
ask: "What progress have I made in the last five years,
the last ten, the last fifteen years in taming my mind?"
If we can see that we have indeed made a little improvement then this can encourage us. Do not be proud, or
anything like that, but if we realise that over five or ten
years we can progress a little then we will not be discouraged over short periods of time.

The actual practice is to hear, think and meditate
about the teachings. But when we hear teachings or
study them, we should always check our attitude about
them. Whatever we hear we should immediately put
into practice. We should never have our practice of
hearing, thinking and meditating be separate from
each other or have any of them missing.

(2) "A Bodhisattvas' practice is to leave our homeland, where desire for our friends shakes us up like water, anger towards enemies burns us like fire and the closed-minded ignorance of forgetting what is to be adopted and abandoned cloaks us in darkness."

Best is to leave our country, but even if we do not or cannot, we should not have attachment or aversion over it. Do not think, "This is my country, my family," as though there were a findable, inherently existent country for which we could have attachment or hatred of its enemies. Attachment and aversion bring much non-virtue and suffering. These two are the chief of all our delusions and both come from ignorance. But even if we leave our country and go to another, make new friends and then develop attachments and aversions there, this will not do. This is no good. The main point is to abandon attachment and aversion and replace it with an attitude of wishing to help everyone. If there are people to whom we feel attracted and for whom we have attachment, then with just a slight change in their behaviour all of a sudden we hate them. But if, instead, we have an attitude of love and compassion to help these persons, then even if they behave badly we will still wish for them to be happy. Thus, we must replace our attachment with an attitude of wishing to help others.

Most of us here have left our country, but there is nothing wonderful or extraordinary about that if we still have attachment and aversion. We must abandon these.

(3) "A Bodhisattvas' practice is to rely on seclusion where, by abandoning negative objects our delusions gradually become stymied, by lacking distractions our

virtuous practices naturally increase, and by clearing up our awareness our certainty grows in the Dharma."

If we are away from those who disturb us and we do not have a head full of busy work, then automatically we turn to virtue more easily. Therefore it is most helpful to live in seclusion and quietude. But to be able to meditate in solitude we need the full force of having heard and thought about the teachings, and this without any attachment or aversion. Thus we have attained a precious human rebirth and now we must use it properly and not lose this opportunity because it is impermanent. We must turn away then from our obsessive concern with mainly this life, as it says in "The Three Principal Paths". If we put our main emphasis on future lives, then things will go well in this life also. But if all our emphasis is on this life, it will not help our future lives at all. Therefore we must turn from being only involved in this life and work to improve our future ones. To do this we must think about impermanence.

(4) "A Bodhisattvas' practice is to give up total concern with this lifetime in which friends and relations a long time together must part their own ways, wealth and possessions gathered with effort must be left behind, and our consciousness, the guest, must depart from our body, its guest house."

If we look at world history, no one in the Three Realms has lived forever. Look at the great places of the past, Nalanda, where great Atisha and others flourished. Now only its ruins are left, but this helps to show us impermanence. Look at the customs and so forth of Tibet of the past. These circumstances are past, they are impermanent and have finished. A hundred years from now it is certain that none of us here will be alive. Our mind-stream of mere awareness and clarity will have gone on; the existence of past and future lifetimes is for certain. But what we experience now will not— our wealth, our prosperity, all of these things which have come from causes in past lifetimes. No matter how close we are with others, our family and so on, we will all have to part and go our own ways. Those who have accumulated virtue will experience happiness; those who haven't, will not. The continuity of the mere "I" labelled on the subtle energy and consciousness goes on for sure and thus we shall experience the fruits of the actions we commit now. Therefore it is crucial what we do.

When we die, we all go alone. Even the Dalai Lama, when he dies, has to go alone. When Mao Tse-tung died, he went alone. Jiang Qing did not accompany him, nor did his masses. All his fame while alive did not help him at all. We can see what happened afterwards. Even such a great man as Mahatma Gandhi went alone. He had to leave his staff, his sandals, his round wire glasses behind. We can see them in his memorial; he has taken nothing along. External material possessions, friends, relatives, nothing helps, not even the body we have received from our parents. As Ghungthang Rinpoche explained, we all have to go alone.

Look at us Tibetans, look at yourselves. Even if we are in such difficult times, we are still human and when we die there is no certainty that we will be human again. If we do not make some progress now while we are human what can we do later in another lifetime not as a human. Now, of course, we have to eat. Except for great beings

who live on single-minded concentration, all of us have
to eat solid meals. So obviously we have to plant food
and do things for this lifetime. But we should not have
this to be our total obsession. We should devote
maybe 30% of our time to this lifetime and 70% to
the future, or better 50/50. But the main point is
not to be totally involved with this life alone.

(5) "A Bodhisattvas' practice is to abandon bad friends
with whom, when we associate, our three poisonous
attitudes increase, our actions of listening, thinking
and meditating decrease and our love and compassion
turn to nil."

We must think then mostly of our future lives and to
do so we need friends. They are important because they
influence us very much. Even if our own hearing and
thinking of teachings is quite meagre their good
example can influence us to do more. It is important
then to have friends of the same disposition as ourselves. Why? Because as it says in the verse, bad friends
or misleading ones can harm us by their company,
therefore we must abandon them. But of course this
means that we should still have love for them; just stay
out of their influence.

(6) "A Bodhisattvas' practice is to cherish more than
our own body our holy, spiritual teachers by devoting
ourselves to whom our faults become eliminated and our
good qualities come to increase like the waxing moon."

If we have positive-minded friends and keep the
good company of Gurus or Spiritual Teachers, they
exert the best influence on us. Of course we need a
Guru who suits us, but even if such a person is pleasing

to our mind, he must be fully qualified. We Tibetans have Tulkus or Incarnate Lamas with famous names, but they must be fully qualified otherwise it is meaningless. Therefore we should put aside the person's title as a Tulku and check his own personal qualifications. If he is fully qualified then he is a Guru or a Lama. But many Tulkus in fact are not Lamas. They have no qualifications, even though they might have a very large estate and a great deal of wealth. Money, a big name and fame, however, do not make someone a Lama. Therefore we must check their actual qualifications, their studies and so forth. Such careful scrutiny is extremely important. Buddha emphasised it, as did Je-Tzong-kha-pa. Guru-devotion between disciples and their Spiritual Teachers is extremely crucial. If the Guru is fully qualified then we can fully entrust ourselves to him and do whatever he says, as was the case with Naropa and Tilopa. If Tilopa told him to jump, Naropa did so without hesitation. But if he is not such a person, we should not just do anything that just anyone tells us. We do not go out and jump off this stupa monument simply because some fool tells us to do that, do we?

The main point is for us beginners to have a firm basis or foundation in moral discipline upon which we can build. The way we Tibetans practise is very good. We have a basis of morality, on top of which we have the Mahayana practice of love and compassion. Then at the peak we have the practice of tantra, and this is of all four of its classes. In fact, we Tibetans are the only Buddhists who practise the entire path of the Buddha's teachings and this on the basis of one person practising it all. In Thailand, Burma and Sri Lanka, for instance, they have only the discipline part and lack the Mahayana as well as the tantras. In Japan, Korea and some other places where there is Mahayana, they have the tantras but only the first three classes: kriya, charya and yoga. They have nothing of anuttarayoga tantra, the fourth class. Some places have a view of Voidness but only that of the Chittamatra or of the Yogacharya Svatantrika systems and not the Prasangika view. Some places seem to have Mahayana with no basis of discipline and others even try to have Tantrayana with both of the other two missing. It is only among the Tibetans that we have the full, entire path and practice incorporated into one person, and this person should be each of us ourselves.

(7) "A Bodhisattvas' practice is to take refuge in the Precious Gems by seeking protection from whom we are never deceived—since who can worldly gods protect when they themselves are still bound in the prison of cyclic existence."

This brings us to refuge, and when we do so we must be mindful of the good qualities of the Three Jewels of Refuge. The word for Buddha in Tibetan is "Sangyay". "Sang" means to eliminate everything that is to be abandoned, to eliminate all faults, and "gyay" means to realise and achieve all good qualities. The Sanskrit word "Dharma" means to hold, to hold one back from what is non-conducive. In other words, following the Dharma holds us back from suffering. Actually, the Dharma Refuge refers to the Noble Truths of Cessation and the Path. The cessation of the fleeting taints over our mind, their dissolution into the pure sphere of Voidness, is a true cessation. The pathlike minds that have bare perception of Voidness are true paths.

These two are the Dharma Refuge. The Sangha Refuge refers to Aryas or Noble Ones, those who have such bare perception of Voidness. Thus these are the Three Jewels of Refuge. Buddha is like a doctor, Dharma is like medicine or, more precisely, the path of the cure and the state of being cured are like the Noble Truths of the Path and Cessation, and the Sangha are like nurses to help.

We all dislike suffering, from the slightest discomfort upwards, and we wish liberation from it. Its state of elimination and the methods to eliminate it are like the Dharma Refuge. We need a teacher of this process and this is the Buddha Refuge, and friends to help, which is the Sangha Refuge. Furthermore, we need to be confident in the refuge objects' ability to give us protection, plus we need to have fear or dread of suffering and the desire for relief. These act as the causes for taking refuge. As Buddha taught a way to eliminate the cause of suffering such that its cessation will come about, he is worthy of being an object of refuge. We have met with the teachings of such a Buddha and thus we must take refuge. We have a resultant refuge, which we can take in our future attainment of the cessation of suffering and Enlightenment, and a causal refuge in the Three Jewels now to bring us to this state. Therefore all of you please take refuge.

Look at all the people around you, whether they are close or distant, rich or poor, all of us are equal in wanting happiness and no suffering. The best way to accomplish this is the practice of Dharma. We have a fully endowed human body and have met with the complete teachings of discipline, Mahayana and tantra and have likewise met with well-qualified Gurus. Therefore we must set a full Mahayana motivation to eliminate all our delusions, attain all good qualities and reach Enlightenment. The basic point is to develop a warm and kind heart. This is the root of all happiness for ourselves and others, both superficially and ultimately. It is the root of Bodhichitta which brings us Enlightenment and thus the ability to bring happiness to everyone. Therefore as much as we can we should develop a kind heart. Do not just say words like "May I develop a kind heart." What we have to do is actually train and practise in the stages to attain it. We must know the methods and then put them into practice. The full teachings are found in the 100 volumes of the Kangyur and the 200 of the Tengyur commentaries by the Indian masters. The main Lama who brought the full Lam-rim stages of training the mind to Tibet was Atisha, and his "Bodhipathapradipa", or "Lamp, for the Path to Enlightenment", is the root source of this text, "Thirty-Seven Bodhisattva Practices". As it is short and easy to understand, we should try to memorise and then often recite it, thinking of the meaning, and put it into practice.

Now listen to the teachings on this text. First we must recognise the precious human body and think to take advantage of it. As it is certain that we will die and lose it, we must turn from our obsession with this life and eventually turn from that with future lives as well. To do so we should initially think about death and impermanence and that when we die we can be reborn in one of the three lower realms. We cannot see the hell beings or hungry ghosts but we know about the animals and their sufferings. We see how they are abused, beaten, exploited for their labour, used cruelly in medical experiments, sacrificed for their meat, and so forth. In Buddhism we must develop kindness for them. In other religions they feel killing animals is not much different from chopping down a tree or picking a vegetable, but in Buddhism it is different. We actually look at and take their suffering seriously and consider how we could easily be reborn as one of them.

The person who teaches the path of how to avoid being reborn as an animal is the Fully Enlightened Buddha. He taught the path of cause and effect, of what actions are to be abandoned and which are to be practised. We should try to learn as much as we can of the Buddha's perfect teachings, for they are without any faults and they offer a total refuge. As we were saying yesterday, the Buddha, Dharma and Sangha are the Three Jewels of Refuge. Only these three offer a never-failing refuge and protection. Although there is no fault in going to worldly gods for help as friends, it is improper to seek our ultimate refuge in them.

Look at the monks in the monasteries of Thailand and Burma; they are really excellent. In their temples they have only representations of the Buddha Sakyamuni and no one else. In Tibetan temples we may have a picture of Buddha Sakyamuni but also there are various exotic-looking protectors and so forth. In Japan there are pictures of just the main teachers and almost no representations of Sakyamuni Buddha. Of course there is the fact of the Buddha's being inseparable from the Gurus and appearing in many forms, but this is something different. The point is that the main one to whom we should turn for blessings and virtuous conduct is the Buddha Sakyamuni. Often people criticise us and say that we Tibetans forget about the Buddha and just beat drums before pictures of protectors. There is much danger in this, so be careful. But enough on this point.

Concerning the Sangha Refuge, the practice in Thailand and Burma also is excellent. The monks are treated with great respect and are supported by the householders and given alms. This is excellent. Often people feel that there are actually only two Jewels of Refuge, the Buddha and the Dharma, and that the Sangha is unnecessary. We can forget about them. There is no need, of course, for everyone to be monks and nuns, but we should check our own disposition and if it suits us, being ordained is best. But at least never criticise monks and nuns. We should examine and criticise only ourselves. The Sangha is very important for setting examples and for symbolising the Buddha's teachings. We must be very careful about our own karma and about what we say and do.

(8) "A Bodhisattvas' practice is never to commit any negative actions even at the cost of our life, because the Sage Buddha has said that the extremely difficult to endure sufferings of the unfortunate rebirths are the result of negative actions."

In short, if we do good, good comes from it and if we do bad, bad comes from it. It is very simple. The effect follows in the same category as the cause. It never fails and moreover, from small causes we can experience extensive results. In countries as well, any horrible conditions that happen come from past karmic debts due to negative actions. In Tibet for instance, we sometimes have drought, our crops fail, sometimes there are wars, invasions and so forth. All of these are due to our lack of merit and past negative actions. If we do not have any merit then no matter what we do it will not bring about good conditions. Therefore we should always wish for others' happiness. Like concerning the Chinese, we can only wish them well. We should not wish that bad things befall them. What they experience will be the results of their own actions.

Negative behaviour comes from our delusions and from these we collect black karmic debts which bring us nothing but suffering. Negative actions can be of body, speech or mind. An example for one of the body would be, for instance, killing, which is taking the life of anything from a human down to an insect. It is very bad to kill, so we should refrain ourselves as much as we can. All beings have an equal right to life and cherish their life as much as we do. If we prick our finger with a thorn, we say "Ouch, I hurt". Everybody feels exactly the same, all beings. It is especially terrible to sacrifice animals; they do that in some lands. In the past they did this in Kinnaur and Spiti and some places in Nepal and even in certain districts in Tibet. Superficially the people there take refuge in me, the Dalai Lama, and then sacrifice animals. This is very bad. Saying the mantra of compassion "Om mani padme hum" and yet sacrificing, that will never, never do.

Next is stealing. This also is very negative. Sexual misconduct is to have relations with another person's spouse, or with someone who has a relation with someone else, and not seeing anything wrong in so doing. When we look at the historical literature, most of the various discords and fights in royal families came from sexual misconduct. It is very destructive. Next is lying. This, too, is extremely negative. Of course to lie to protect someone's life is something else, but we should always be honest. If we lie, it brings only unhappiness. We sit in fear that somebody is going to find us out. That always makes for a very uneasy mind, doesn't it? Next is divisive language, causing others to be unfriendly and apart. We hear bad things about someone and then spread it; this is very destructive. We must try to bring other people together When people live and work together, their harmony is based on their mutual confidence. When we look at the Chinese, for instance, they speak of everybody as being comrades, but this is only at the discussion table. Outside they will not even share a bar of soap with each other. This is because they have no confidence, they do not trust one another. And this comes from causing divisiveness among others. Therefore never use divisive language.

Next is abusive language, calling other people bad names like "beggar" and so forth. It hurts them, it does not bring happiness at all. Gossip is chattering always meaningless things; it is a complete waste of time. Then there is covetous thought. Someone else has something nice which we would like, and we walk along directing all our attention at this object and wishing only to have it. If we are not careful we will walk right into a wall! Ill-will is next. This is also very bad. It just makes us unhappy. It usually does not hurt the other person, it hurts only ourselves. It is very self-destructive to hold grudges and to wish others ill. We can never solve problems by holding a grudge. Problems can only be solved through compassion, love and patience so never harbour ill-will. Next is distorted views, denying what exists or making up something which does not.

These ten then, from killing to holding distorted views, are the ten negative actions. We should realise their disadvantages and refrain from them. The actual practice then is, from seeing their drawbacks, to refrain ourselves, with enthusiasm and conscious effort, from killing, lying and so forth. Even if we cannot refrain completely we should try to lessen them as much as we can. This is what follows from taking refuge.

Now comes the teaching for a person on the intermediate level of motivation.

(9) "A Bodhisattvas' practice is to work with keen interest for the supreme, never-changing state of Liberation, as the pleasures of the Three Realms are phenomena that perish in a moment, all at once, like dew on the tips of grass."

No matter where we are born in the Three Realms, it is like merely being on different floors of a burning building. Everywhere is suffering, so we must by all means attain liberation from it. Samsara, or cyclic existence refers to the suffering contaminated aggregates that we receive from karma and delusions. We should think about this. Although we have a precious human rebirth, yet if we are under the power of karma and delusions and have no independence, we can only create more suffering. Therefore, we must try to free ourselves from these repeating syndromes. Whatever worldly pleasures we have are not ultimate. They are merely superficial and only temporary. We can fall to a lower rebirth at any time.

If our suffering comes from our very own aggregate physical and mental faculties, which are under the power of karma and delusions, then where can we run from our contaminated aggregates? Think about that. If our own aggregates themselves are in the nature of suffering, how can we escape them? The source of suffering is our delusions, the main ones of which are attachment and aversion. These both come from ignorance, the ignorance of grasping for inherent existence, but this is a distorted view. On the other hand, by cultivating the opponent for this, namely the opposite view, that inherent existence does not exist, and by accustoming ourselves to it, then the more familiar we are with it, the less will be our ignorance. The stains of ignorance over the mind are fleeting; they can be removed. The ignorance of grasping for inherent existence and the understanding of the lack of inherent existence are both aimed at the same object. Thus when we have one we cannot have the other at the same time. It is in this way that the discriminating awareness or wisdom of Voidness acts as the opponent to ignorance. With this wisdom we eliminate attachment and aversion and thus gain liberation from suffering.

Some people say that attachment and aversion or hostility are the nature of the mind and that it is almost as if a person is not alive if he does not have such feelings. But if these were the nature of the mind, then just as is the case when we accept mere awareness and clarity as its nature, these feelings of attachment and hostility should be present all the time. But we see that anger can be quelled, it does not last forever. Thus it is a mistaken view to feel that it is a natural part of life and the nature of the mind to have attachment and aversion.

We need discriminating awareness or wisdom then to see the two levels of truth, that ultimately all is void of inherent existence, yet on a conventional level dependent arising is never false. This is the training in higher wisdom and for it we need the training in higher concentration as its base in order not to have any mental wandering and so forth. For this we need the training in higher discipline, either as an ordained person or even as a householder. For instance there are the householder vows, the five lay vows, and it is important at least to keep these. Thus we need the practice of the three higher trainings.

Next are the teachings for a person on the advanced level of motivation.

(10) "A Bodhisattvas' practice is to develop an Enlightened Motive of Bodhichitta in order to liberate limitless sentient beings because if our mothers, who have been kind to us from beginningless time, are suffering, what can we do with just our own happiness."

All sentient beings, as widespread as space, wish for happiness and no suffering, the same as we do. They are so numerous and if we ignore them and think only of our own purpose, it is pathetic, not to mention unfair. We should place ourselves on one side and all other beings on the other. We all wish happiness and not suffering; the only difference is that we are one and they are numberless. So who could see it as fair or reasonable to favour one over everybody else? Bodhisattvas work and wish only for other people's happiness. There is no need to mention that of course they achieve Enlightenment, but besides that, while on the path they do not become unhappy. The harder they work for others and the more they ignore themselves, the happier they become, which then encourages them to work even harder. But if we work only for our own purposes and ignore others, all we obtain is unhappiness, dissatisfaction and discouragement. It is funny it is like that. So we must try to lessen our selfishness and increase our concern for others as much as we can and by so doing we will find that, on the side, we will be a happier person.

If we are working only for the purpose of others then, as is described in "Engaging in the Bodhisattvas' Conduct", we will never be afraid where or in what conditions we might be reborn. Wherever we find ourselves we will work there for the sake of helping others. The same is emphasised in "The Precious Garland" by Nagarjuna. To work only for the sake of others and ignore our own purposes is the way to attain Buddhahood. We say we are Mahayanists, but as Je Tzong-kha-pa has said, we must have a Mahayana personality in order to be considered a Mahayanist. Therefore we must work for the sake of others. If we look around for ways to be helpful and if we develop an Enlightened Motive of Bodhichitta, then automatically things will work out to benefit everyone. So as much as we can we should follow the Mahayana training and practice. Understand?

Now what is a Bodhisattva? Similar to what was explained about the word "Buddha", the first syllable of the Tibetan for "Bodhi" is "Jhang" which means to eliminate faults, while the second, "chub", means to attain all good qualities. Actually there are two "Bodhis" or states of Perfection and what is being referred to here is not the lesser one of the Arhats but the higher one of a Buddha's Enlightenment. "Sattva" means one who has his mind aimed at this attainment of Bodhi or Perfection, to benefit all. Thus we need two aims together. We need to be aimed at sentient beings in order to benefit them and to be aimed at Enlightenment to be able to do that. That is Bodhichitta and this is what we must develop. How do we do that?

(11) "A Bodhisattvas' practice is to purely exchange our own happiness for the suffering of others because all our sufferings come from desiring our own happiness, while a fully Enlightened Buddha is born from the attitude of wishing others well."

How does all suffering come from wishing only our own happiness? Such a self-centred wish leads us to commit much non-virtue in order to accomplish our selfish aims and as a result we experience suffering. Buddhahood, on the other hand, comes from helping others. Therefore we have to exchange our attitude and instead of wishing for our own happiness and ignoring others' suffering, we should wish only for others' happiness and ignore ourselves. To do this we train in the practice known as "taking and giving", namely taking on others' suffering and giving them our happiness. To help us do this there is a very good and useful visualisation. We should visualise ourselves in our ordinary form on the right, selfish and wishing only our own happiness. On the left visualise infinite, numberless living beings all wanting happiness. Then we should stand back in our mind as a witness and judge: "Which is more important, this selfish person here or all the others?" Think which side we would favour and which would we want to join, the side of the selfish person or that of all these pathetic beings who equally deserve happiness? Such practice like this and others mentioned in "Engaging in the Bodhisattvas' Conduct" are very beneficial.

(12) "A Bodhisattvas' practice is, even if someone under the power of great desire steals or causes others to steal all our wealth, to dedicate to him our body, wealth and virtues of the three times."

Now we have developed Bodhichitta. But to attain Enlightenment we must engage in the Bodhisattva actions. If someone steals from us there is the danger of becoming angry. But if we are practising to attain Enlightenment and are giving away everything to others, then this so-called thief already owns our former possessions. He has taken them now because in fact they already are his. Thus we should dedicate to him not only these possessions that he has taken or which we think he has stolen from us, but even further our body and virtues of the three times.

(13) "A Bodhisattvas' practice is, even if while we have not the slightest fault ourselves, someone were to chop off our heads, to accept on ourselves these black karmic debts with the power of compassion."

If others harm us we must have compassion towards them and accept on ourselves all these harms of others.

(14) "A Bodhisattvas' practice, is, even if someone were to publicise throughout the billion worlds all sorts of unpleasant things about us, to speak in return about their good qualities with an attitude of love."

When others abuse or say bad things about us, we must never return it. Never say nasty things back, but only speak kindly of them, as it says in "Engaging in the Bodhisattvas' Conduct".

(15) "A Bodhisattvas' practice is, even if someone exposes our faults or says foul words about us in the midst of a crowd of many beings, to bow to him respect-fully, recognising him as our teacher."

Even if others humiliate or embarrass us in front of others, we should act as taught in the training of the mind. If others disgrace us or point out our faults, they are in fact our teachers. Thus we should thank them for making us aware of our shortcomings and show them great respect.

(16) "A Bodhisattvas' practice is, even if someone whom we have raised and cherished like our own child, were to regard us as his enemy, to have special loving kindness for him like a mother towards her child stricken with an illness."

If a child is naughty when he is ill, no matter how bad he is, his mother would still love him. This is the way we should view all beings.

(17) "A Bodhisattvas' practice is, even if someone our equal or inferior were to try to demean us out of the power of his pride, to receive him on the crown of our head respectively, like a Guru."

The same is true when others try to compete with us. We must develop patience. As it says in "Engaging in the Bodhisattvas' Conduct", if we had no enemies we could not develop patience. Thus we need someone annoying towards whom to develop a tolerant attitude. We cannot develop patience with our mind aimed at our Guru or at a Buddha. We need an enemy at whom to aim it. For instance, I think about myself. If someone writes in the newspaper or calls the Dalai Lama a weak refugee and so on, if I am practising sincerely I try to develop patience with him. Since we need a teacher to help train us in patience, an enemy or someone who hates us is very important as this teacher. If we think more about it, enemies are extremely important, aren't they? If we are practising Mahayana we must cultivate patience and endure difficult situations, but how can we really practise Mahayana without enemies? In short, to exchange our attitudes concerning self and others we need many trials and tribulations, many trying situations. Therefore enemies or people who are very annoying and difficult are extremely important and precious.

(18) "A Bodhisattvas' practice is, even if we are destitute in our livelihood and always abused by people, sick with terrible diseases or afflicted by ghosts, to accept on ourselves the sufferings of all beings and not be discouraged."

There are two very difficult situations for Dharma practice. One is when, due to past causes, we are in very difficult straits, poor and so on. Then we become discouraged. The other is if we are extremely comfortable and rich and then we become prideful and arrogant. We must be careful in both cases. If we are very sick, for instance, then if we practise exchanging self with others and also taking and giving, we will become very happy that we are sick. In fact, we will wish to take on the sicknesses and suffering of others.

(19) "A Bodhisattvas' practice is, even we are sweetly praised, bowed to with their heads by many beings, or

have obtained riches like those of the children of the Lord of Wealth, never to be conceited by seeing that worldly prosperity has no essence."

This is the other extreme, the other crucial situations. If we are very well-esteemed and everything goes well for us, we can become very prideful about that, lazy and arrogant. As this blocks our practice, we must see that such worldly good fortune has no essence at all.

(20) "A Bodhisattvas' practice is to tame our own mind-stream with the martial arts of love and compassion because, if we do not subdue the enemy which is our own hostility, then even if we have subdued an external enemy, more will come."

There is no enemy worse than anger. If we look at the world, like for instance the situation of World War Two, we can see that it all came about because of anger and hatred. At that time the Western nations and Russia were allies and even though they won the war that did not conquer their own hostility! As they are now still left with this poison, we find the Soviet Union pitted against the West as enemies. If war comes again in the future, it will occur once more because of anger and hatred. But if we wish peace and happiness, this can never come about without the elimination of these negative attitudes. Peace and happiness will come only if we develop love and compassion. Therefore we must train in the martial art of love to overcome hatred.

(21) "A Bodhisattvas' practice is immediately to abandon whatever objects cause our attachment and desires to increase, for objects of our desire are like salt

water, the more we indulge in them our thirst for them increases in turn."

No matter what we are attracted to we are never satisfied with it, we never have enough. It is like drinking salt water, we are never quenched as is described in "The Precious Garland". Think of an example, for instance, like when we have a rash. If we scratch it, it feels nice, but if we are attached to that nice feeling, then the more we scratch, it just makes it worse. It gets sore, it starts to bleed, becomes infected and is a mess. The best thing is to cure the rash from its base so that we will have no desire to scratch it at all.

(22) "A Bodhisattvas' practice is not to apply ourselves mentally to any signs of takers of objects and objects taken, by realising that however things appear, they are from our own mind and that the nature of mind is, from the beginning, free of extremes of fabricated modes of existence."

This seems to be Svatantrika vocabulary, but that is not necessarily so. When it says here that these appearances are "from our own mind", this means that they are the play of our mind in the sense that the karma accumulated through our mind brings about all appearances. The mind itself, from the beginning, is free of extremes of inherent existence. If we understand this, then we will not apply our mind to considering that this is the consciousness that understands Voidness and that is the object of this consciousness, namely Voidness, Rather we will simply place our mind in meditative equipoise on the pure, non-affirming negation which is Voidness. This is the practice that is outlined here.

(23) "A Bodhisattvas' practice is to abandon attachment and desire through, when we meet with a pleasing object, not regarding it as truly existent even though it appears beautifully, like a summer's rainbow."

Although things appear beautifully like a rainbow, we should see that they are void of inherent existence and not be attached.

(24) "A Bodhisattvas' practice is, at the time when meeting with adverse conditions, to see them as deceptive, for various types of suffering are like the death of our child in a dream and to take such deceptive appearances to be true is a tiresome waste."

Thus, we should see everything as deceptive appearances and not be depressed by difficult conditions.

These are the teachings on developing Bodhichitta. Next is the practice of the perfections.

(25) "A Bodhisattvas' practice is to give generously without hope for anything in return or something to ripen because, if those who would wish Enlightenment must give away even their body what need to mention our own external possessions."

This is the practice of generosity.

(26) "A Bodhisattvas' practice is to safeguard morality without worldly intents because, if we cannot fulfil our own aims without moral discipline, to wish to fulfil the aims of others is a joke."

Most important is to have moral discipline, especially the discipline of refraining from negative actions. Without it, how can we help anyone?

• • •

(27) "A Bodhisattvas' practice is to meditate on patience, without anger or resentment for anyone because, for a Bodhisattva wishing to make use of virtue, all those who do harm are the same as treasures of great gems."

We need much patience. For a Bodhisattva wishing to create the merit to be able to attain Enlightenment, those who do harm, our enemies, are as precious as gems because with them we can practise patience. This brings about a collection of merit which will bring about our Enlightenment.

(28) "A Bodhisattvas' practice is to exert joyous effort, the source of good qualities for the sake of all beings, as we see the effort of Shravakas and Pratyekabuddhas who, in working only for their own sake, are not swayed even if their heads were to be in flames."

This refers to exerting enthusiastic perseverance with joyous effort. If the Hinayana practitioners can work so hard to attain their goal for themselves, then we as Mahayanists working for the sake of all must work even harder.

(29) "A Bodhisattvas' practice is to meditate on meditative concentration which surpasses the four formless absorptions, by realising that penetrative insight possessing perfect mental quiescence can destroy the delusions completely."

This refers to the perfection of meditative concentration and here in the sutra context. Thus in order to be able to realise penetrative insight or "vipashyana", we need to have beforehand mental quiescence, or "samatha", to hold it. Then we will have inseparable mental quiescence and penetrative insight.

(30) "A Bodhisattvas' practice is to meditate on wisdom which possesses methods and has no conceptions about the inherent existence of the three spheres, because without wisdom the five perfections cannot bring us complete Enlightenment."

We cannot attain Enlightenment with only the method side, namely the first five perfections alone. We need the wisdom aspect as well. Thus we must cultivate inseparable method and wisdom with which we see that the three spheres of any virtuous action of these perfections, namely the action, the actor and the act itself, and all avoid of inherent existence.

Next concerns the Bodhisattvas' daily practice.

(31) "A Bodhisattvas' practice is continually to examine our own mistakes and abandon them because, if we do not examine our own mistakes ourselves, it is possible that with a Dharmic external form we can commit something non-Dharmic."

In other words, we must always check our own delusions each day, because as it says here it is quite possible externally to appear to be proper but in fact not to be proper at all.

(32) "A Bodhisattvas' practice is not to say that any person who has entered the Mahayana Great Vehicle has any faults because, if under the power of delusions we find fault with someone else who is a Bodhisattva, we ourselves will get the worst."

We should never look at others with the idea of trying to pick or find faults in them. We never know who others might be or what their attainment is. Especially as a Mahayana practitioner we should only have thoughts of helping and benefiting others, not faulting them.

(33) "A Bodhisattvas' practice is to abandon attachment to homes of relatives and friends and homes of patrons because, under the power of wanting gain and respect, we will fight with each other and our activities of hearing, thinking and meditating will decline."

There is much danger if we always stay in the homes of patrons, relatives and so forth. We inevitably become entangled in very complicated situations of arguments, disputes and so on. Therefore we should avoid attachment to such places.

(34) "A Bodhisattvas' practice is to abandon harsh language displeasing to the minds of others because harsh words disturb others' minds and cause our ways of Bodhisattva behaviour to decline."

The root of anger is attachment to our own side. But here the anger itself is stressed especially when it leads to abusive language. Such harsh sounding words destroy our merit, disturb others and cause great harm.

(35) "A Bodhisattvas' practice is to have the soldiers of mindfulness and alertness hold the opponent weapons and forcefully to destroy delusions like attachment and so forth as soon as they first arise because, when we are habituated to delusions, it is difficult for opponents to reverse them."

As soon as attachment or aversion arises, we should immediately employ mindfulness and awareness to oppose them.

(36) "In short, a Bodhisattvas' practice is to work for others' purposes by continually possessing mindfulness and alertness to know, no matter what our activity, how we are acting and further how is the condition of our minds."

As it says in "Engaging in the Bodhisattvas' Conduct" we must continually examine our mind and see its condition. Then with mindfulness we should immediately apply the various opponents to any delusions. For instance, if we were on a caravan and reached the northern plateau of Tibet, we would be very mindful not to go just anywhere but would choose the correct path very carefully. In the same way, we should not allow our mind to go just anywhere.

(37) "A Bodhisattvas' practice is, with the wisdom that purifies the three spheres, to dedicate for Enlightenment, in order to eliminate the suffering of limitless beings, the virtue realised by these efforts."

Thus, the last Bodhisattva practice mentioned here is to dedicate the merit of all these actions. This completes the actual body of the text and next is the third part of the outline, the conclusion.

"Having followed the words of the holy beings and the meaning of what has been spoken in the sutras, tantras and treatises, I have arranged these thirty-seven Bodhisattva practices for those who wish to train in the Bodhisattvas' path."

The author has taken these teachings from various sources and condensed them into these thirty-seven practices.

"Because my intelligence is feeble and my learning small, I may not have written this in a poetic fashion that would please the erudite. But because I have relied on the sutras and the words of the holy ones, I believe these are unmistakenly a Bodhisattvas' practice."

Next the author apologises if he has committed any faults.

"But since it is difficult for someone dull-witted like myself to fathom the depth and extent of the great waves of a Bodhisattvas' actions, I request the holy ones to be patient with my mass of faults such as contradictions and unconnected lines."

Then he ends with the dedication.

"By the virtue from this may all beings never abide in the extremes of Samsara and Nirvana but with supreme, ultimate and conventional Bodhichitta, become equals of the Protector Avalokiteshvara."

This concludes "Thirty-seven Bodhisattva Practices" by Thogmey zangpo.

from My Land and My People

by *the Dalai Lama*

The Dalai Lama considers himself to be "just a simple monk." Here he tells the story of the early years of his religious education.

*M*y education began when I was six, and as I was taught entirely by the traditional system of Tibet, I must explain its methods and purposes. Our system has proved effective, so far, in maintaining a fairly high moral and intellectual standard among Tibetans, although it was established many centuries ago. By modern standards, it has the defect of entirely ignoring the scientific knowledge of recent centuries, but the reason for that, of course, is that Tibet remained entirely isolated until very recent times.

The basic purpose of the Tibetan system is to broaden and cultivate the mind by a wide variety of knowledge. For the advanced standard of secular education, the curriculum includes drama, dance and music, astrology, poetry, and composition. These are known in Tibet as the "five minor subjects." They are not reserved for lay pupils alone, but pupils receiving religious education can also choose one or more of them, and most of them choose astrology and composition.

For higher education, the course includes the art of healing, Sanskrit, dialectics, arts and crafts, and metaphysics and the philosophy of religion. Of these "five higher subjects," as they are called, the last is the most important and fundamental. Together with dialectics, it is divided in turn into five branches. These, with their Sanskrit names, are *Prajnaparamita*, the Perfection of Wisdom; *Madhyamika*, the Middle Path, which urges the avoidance of extremes; *Vinaya*, the Canon of Monastic Discipline; *Abhidharma*, Metaphysics; and *Pramana*, Logic and Dialectics. Strictly speaking, the last of these is not one of the branches or scriptures, but it is included in these Five Great Treatises to emphasize the importance of logic in developing mental powers. The *Tantric* part of *Mahayana* is not included among them; it is studied separately.

This religious education is followed mainly by the monks of Tibet. It is a profound study, and effort is needed to understand its difficult subject matter.

Beside providing a pupil with information, the Tibetan system lays down various methods for developing his mental faculties. To begin with, children learn to read and write by imitating their teacher. This, of course, is a natural method which one uses all one's life. To train the memory, there are rigorous courses for learning the scriptures by heart. The third method, explanation, is used throughout the world, and some of our monastic colleges depend on it for teaching their students. But many monasteries prefer the method of dialectical discussions between pupil and teacher or between pupils alone. Finally, there are the methods of meditation and concentration, which are especially used for training the mind for the advanced study and practice of religion.

Like most children, I started by learning to read and write, and I felt what I suppose young boys of that age generally feel—a certain reluctance and some resistance. The idea of being tied down to books and the company of teachers was not very interesting. However, I found myself doing my lessons to my teachers' satisfaction, and as I got used to the strict course of study, they began to mark my progress as rather unusually rapid.

There are four different forms of Tibetan script. For the first two years, I learned from my Senior and Junior Tutors to read the form which is used for printing—it is known as *U-chhen*. At the same time I learned a verse from the scriptures by heart every day and spent another hour in reading the scriptures. Then, when I was eight, I began to learn the ordinary written form of Tibetan, which is called *U-me*. I was taught this by an old companion, Khenrab Tenzin, who had been with the search party and came back with me from Dokham to Lhasa. He was a monk official and a man of character, who had a special gift for teaching small children. He followed the method which is always used in Tibet—he wrote the Tibetan characters without any ink on a small wooden board which had been covered with chalk dust, and then I had to write over the characters with ink, beginning with large characters and later, as I progressed, writing them smaller. After a time, I began to copy words which he had written at the top of the board. For about eight months I wrote on wooden boards to acquire the proper form of script, and then Khenrab Tenzin began to allow me to write on paper. Later, my Junior Tutor, Trijang Rinpoché, taught me grammar and spelling. Altogether I spent about five years on writing Tibetan. This was in addition, of course, to my daily study of the scriptures, morning and evening, for religious training was the main purpose of my education, and reading, writing, and grammar were only a means to that end.

My religious education in dialectical discussion did not begin in earnest till I was twelve. At first it was not very easy, because I felt again a certain mental resistance, more intense than the similar experience six years earlier. But soon the difficulties disappeared, and the subjects became most agreeable. I had to study and learn by heart the treatises on the "higher subjects," and take part in discussions of them, at times debating with the most learned scholars. I began on the *Prajnaparamita* (the Perfection of Wisdom). There are over thirty volumes of commentaries on this treatise, and the monastic universities make their own choice. I chose for myself, beside the fundamental principles of the treatise, two of its commentaries, one by the great Indian Pandit Singhabhadra, and the other, consisting of 302 pages, by the Fifth Dalai Lama. Henceforth I had to learn about a third of a page by heart every day and read and understand much more. At the same time my training in the art of dialectical argument began with elementary logic. Seven learned scholars from the seven monastic colleges of the Drepung, Sera, and Gaden monasteries were selected to help me for this purpose.

When I was just over thirteen, in the eighth month of the Fire Hog Year, I was formally admitted to the two large monasteries of Drepung and Sera. On this occasion, I had to attend congregational debates at the five monastic colleges of these two monasteries. This was the first time I had taken part in public dialectical discussions on the Great Treatises, and naturally I felt shy, excited, and a little worried. My opponents were learned abbots, who were formidable contestants in debate, and the meetings were attended by hundreds of religious dignitaries, all of whom were scholars, and by thousands of monks. However, the learned lamas told me afterwards that I had conducted myself to their satisfaction.

I will not ask all my readers of other religions to follow me throughout my further studies of Buddhist thought, for Buddhism is an intellectual rather than an emotional religion, and it has a literature of thousands of volumes, of which I studied hundreds. However, I have given a short explanation of the Buddhism of Tibet in the Appendix of this book. And I will confess that when I was introduced to metaphysics and philosophy soon after I was thirteen, they unnerved me so that I had the feeling of being dazed, as though I were hit on the head by a stone. But that phase did not linger beyond the first few days, and after that the new studies, like the earlier courses, became simpler and clearer. "Nothing remains difficult once you get used to it," an Indian seer has said, and I certainly found this was so in my education. One by one, other subjects were added to my curriculum, and as I went on I found less and less difficulty in learning all that was required of me. In fact, I began to feel a growing inquisitiveness to know more and more. My interest reached beyond my allotted studies, and I found satisfaction in reading advanced chapters of the books and wanting to know from my teachers more than I was supposed to at my age.

This increase in one's intellectual powers is associated with spiritual development. At each stage in my training, I received consecration of the mind and body in preparation for the higher doctrines. I had the first of these initiations when I was eight, and I still remember it vividly, and the feeling of peace and happiness it brought me. At each of the later ceremonies, I could feel the spiritual experience which has always been associated with them. My belief and faith in my religion became deeper, the assurance in my mind that I was following the right path became firmer.

As I grew more accustomed to these experiences and reached the age of about fifteen, I was able to sense a spontaneous feeling growing within me of gratitude to Lord Buddha. I also felt an immense debt to those teachers, mostly Indians, who had given the Tibetans their invaluable religious doctrines, and to those Tibetan scholars who had interpreted and preserved them in our language. I began to think less of myself and more of others and became aware of the concept of compassion.

It was this sense of spiritual elevation which was attended on the mental plane by a sense of improved intellect, by better powers of memory, greater proficiency in debate, and increased self-confidence.

Political and other circumstances, as I shall tell, did

not allow me to carry on my studies like the scholars of great talent and learning who devote their whole lives to the pursuit of religious knowledge and spiritual enlightenment. But for a period of thirteen years I was able to give a good part of my time and attention to these serious studies, and when I was twenty-four I took the preliminary examination at each of the three monastic universities.

These examinations are always in the form of congregational debates. The rules of procedure are simple, but dignified. Each student has to face a large number of opponents who choose whatever subject and whatever disputable point they think necessary to defeat their adversary, and all the standard works of Indian and Tibetan scholars, as well as Lord Buddha's words embodied in the Sutras, are quoted to refute the contentions of the opposing party. At each of my preliminary examinations, I had to compete with fifteen learned scholars in these debates, three for each of the five treatises, and defend my thesis and refute their arguments. Then I had to stand before two very erudite abbots and initiate a dialectical discussion on any of the five principal subjects. In all these debates, strong formal gestures are made to emphasize each point, so that the arguments appear like battles of intellect, which indeed they are.

A year later, I appeared for my final examination, during the annual Monlam Festival in Lhasa, when many thousands of monks come into the city to attend the special Buddhist festival of prayer which is held in the first month of each year. This examination was held in three sessions. In the morning I was examined on *Pramana*, or logic, by thirty scholars turn by turn in congregational discussion. In the afternoon, fifteen scholars took part as my opponents in debate on *Madhyamika* (the Middle Path), and *Prajnaparamita* (the Perfection of Wisdom). In the evening there were thirty-five scholars to test my knowledge of *Vinaya*, the canon of monastic discipline, and *Abhidharma*, the study of metaphysics. And at each session hundreds of learned lamas in their brilliant red and yellow robes—my own tutors anxiously among them—and thousands of monks sat round us on the ground, eagerly and critically listening. I found these examinations extremely difficult, because I had to concentrate so hard on the subject with which I was dealing, and had to be so prompt in answering any questions. Several hours of debate seemed like an instant. Of course, I was proud and happy to be taking the final examination and to receive the degree of Master of Metaphysics, after so many years of studying the great teachings of Lord Buddha. But I knew that there is really no end to one's need for continual learning until one can reach the highest stages of spiritual attainment.

Such a religious training, in my view, brings a certain unique equanimity of mind. The practical test comes when occasions of sorrow or suffering arise. The person whose mind is conditioned by the study and practice of religion faces these circumstances with patience and forbearance. The person who does not follow the path of religion may break under the impact of what he regards as calamities, and may end in either self-frustration, or else in pursuits which inflict unhappiness on others. Humanitarianism and true love for all beings can only stem from an awareness of the content of religion. By whatever name religion may be known, its understanding and practice are the essence of a peaceful mind and therefore of a peaceful world. If there is no peace in one's mind, there can be no peace in one's approach to others, and thus no peaceful relations between individuals or between nations.

Here I must give a brief explanation of our beliefs, and the significance of my own position as the Dalai Lama, because these beliefs had a most profound influence on all that I did and all that our people did when our time of trouble came. But I must also add that it is impossible to describe the complexities of the Buddhist doctrine in a few lines, and so I shall not try to indicate more than the general trend of it, for the sake of those to whom it is quite unfamiliar.

We believe, with good reason, that all beings of various forms (both animal and human) are reborn after death. In each life, the proportion of pain and joy which they experience is determined by their good or evil deeds in the life before, although they may modify the proportion by their efforts in their present life. This is known as the law of Karma. Beings may move up or down in the Kure realms, for example, from animal to human life or back. Finally, by virtue and enlightenment, they will achieve Nirvana, when they cease to be reborn. Within Nirvana, there are stages of enlightenment: the highest of all—the perfection of enlightenment—is Buddhahood.

Belief in rebirth should engender a universal love, for all living beings and creatures, in the course of their numberless lives and our own, have been our beloved parents, children, brothers, sisters, friends. And the virtues our creed encourages are those which arise from this universal love—tolerance, forbearance, charity, kindness, compassion.

Incarnations are beings who have either achieved various stages of Nirvana or have achieved the highest stage below Nirvana—the Buddhas, Bodhisattvas and Arahats. They are reincarnated in order to help other beings to rise toward Nirvana, and by doing so the Bodhisattvas are themselves helped to rise to Buddha-hood, and the Arahats also reach Buddhahood finally. Buddhas are reincarnated solely to help others, since they themselves have already achieved the highest of all levels. They are not reincarnated through any active volition of their own; such an active mental process has no place in Nirvana. They are reincarnated rather by the innate wish to help others through which they have achieved Buddhahood. Their reincarnations occur whenever conditions are suitable, and do not mean that they leave their state in Nirvana. In simile, it is rather as reflections of the moon may be seen on earth in placid lakes and seas when conditions are suitable, while the moon itself remains in its course in the sky. By the same simile, the moon may be reflected in many different places at the same moment, and a Buddha may be incarnate simultaneously in many different bodies. All such incarnate beings, as I have already indicated, can influence, by their own wishes in each life, the place and time when they will be reborn, and after each birth, they have a lingering memory of their previous life which enables others to identify them.

I worked hard at my religious education as a boy, but my life was not all work. I am told that some people in other countries believe the Dalai Lamas were almost prisoners in the Potala Palace. It is true that I could not go out very often because of my studies; but a house was built for my family between the Potala and the city of Lhasa, and I saw them at least every month or six weeks, so that I was not entirely cut off from family life. Indeed, I saw my father very often, for one of the minor daily ceremonies (either in the Potala or the Norbulingka— the summer palace) was the morning tea ceremony, when all the monk officials met for their early bowls of tea—and both my father and I often attended this meeting. Despite our changed circumstances, he still kept up his interest in horses. He would still go out to feed his own horses every morning before he took any food himself, and now that he could afford it, he gave them eggs and tea to strengthen them. And when I was in the summer palace, where the Dalai Lama's stables were situated, and my father came to see me there, I think he often went to call on my horses before he came to call on me.

About a year after we arrived in Lhasa, my elder sister came to join us, and then my eldest brother left the monastery at Kumbum and came to Lhasa too, so that we were all united again. Soon after my elder sister arrived, my younger sister was born, and after her a baby boy. We were all very fond of this baby, and it delighted me to have a younger brother, but to our grief he died when he was only two years old. It was a grief only too familiar to my parents, because so many of their children had already died. But a curious thing happened on the death of the baby. It is the custom in Tibet to consult the lamas and astrologers before a funeral, and sometimes the oracles too. The advice which was given on this occasion was that the body should not be buried but preserved, and he would then be reborn in the same house. As proof, a small mark was to be made on the body with a smear of butter. This was done, and in due course my mother had another baby boy—her last child. And when he was born, the pale mark was seen on the spot of his body where the butter had been smeared. He was the same being, born again in a new body to start his life afresh.

In all these family matters I was able to take some part, but I will agree that most of my time in my boyhood was spent in the company of grown-up men, and there must inevitably be something lacking in a childhood without the constant company of one's mother and other children. However, even if the Potala had been a prison for me, it would have been a spacious and fascinating prison. It is said to be one of the largest buildings in the world. Even after living in it for years, one could never know all its secrets. It entirely covers the top of a hill; it is a city in itself. It was begun by a king of Tibet 1,300 years ago as a pavilion for meditation, and it was greatly enlarged by the Fifth Dalai Lama in the seventeenth century of the Christian era. The central part of the present building, which is thirteen stories high, was built on his orders, but he died when the building had reached the second story. But when he knew that he was dying, he told his Prime Minister to keep his death a secret, because he feared that if it were known that he was dead, the building would be stopped. The Prime Minister found a monk who resembled the Lama and succeeded in concealing the death for thirteen years until the work was finished, but he secretly had a stone carved with a prayer for a reincarnation and had it built into the walls. It can still be seen on the second story today.

This central part of the building contained the great halls for ceremonial occasions, about thirty-five chapels richly carved and painted, four cells for meditation, and the mausoleums of seven Dalai Lamas— some 30 feet high and covered in solid gold and precious stones.

The western wing of the building, which is of later date, housed a community of 175 monks, and in the eastern wing were the government offices, a school for monk officials, and the meeting halls of the National Assembly—the houses of Parliament of Tibet. My own apartments were above the offices, on the top story— 400 feet above the town. I had four rooms there. The one which I used most often was about 25 feet square, and its walls were entirely covered by paintings depicting the life of the fifth Dalai Lama, so detailed that the individual portraits were not more than an inch high. When I grew tired of my reading, I often used to sit and follow the story told by this great and elaborate mural which surrounded me.

But apart from its use as office, temple, school, and habitation, the Potala was also an enormous storehouse. Here were rooms full of thousands of priceless scrolls, some a thousand years old. Here were strong rooms filled with the golden regalia of the earliest kings of Tibet, dating back for a thousand years, and the sumptuous gifts they received from the Chinese or Mongol emperors, and the treasures of the Dalai Lamas who succeeded the kings. Here also were stored the armor and armament from the whole of Tibetan history. In the libraries were all the records of Tibetan culture and religion, 7,000 enormous volumes, some of which were said to weigh eighty pounds. Some were written on palm leaves imported from India a thousand years ago. Two thousand illuminated volumes of the scriptures were written in inks made of powdered gold, silver, iron, copper, conch shell, turquoise, and coral, each line in a different ink.

Down below the building there were endless underground storehouses and cellars, containing government stocks of butter, tea, and cloth which were supplied to the monasteries, the army, and government officials. At the eastern end was a prison for wrong-doers of high rank—corresponding perhaps to the Tower of London. And on the four corners of the building were defensive turrets where the Tibetan army used to keep watch.

In these unique surroundings I pursued my studies and also pursued my childish interests. I was always fascinated by mechanical things, but there was nobody who could tell me anything about them. When I was small, kind people who knew of this interest sometimes sent me mechanical toys, such as cars and boats and airplanes. But I was never content to play with them for long—I always had to take them to pieces to see how they worked. Usually I managed to put them together again, though sometimes, as might be expected, there were disasters. I had a set of Meccano, and I built cranes and railroad cars with it long before I had ever seen such things. Later on, I was given an old movie projector which was operated by turning a handle, and when I took that to pieces I found the batteries which worked its electric light. That was my first introduction to electricity, and I puzzled over the connections all alone until I found the way to make it go. I had a success, though this was later, with my wristwatch. I took that entirely to pieces, to study its principles, and it still worked when I put it together again.

In the Potala, each year began with a ceremony on the highest roof before sunrise on New Year's Day (a bitterly cold occasion, when I was not the only one who thought with longing of the tea ceremony later in the morning) and religious activities continued day by day throughout the year until the great Dance of the Lamas the day before New Year's Eve. But in the spring, I myself and my tutors and attendants and some of the government departments moved to the Norbulingka, in a procession which all the people of Lhasa came to see. I was always happy to go to the Norbulingka. The Potala made me proud of our inheritance of culture and craftsmanship, but the Norbulingka was more like a home. It was really a series of small palaces, and chapels, built in a large and beautiful walled garden. Norbulingka means "The Jewel Park." It was started by the Seventh Dalai Lama in the eighteenth century, and successive Dalai Lamas have added their own residences to it ever since. I built one there myself. The founder chose a very fertile spot. In the Norbulingka gardens we grew a radish weighing twenty pounds, and cabbages so large you could not put your arms round them. There were poplars, willows, junipers, and many kinds of flowers and fruit trees: apples, pears, peaches, walnuts, and apricots. We introduced plums and cherry trees while I was there.

There, between my lessons, I could walk and run among the flowers and orchards, and the peacocks and the tame musk deer. There I played on the edge of the lake and twice nearly drowned myself. And there, also in the lake, I used to feed my fish, which would rise to the surface expectantly when they heard my footsteps. I do not know now what has happened to the historical marvels of the Potala. Thinking about them, I sometimes also wonder whether my fish were so unwise as to rise to the surface when they first heard the boots of Chinese soldiers in the Norbulingka. If they did, they have probably been eaten.

One of the minor pleasures of the Norbulingka was that it had a motor generator for electric light, which often broke down, so that I had every excuse to take it to pieces. From that machine, I discovered how internal combustion engines work, and also noticed how the dynamo created a magnetic field when it turned—and I must say that I managed to mend it more often than not.

I tried to make use of this knowledge on three old motor cars, the only ones in Lhasa. There were two 1927 Baby Austins, one blue and the other red and yellow, and a large Dodge of 1931, painted orange. They had been been presented to my predecessor and carried over the Himalayas in pieces and then reassembled. However, they had never been used since his death and had stood and been allowed to rust. I longed to make them work. At last I found a young Tibetan who had been trained as a driver in India, and with my eager assistance he managed to put the Dodge in working order, and also one of the Austins, by borrowing parts from the other. These were exciting moments.

I was curious also about the affairs of the world

outside Tibet, but naturally much of that curiosity had to go unsatisfied. I had an atlas, and I pored over maps of distant countries and wondered what life was like in them, but I did not know anyone who had ever seen them. I started to teach myself English out of books, because Britain was the only country beyond our immediate neighbors with which we had friendly ties. My tutors read in a Tibetan newspaper, which was published in Kalimpong in India, of the progress of the Second World War, which started in the year I was taken to Lhasa—and they told me about it. Before the end of the war, I was able to read such accounts myself. But few world events affected us in Lhasa. I have sometimes been asked if we followed with interest the attempts of the British to climb Mount Everest. I cannot say that we did. Most Tibetans have to climb too many mountain passes to have any wish to climb higher than they must. And the people of Lhasa, who sometimes climbed for pleasure, chose hills of a reasonable size—and when they came to the top, burned incense, said prayers, and had picnics. That is a pleasure I also enjoy when I have an opportunity.

All in all, it was not an unhappy childhood. The kindness of my teachers will always remain with me as a memory I shall cherish. They gave me the religious knowledge which has always been and will always be my greatest comfort and inspiration, and they did their best to satisfy what they regarded as a healthy curiosity in other matters. But I know that I grew up with hardly any knowledge of worldly affairs, and it was in that state, when I was sixteen, that I was called upon to lead my country against the invasion of Communist China.

from Seven Years in Tibet

by *Heinrich Harrer*

Austrian mountain climber Heinrich Harrer (born 1912) was a prisoner in a British India POW camp before escaping to Tibet in 1944. His journey took two years, and he remained in Lhasa for another five years. There he befriended the teenage Dalai Lama and became his tutor.

L obsang Samten [the Dalai Lama's brother] surprised me one day by asking me if I would undertake to build a room for showing films. His brother had expressed the wish that I should do so. Life in Lhasa had taught me that one should not say no even when asked to do things with which one is completely unfamiliar. Aufschnaiter and I were known as "Jacks of all trades" and we had already solved a lot of difficult problems. When I had ascertained what amount of current the Dalai Lama's projector would need and how far the projector would have to be from the screen, I declared myself ready to undertake the work. I was then

officially commissioned to execute it by the Dalai
Lama's abbot guardians. From that time the gates of the
Inner Garden at the Norbulingka were always open to
me. I started the job in the winter of 1949-50 after the
young king had already returned to the Potala. After
looking at all the buildings I chose an unused house
adjacent to the inner side of the garden wall, which I
thought I could transform into a motion-picture theater. The best masons in Lhasa and the soldiers of the
bodyguard were placed at my disposal. I was not allowed
to employ women, whose presence would have pro-
faned the holy place. I used short lengths of iron
screwed together into girders to support the ceiling, so
as to dispense with the customary pillars. The theater
was sixty feet long and I had to build a platform for the
projector. This was accessible both from the inside of
the room and from the outside of the building. Some
distance away from the theater I erected a powerhouse
for the motor and the generator. I did this at the express
wish of the Dalai Lama, who did not want the sound of
the motor to be audible in the theater, as he was anxious
not to upset the old regent (the installation of a motion
picture in the Norbulingka was already revolutionary
enough). I built a special room for the exhaust pipes,
the noise of which was effectively deadened. As the old
gasoline motor was not altogether reliable, I proposed
that the engine of the jeep should be made available to
propel the generator in case of need. The Dalai Lama
approved the suggestion, and as his will was law, the jeep
was adapted to this purpose. We had some trouble at the
outset because the garden gate was just too narrow to
admit the jeep. However the young ruler, regardless of
tradition, ordered the gateway to be widened. A new

gate replaced the old one and all traces of the operation were removed as soon as possible, so that there should be nothing visible to attract the criticism of reactionary spirits. The strong point about this boy was that he was able to get his ideas put into action without alienating the sympathies of those around him.

So the jeep got its own house and often came to the rescue when the old motor went on strike. The chauffeur of the thirteenth Dalai Lama helped me to do the wiring and soon the whole machine was going like clockwork. I took great pains to remove all traces of our building activities from the garden, and made new flower beds and paths on the ground which had been trampled by the workmen. And, of course, I took this unique opportunity to explore the closed garden thoroughly, little thinking that in the future I should often be in it as a guest.

When the spring came the Norbulingka was a vision of loveliness. The peach and pear blossoms were in full bloom. Peacocks strutted proudly through the grounds and hundreds of rare plants stood in pots in the sunshine. In one corner of the park there was a small zoo, but most of the cages were empty. Only a few wildcats and lynxes remained. Formerly there were panthers and bears, but these had soon succumbed in their narrow dens. The Dalai Lama received many presents of wild animals, especially injured ones, which found a safe refuge in the Jeweled Garden.

In addition to the temples there were many small houses scattered about under the trees. Each was used for a special purpose—one was for meditation, another for reading and study, and others served as meeting places for the monks. The largest building, several stories high, stood in the center of the garden and was half a temple and half a residence for His Holiness. The windows were too small for my liking, and I found the title "palace" too flattering for this ordinary house. It was certainly more attractive as a residence than the Potala, which was more like a prison than a palace, but it was rather dark. So was the garden. The trees had been allowed to grow untended for many years and in places they resembled a dense jungle. No one had ever attempted to clear them out. The gardeners complained that flowers and fruit simply would not grow in the shade of the big trees. I would have been very happy if they had allowed me to tidy up and rearrange the Inner Garden. There were many gardeners, but none with a sense of style. I did succeed in convincing the high chamberlain that certain trees had to be cut down and I was allowed to supervise the work of felling them. The gardeners had little understanding of this sort of thing, and occupied themselves mainly with cultivating pot flowers, which were left out in the open all day and placed under cover at night.

One of the doors in the wall of the Inner Garden led directly to the stables, which housed the favorite horses of the Dalai Lama and an onager which had been presented to him. These animals lived a contemplative, peaceful life tended by many grooms. They grew fat and soft as their master never rode or drove them.

The teachers and personal servants of the Dalai Lama lived outside the yellow wall in the Norbulingka park. They and the bodyguard, five hundred strong, lived in comfortable and (for Tibet) extraordinarily clean blocks of houses. The thirteenth Dalai Lama had taken a personal interest in the welfare of his troops.

He had dressed them in uniforms of European cut and used to watch them exercising from one of his pavilions. I was struck by the fact that these soldiers had their hair cut in Western fashion in contrast to all other Tibetans. The thirteenth Dalai Lama had probably been favorably impressed by the appearance of British and Indian troops during his stay in India and had modeled his bodyguard on them. The officers lived in nice little bungalows with flower beds blooming all around them. The duties of officers and men were easy. They consisted mainly in mounting guard and turning out to march in ceremonial processions.

Long before the Dalai Lama moved into the Summer Residence I had finished my building. I wondered if he would be pleased with the theater. I could count on learning his opinion of it all from Lobsang Samten, who was certain to be present at the first performance. The Dalai Lama would probably call on the film man of the Indian Legation to work the apparatus. The legation used frequently to show films, Indian and English, at its pleasant parties and it was a joy to see the childish enthusiasm with which the Tibetans watched these performances and especially the films showing scenes from distant lands. The question was how the young ruler would react to the pictures.

I was naturally present with my moving-picture camera to see the procession from the Potala to the Norbulingka. I had the usual difficulty in finding a suitable place from which to film the ceremony, but my attendant, a pock-marked giant of formidable aspect, made things easier for me. He carried my cameras and the crowds opened to let us through. He not only looked forbidding, but was in fact a very gallant fellow as the following anecdote shows.

It sometimes happens that leopards stray into the gardens of Lhasa. They must not be killed, so the people try to lure them into traps or catch them by any sort of device. One day a leopard got through into the Garden of Jewels. Harried on all sides and wounded in the foot by a bullet, it was driven into a corner where it stood at bay spitting at anyone who dared to approach it. Suddenly my attendant went for it with his bare hands and held it until other soldiers rushed up with a sack into which they forced it. The man was badly clawed and the leopard was lodged in the Dalai Lama's zoo, where it soon died.

When the Dalai Lama passed by me in his sedan chair and found me filming he gave me a smile. My private thought was that he was congratulating himself on his little motion-picture theater, but I am sure that no one else thought as I did; though what could be more natural for a lonely fourteen-year-old boy? Then a look at the humble and rapturous face of my attendant reminded me that for everyone else except myself, he was not a lonely boy but a god.

After filming the scenes in the Norbulingka I was riding slowly home when, a little way out of Lhasa, I was overhauled by an excited soldier of the bodyguard, who told me that they had been looking for me everywhere and that I must at once ride back to the Summer Garden. My first thought was that the motion-picture apparatus was out of order, as I could hardly imagine that the young ruler, still a minor, would override all conventions and summon me directly to see him. I immediately turned around and was soon back at the Norbulingka, where everything was now peaceful and still. At the door of the yellow gate a couple of monks were waiting. As soon as they saw me they signaled to me to hurry up and when I reached them they ushered me into the Inner Garden. There Lobsang Samten awaited me. He whispered something to me and put a white scarf in my hand. There was no doubt about it. His brother was going to receive me.

I at once went toward the motion-picture theater, but before I could enter the door opened from the inside and I was standing before the Living Buddha. Conquering my surprise I bowed deeply and handed him the scarf. He took it in his left hand and with an impulsive gesture blessed me with his right. It seemed less like the ceremonial laying on of hands than an impetuous expression of feeling on the part of a boy who had at last got his way. In the theater three abbots were waiting with bowed heads—the guardians of His Holiness. I knew them all well and did not fail to observe how coldly they returned my greeting. They certainly did not approve of this intrusion into their domain, but they had not dared openly to oppose the will of the Dalai Lama.

The young ruler was all the more cordial. He beamed all over his face and poured out a flood of questions. He seemed to me like a person who had for years brooded in solitude over different problems, and now that he had at last someone to talk to, wanted to know all the answers at once. He gave me no time to think over my answers, but pressed me to go to the projector and put on a film which he had long been wanting to see. It was a documentary film of the capitulation of Japan. He came with me to the apparatus and sent the abbots into the theater to act as spectators.

I must have seemed slow and clumsy in handling the projector as he impatiently pushed me on one side and, taking hold of the film, showed me that he was a much more practiced operator than I was. He told me that he had been busy the whole winter learning how to work the apparatus and that he had even taken a projector to pieces and put it together again. I observed then, for the first time, that he liked to get to the bottom of things instead of taking them for granted. And so, later on, like many a good father who wishes to earn the respect of his son, I often spent the evening reviving my knowledge of half-forgotten things or studying new ones. I took the utmost trouble to treat every question seriously and scientifically, as it was clear to me that my answers would form the basis of his knowledge of the Western world.

His obvious talent for technical things astonished me at our first meeting. It was a masterly performance for a boy of fourteen years to take a projector to pieces and then to reassemble it without any help, for he could not read the English prospectus. Now that the film was running well, he was delighted with the arrangements and could not praise my work too highly. We sat together in the projecting room and looked at the picture through the peep holes in the wall and he took the greatest pleasure in what he saw and heard, often clasping my hands excitedly with the vivacity of youth. Although it was the first time in his life that he had been alone with a white man he was in no way embarrassed or shy. While he was putting the next film on the reel, he pressed the microphone into my hands and insisted on my speaking into it. At the same time he looked through the peep holes into the electrically lit theater in which his tutors sat on carpets. I could see how keen he was to observe the wondering faces of the worthy abbots when a voice should suddenly come out of the loudspeaker. I did not want to disappoint him so I invited the nonexistent public to remain in their seats as the next film would present sensational scenes from Tibet. He laughed enthusiastically at the surprised and shocked faces of the monks when they heard my cheerful, disrespectful tones. Such light, unceremonious language had never been used in the presence of the Divine Ruler, whose gleaming eyes showed how he enjoyed the situation.

He made me turn the film which I had made in Lhasa while he looked after the switches. I was as curious as he was to see the results, as this was my first full-length picture. An expert could have picked out faults in it, but it seemed quite satisfactory to us. It contained my shots of the "little" New Year Festival. Even the formal abbots forgot their dignity when they recognized themselves on the flickering screen. There was a burst of laughter when a full-length picture appeared of a minister who had gone to sleep during the ceremonies. There was no malice in their laughter, for each of the abbots had sometimes to struggle to keep awake during these endless festivities. All the same the upper classes must have got to know that the Dalai Lama had witnessed his minister's weakness, for afterwards whenever I appeared with my camera, everyone sat up and posed.

The Dalai Lama himself took more pleasure than anyone in the pictures. His usually slow movements became youthful and lively and he commented enthusiastically on every picture. After a while I asked him to turn a film which he had made himself. He very modestly said that he would not dare to show his apprentice efforts after the pictures we had already seen. But I was anxious to see what subjects he had chosen for filming and persuaded him to put his roll onto the screen. He had not, of course, had a large choice of subjects. He had done a big sweeping landscape of the valley of Lhasa, which he turned much too fast. Then came a few underlighted long-distance pictures of mounted noblemen and caravans passing through Shö. A close-up of his cook showed that he would have liked to take film portraits. The film he had shown me was absolutely his first attempt and had been made without instructions or help. When it was over he got me to announce through the microphone that the performance was over. He then opened the door leading into the theater, told the abbots that he did not need them any more and dismissed them with a wave of the hand. It was again clear to me that here was no animated puppet, but a clear-cut individual will capable of imposing itself on others.

When we were alone we cleared away the films and put the yellow covers on the machines. Then we sat down on a magnificent carpet in the theater with the sun streaming through the open windows. It was fortunate that I had long acquired the habit of sitting cross-legged, as chairs and cushions are not included in the

Dalai Lama's household furniture. At the start I had wished to decline his invitation to sit down, knowing that even ministers were not supposed to sit in his presence, but he just took me by the sleeve and pulled me down, which put an end to my misgiving.

He told me that he had long been planning this meeting as he had not been able to think of any other way of becoming acquainted with the outside world. He expected the regent to raise objections but he was determined to have his own way and had already thought up a rejoinder in case of opposition. He was resolved to extend his knowledge beyond purely religious subjects, and it seemed to him that I was the only person who could help him to do so. He had no idea that I was a qualified teacher, and had he known this it would probably not have influenced him. He asked my age and was surprised to learn that I was only thirty-seven. Like many Tibetans he thought that my "yellow" hair was a sign of age. He studied my features with childish curiosity and teased me about my long nose, which, though of normal size as we reckon noses, had often attracted the attention of the snub-nosed Mongolians. At last he noticed that I had hair growing on the back of my hands and said with a broad grin: "Henrig, you have hair like a monkey." I had an answer ready, as I was familiar with the legend that the Tibetans derive their descent from the union of their god Chenrezi with a female demon. Before coupling with his demon lover Chenrezi had assumed the shape of a monkey, and since the Dalai Lama is one of the Incarnations of this god, I found that in comparing me with an ape he had really flattered me.

With remarks such as this our conversation soon

became unconstrained and we both lost our shyness. I now felt the attraction of his personality, which at our earlier fleeting contacts I had only guessed at. His complexion was much lighter than that of the average Tibetan. His eyes, hardly narrower than those of most Europeans, were full of expression, charm, and vivacity. His cheeks glowed with excitement, and as he sat he kept sliding from side to side. His ears stood out a little from his head. This was a characteristic of the Buddha and, as I learned later, was one of the signs by which as a child he had been recognized as an incarnation. His hair was longer than is customary. He probably wore it so as a protection against the cold of the Potala. He was tall for his age and looked as though he would reach the stature of his parents, both of whom had striking figures. Unfortunately, as a result of much study in a seated posture with his body bent forward, he held himself badly. He had beautiful aristocratic hands with long fingers which were generally folded in an attitude of peace. I noticed that he often looked at my hands with astonishment when I emphasized what I was saying with a gesture. Gesticulation is entirely foreign to the Tibetans, who in their reposeful attitudes express the calm of Asia. He always wore the red robe of a monk, once prescribed by Buddha, and his costume differed in no way from that of the monastic officials.

Time passed swiftly. It seemed as if a dam had burst, so urgent and continuous was the flood of questions which he put to me. I was astounded to see how much disconnected knowledge he had acquired out of books and newspapers. He possessed an English work on the Second World War in seven volumes, which he had had translated into Tibetan. He knew how to distinguish between different types of airplanes, automobiles, and tanks. The names of personages like Churchill, Eisenhower, and Molotov were familiar to him, but as he had nobody to put questions to, he often did not know how persons and events were connected with each other. Now he was happy, because he had found someone to whom he could bring all the questions about which he had been puzzling for years.

It must have been about three o'clock when Sopön Khenpo came in to say that it was time to eat. This was the abbot whose duty it was to look after the physical welfare of the Dalai Lama. When he gave his message, I immediately rose to my feet meaning to take my leave, but the God King drew me down again and told the abbot to come again later. He then, very modestly, took out an exercise book with all sorts of drawings on the cover and asked me to look at his work. To my surprise I saw that he had been transcribing the capital letters of the Latin alphabet. What versatility and what initiative! Strenuous religious studies, tinkering with complicated mechanical appliances, and now modern languages! He insisted that I should immediately begin to teach him English, transcribing the pronunciation in elegant Tibetan characters. Another hour must have passed, when Sopön Khenpo came in again and this time insisted that his master should take his dinner. He had a dish of cakes, white bread, and sheep's cheese in his hand which he pressed on me. As I wanted to refuse it, he rolled the food up in a white cloth for me to take home with me.

But the Dalai Lama still did not want to end our conversation. In wheedling tones he begged his cupbearer to wait a little longer. With a loving look at his charge the abbot agreed and left us. I had the feeling that he was as fond of the boy and as devoted as if he had been his father. This white-haired ancient had served the thirteenth Dalai Lama in the same capacity and had remained in the service. This was a great tribute to his trustworthiness and loyalty, for in Tibet when there is a change of masters, there is a change of servants. The Dalai Lama proposed that I should visit his family who lived in the Norbulingka during the summer. He told me to wait in their house till he should send for me. When I left him he shook my hand warmly—a new gesture for him.

As I walked through the empty garden and pushed back the gate bolts, I could hardly realize that I had just spent five hours with the God-King of Lama Land. A gardener shut the gate behind me and the guard, which had been changed more than once since I came in, presented arms in some surprise. I rode slowly back to Lhasa and, but for the bundle of cakes which I was carrying, I would have thought it was all a dream. Which of my friends would have believed me if I had told him that I had just spent several hours alone in conversation with the Dalai Lama?

Needless to say I was very happy in the new duties that had fallen to my lot. To instruct this clever lad— the ruler of a land as big as France, Spain, and Germany put together—in the knowledge and science of the Western world, seemed a worthwhile task, to say the least.

On the same evening I looked up some reviews which contained details of the construction of jet planes, about which my young pupil had that day asked me questions to which I did not know the answers. I had promised to give him full explanations at our next meeting. As time went on I always prepared the materials for our lessons, as I wanted to introduce some system into the instruction of this zealous student.

I had many setbacks on account of his insatiable curiosity, which drove him to ask me questions that opened up whole new fields. Many of these questions I could answer only to the best of my knowledge. In order, for example, to be able to discuss the atom bomb, I had to tell him about the elements. That led to a formal discussion on metals, for which there is no generic word in Tibetan, so I had to go into details about the different sorts of metals—a subject which, of course, brought down an avalanche of questions.

My life in Lhasa had now begun a new phase. My existence had an aim. I no longer felt unsatisfied or incomplete. I did not abandon my former duties. I still collected news for the ministry: I still drew maps. But now the days were all too short and I often worked till late into the night. I had little time for pleasures and hobbies, for when the Dalai Lama called me, I had to be free. Instead of going to parties in the morning, as others did, I came late in the afternoon. But that was no sacrifice. I was happy in the consciousness that my life had a goal. The hours I spent with my pupil were as instructive for me as they were for him. He taught me a great deal about the history of Tibet and the teachings of Buddha. He was a real authority on these subjects. We often used to argue for hours on religious subjects and he was convinced that he would succeed in converting me to Buddhism. He told me that he was making a study of books containing knowledge of the

ancient mysteries by which the body and the soul could
be separated. The history of Tibet is full of stories
about saints whose spirits used to perform actions
hundreds of miles away from their physical bodies.
The Dalai Lama was convinced that by virtue of his
faith and by performing the prescribed rites he would
be able to make things happen in far-distant places
like Samye. When he had made sufficient progress,
he said he would send me there and direct me from
Lhasa. I remember saying to him with a laugh "All
right, Kundün, when you can do that, I will become a
Buddhist too."

Unfortunately we never got as far as making this exper-
iment. The beginning of our friendship was darkened
by political clouds. The tone of the Peiping radio
became more and more arrogant and Chiang Kai-shek
had already withdrawn with his government to Formosa.
The National Assembly in Lhasa held one sitting after
another; new troops were raised; parades and military
exercises were carried out in Shö, and the Dalai Lama
himself consecrated the army's new colors.

Fox, the English radio expert, had much to do, as
every military unit had to have at least one trans-
mitting set.

The Tibetan National Assembly, by whom all
important political decisions are taken, is composed of
fifty secular and monastic officials. The assembly is
presided over by four abbots from Drebung, Sera, and
Ganden, each of whom has a monk and a finance secretary attached to him. The other members of the
National Assembly, whether secular or religious,
belong to the different government offices but none of

the four cabinet ministers is a member. The constitution provides that the cabinet should meet in an
adjoining chamber and should see all the decisions of
the assembly, without possessing the right of veto. The
final decision in all questions belongs to the Dalai
Lama or, if he is still a minor, to the regent in his
stead. Of course no one would dare even to discuss a
proposal coming from such a high authority.

Until a few years ago the so-called Great National
Assembly was convoked every year. This body was composed of officials together with representatives of the
guilds of craftsmen—tailors, masons, carpenters, and
so on. These annual meetings of about five hundred
persons were quietly discontinued. They had really no
value except to satisfy the letter of the law. In effect the
power of the regent was supreme.

In these difficult times the State Oracle was frequently consulted. His prophecies were dark and did
not help to raise the morale of the people. He used to
say "A powerful foe threatens our sacred land from the
north and the east." Or "Our religion is in danger."
All the consultations were held in secret but the orac-
ular utterances seeped through to the people and were
spread abroad by whisperers. As is usual in times of war
and crisis, the whole town buzzed with rumors like a
beehive, and the strength of the enemy was swelled to
fabulous dimensions. The fortunetellers had a good
time, for not only was the fate of the country in the
balance but everyone was interested in his own personal welfare. More than ever men sought counsel of
the gods, consulted the omens and gave to every happening a good or bad meaning. Farsighted people
already began to send away their treasures to be stored

in the south or in remote estates. But the people as a whole believed that the gods would help them and that a miracle would save the country from war.

The National Assembly had soberer views. It had at last become clear to them that isolationism spelled a grave danger for the country. It was high time to establish diplomatic relations with foreign states and to tell the whole world that Tibet wished to be independent. Hitherto China's claim that Tibet was one of her provinces had remained without contradiction. Newspapers and broadcasters could say what they liked about the country: there was never an answer from Tibet. In conformity with their policy of complete neutrality the government had refused to explain themselves to the world. Now the danger of this attitude was recognized and people began to grasp the importance of propaganda. Every day Radio Lhasa broadcasted its views in Tibetan, Chinese, and English. Missions were appointed by the government to visit Peiping, Delhi, Washington, and London. Their members were monastic officials and young noblemen who had learned English in India. But they never got farther than India, thanks to the irresolution of their own government and the intrigues of the great powers.

The young Dalai Lama realized the gravity of the situation but he did not cease to hope for a peaceful outcome. During my visits I observed what a lively interest the future ruler took in political events. We always met alone in the little motion-picture theater, and I was able to understand often from trifling indications how much he looked forward to my coming. Sometimes he came running across the garden to greet me, beaming with happiness and holding out his hand. In spite of my warm feelings toward him and the fact that he called me his friend, I always took care to show him the respect due to the future king of Tibet. He had charged me to give him lessons in English, geography, and arithmetic. In addition I had to look after his motion-pictures and keep him conversant with world events. He had my pay raised on his own initiative, for although he was not yet constitutionally entitled to give orders, he had only to express a wish for them to be executed.

He continually astonished me by his powers of comprehension, his pertinacity, and his industry. When I gave him for homework ten sentences to translate, he usually showed up with twenty. He was very quick at learning languages, as are most Tibetans. It is quite common for people of the upper class and businessmen to speak Mongolian, Chinese, Nepalese, and Hindi. My pupil's greatest difficulty was to pronounce the letter "F," which does not occur in Tibetan. As my English was far from being perfect, we used to listen to the English news on a portable radio and took advantage of the passages spoken at dictation speed.

I had been told that in one of the government offices there were a number of English schoolbooks stored in sealed cases. A hint was given to the ministry and on the same day the books were sent up to the Norbulingka. We made a little library for them in the theater. My pupil was delighted at this discovery, which was something quite out of the ordinary for Lhasa. When I observed his zeal and thirst for knowledge I felt quite ashamed at the thought of my own boyhood.

There were also numerous English books and maps from the estate of the thirteenth Dalai Lama but I noticed that they looked very new and had obviously not been read. The late ruler had learned much during his long journeys in India and China, and it was to his friendship with Sir Charles Bell that he owed his knowledge of the Western world. I was already familiar with the name of this Englishman and had read his books during my internment. He was a great champion of Tibetan independence. As political liaison officer for Sikkim, Tibet, and Bhutan, he had got to know the Dalai Lama on his flight to India. This was the beginning of a close friendship between the two men which lasted for many years. Sir Charles Bell was, doubtless, the first white man to come into contact with a Dalai Lama.

My young pupil was not yet in a position to travel, but that did not diminish his interest in world geography, which was soon his favorite subject. I drew for him great maps of the world and others of Asia and Tibet. We had a globe, with the help of which I was able to explain to him why Radio New York was eleven hours behind Lhasa. He soon felt at home in all countries and was as familiar with the Caucasus as with the Himalayas. He was particularly proud of the fact that the highest summit in the world was on his frontier, and like many Tibetans was astonished to learn that few countries exceeded his kingdom in area.

Our peaceful lessons were disturbed this summer by an untoward event. On August 15th a violent earthquake caused a panic in the Holy City. Another evil omen! The people had hardly got over their fright caused by the comet, which in the previous year had been visible by day and night like a gleaming horsetail in the heavens.

Old people remembered that the last comet had been the precursor of a war with China.

The earthquake came as a complete surprise, without premonitory tremors. The houses of Lhasa began suddenly to shake and one heard in the distance some forty dull detonations, caused no doubt by a crack in the crust of the earth. In the cloudless sky a huge glow was visible to the east. The aftershocks lasted for days. The Indian radio reported great landslides in the province of Assam, which borders Tibet. Mountains and valleys were displaced and the Brahmaputra, which had been blocked by a fallen mountain, had caused immense devastation. It was not till a few weeks later that news came to Lhasa of the extent of the catastrophe in Tibet itself. The epicenter of the earthquake must have been in South Tibet. Hundreds of monks and nuns were buried in their rock monasteries and often there were no survivors to carry the news to the nearest district officer. Towers were split down the middle, leaving ruined walls pointing to the sky, and human beings, as if snatched by a demon's hand, disappeared into the suddenly gaping earth.

The evil omens multiplied. Monsters were born. One morning the capital of the stone column at the foot of the Potala was found lying on the ground in fragments. In vain did the government send monks to the centers of ill-omen to banish the evil spirits with their prayers, and when one day in blazing summer weather, water began to flow from a gargoyle on the cathedral, the people of Lhasa were beside themselves with terror. No doubt natural explanations could have been found for all these happenings, but if the Tibetans lost their superstitiousness they would at the same time lose an asset. One has to remember that if evil portents can demoralize them with fear, good omens inspire them with strength and confidence.

The Dalai Lama was kept informed of all these sinister events. Though naturally as superstitious as his people, he was always curious to hear my views on these things. We never lacked matter for conversation and our lesson time was all too short. He actually spent his leisure hours with me, and few people realized that he was using his free time for further study. He kept punctually to his program, and if he awaited my coming with pleasure, that did not prevent him from breaking off as soon as the clock told him that our conversation time was over, and that a teacher of religion was waiting for him in one of the pavilions.

I once learned by chance what store he set by our lessons. One day, on which many ceremonies were to take place, I did not expect to be called to the Norbulingka and so went with friends for a walk on a hill near the town. Before I started, I told my servant to flash me a signal with a mirror if the Dalai Lama sent for me. At the usual hour the signal came and I ran at top speed back into the town. My servant was waiting with a horse at the ferry but, fast as I rode, I was ten minutes late. The Dalai Lama ran to meet me and excitedly grasped both my hands, calling "Where have you been all this time? I have been waiting so long for you, Henrig." I begged him to pardon me for having disturbed him. It was only then that I realized how much these hours meant to him.

On the same day his mother and youngest brother were present, and I showed them one of the eighty films which the Dalai Lama possessed. It was very interesting for me to see the mother and son together. I knew that from the moment of the official recognition of the boy as the Incarnate Buddha the family had no more claim on him as a son or brother. For that reason his mother's visit was a sort of official event, to which she came in all her finery and jewels. When she left, she bowed before him and he laid his hand on her head in blessing. This gesture well expressed the relation of these two persons to one another. The mother did not even receive the two-handed blessing, which was accorded only to monks and high officials.

It very seldom happened that we were disturbed when we were together. Once a soldier of the bodyguard brought him an important letter. The huge fellow threw himself three times to the ground, drew in his breath with a panting sound as the etiquette demands, and delivered the letter. He then withdrew from the room, walking backwards, and closed the door silently behind him. In such moments, I was very conscious how greatly I myself offended against the protocol.

The letter I have mentioned came from the eldest brother of the Dalai Lama, the abbot of Kumbum in the Chinese province of Chinghai. The reds were already in power there and they were now hoping to influence the Dalai Lama in their favor through his brother Tagtsel Rimpoche. The letter announced that Tagtsel was on the way to Lhasa.

On the same day I visited the Dalai Lama's family. His mother scolded me when I arrived. Her mother's love had not failed to notice how much he depended on me and how often he had looked at the clock as he waited for my coming. I explained why I had not come

in time and was able to convince her that my unpunc-
tuality had not been due to casualness. When I left her
she begged me never to forget how few chances of
enjoying himself in his own way her son had. It was
perhaps a good thing that she herself had seen how
much our lesson hours meant to the Dalai Lama. After
a few months everyone in Lhasa knew where I was
riding about noon. As was to be expected, the monks
criticized my regular visits, but his mother stood up for
her son's wishes.

The next time I came through the yellow gate into
the Inner Garden I thought I noticed the Dalai Lama
looking out for me from his little window, and it
seemed he was wearing glasses. This surprised me as I
had never seen him with spectacles on. In answer to my
question he told me that he had for some time been
having difficulty with his eyes and had therefore taken
to wearing glasses for study. His brother had procured
him a pair through the Indian Legation. He had probably damaged his eyes when he was a child, when his
only pleasure was to look for hours together through
his telescope at Lhasa. Moreover continuous reading
and study in the twilight of the Potala were not exactly
calculated to improve his sight. On this occasion he was
wearing a red jacket over his monastic robe. He had
designed it himself and was very proud of it, but he
allowed himself to wear it only in his leisure moments.
The chief novelty about this garment was the fact that it
had pockets. Tibetan clothes do not have any, but the
designer had noticed the existence of pockets in the
illustrated papers and in my jackets and had realized
how useful they might be. Now, like every other boy of
his age, he was able to carry about with him a knife, a

screwdriver, sweets, etc. He also now kept his colored pencils and fountain pens in his pockets and was, doubtless, the first Dalai Lama to take pleasure in such things. He was also much interested in his collection of watches and clocks, some of which he had inherited from the thirteenth Dalai Lama. His favorite piece was an Omega calendar clock which he had bought with his own money. During his minority he could only dispose of the money which was left as an offering at the foot of his throne. Later on the treasure vaults of the Potala and the Garden of Jewels would be open to him and, as ruler of Tibet, he would become one of the world's richest men.

from Buddha Heart, Buddha Mind:

LIVING THE FOUR NOBLE TRUTHS

by the Dalai Lama

The Dalai Lama here discusses patience and compassion, making reference to Indian Buddhist master Shantideva's *The Bodhicharyavatara* (translated here as *Journey Toward the Awakening*).

*A*nimate beings are innumerable, but, like us, each has but one wish—not to suffer, and to be happy. In this we are all alike. Just as we ourselves deserve to be delivered from suffering, all animate beings deserve to be uncoupled from their individual sufferings.

Each of us has our own way of dissipating sufferings, and our own way of realizing happiness, and the same is true for all animate beings. Each "I" is precious and important, but it counts as one only in relation to the beings whose teeming masses touch the confines of space: animate beings are actually infinite in number.

The most important thing is the greatest number, as one may read in *Journey Toward the Awakening*:

> Since we all have equal need to be happy,
> What privilege would make of me the single
>   object of my efforts toward happiness?
> And since we all dread
> Danger and suffering,
> By what privilege would I have the right to be
>   protected,
> I alone and not others?

Given that all of us, others and myself, have an equal need to be happy, Shantideva wonders why he would be the sole object of his efforts for happiness. Likewise, since none of us wishes to suffer, he asks himself how he could dream of finding a means of protecting himself alone from suffering.

But that is not all. There is a very great bond between our happiness and suffering and that of others. Were there absolutely no connection between the happiness and suffering of each one and the happiness and suffering of others, we should be able never to think of the happiness and sufferings of others, and the happiness and suffering of each one would respond to his or her aspirations alone. But this is scarcely the case. If others are happy, our own happiness is possible. If all others are unhappy, it will be difficult for us to be the only happy being.

And, what is more, the more we think of the happiness and suffering of others, the more strength our mind will have. The more we think only of ourselves, the more hopes and apprehensions we shall have, and in the same proportion. Indeed, it is to the extent of our hopes and apprehensions that we shall be afraid or experience great dreads.

We must also cherish ourselves, since, if we have no self-esteem, we cannot esteem the other. We begin by turning this esteem upon ourselves, after which we shall necessarily cherish others.

Still, as far as self-esteem is concerned, thinking really only of ourselves and disdaining the happiness of others makes one unhappy. We shall be unhappy if we are alone in life, and we shall cause unhappiness to our family, if we have one, and unhappiness to society. In a word, for those who think only of themselves and neglect others, cherish themselves and disdain the happiness of others, that is the origin of the problem.

If, on the contrary, we think that the good of others is far more vast than our own good, we shall only find more courage within ourselves, we shall have no regret, we shall be satisfied in mind, and thus shall think that we are good for something. Even in private we shall think that we have accomplished what is necessary in life, and this kind of thought will bring happiness into the heart of our very family. What is truly useful, then, comes from this kind of state of mind; and the esteem we bear the other, cherishing him or her, will contribute to the general good as well as to our personal good. There we have the basis.

Some may wonder whether, in taking on the happiness and suffering of others, in thinking of the suffering of others more than of our own, we shall not add to our own unhappiness. To this, *Journey Toward the Awakening* answers no. When one has a problem oneself and feels distressed, when one has tried everything in vain, one is helpless, cast down, impotent. But when, by compassion, one experiences a violent sense of the intolerable in the face of the sufferings that torture others, there is no longer room for this sense of impotency.

When, in the mind, we have gained courage, and are willing to take on the suffering of others—once we think of their suffering, we experience a slight discomfort. But once this sense of sadness is past, we are enthusiastic, we feel full of courage, just the opposite of what has occurred before.

We have already spoken of the viewpoint of those who practice the teachings of the Buddha, have we not? The first teaching that they put into practice is discipline, which consists of renouncing the six nonvirtuous acts. The beneficiaries of this practice are animate beings. It is where animate beings are concerned that one forbids oneself to kill, to rob, to abuse sexually, to lie, to slander, to be rough or uncouth. One must begin, then, by no longer doing ill to animate beings, and in this case the object "animate beings" is a necessity: it is in them that discipline finds its support.

The rules of the discipline of individual liberation all consist of renouncing evil done to another, as well as the mental basis of this evil. Once a potential victim appears, one has only to forbid oneself to harm him or her by seeing any harmful act as a great evil. This is how one proceeds in the discipline of individual liberation.

As for the way of the bodhisattvas, generosity, discipline, and patience are necessarily practiced toward animate beings, and patience is the principal practice of the bodhisattvas. Why? Because they must cultivate the spirit of Awakening on the basis of love and

compassion. Meditation on love necessarily blocks
hate, which is the opposite of love, and patience is necessary since it is the antidote of anger. In order to
meditate on patience, then, one needs an object of
patience: an enemy.

If we consider things carefully, enemies are essential,
almost as essential as spiritual masters. We cannot meditate on patience by taking as our object the Buddha.
Patience is addressed only to enemies that agitate your
mind, that make you angry. We need them in order to
make progress in practice. I shall say nothing, then, of
the immense goodness of all beings. It is explained that
those whom we regard as enemies, those on whom
we turn our backs, those whom we wish to harm are
particularly generous with us in this respect.

Likewise, compassion is most essential, and it will have
as its object the ensemble of beings afflicted with misery.
The way of the Lesser and Greater Vehicles, this marvel,
the multiple collections of merits that have been cultivated in them—these practices have as their object living
beings, our dear mothers. And these practices that cul-
minate in the authentic and perfect Awakening—in the
disappearance of every defect, in the possession of all
qualities—these too are reached in taking our brothers
and sisters, living beings, as our object.

Shantideva writes in *Journey Toward the Awakening,*

It is through beings, as if through the buddhas,
That one obtains the virtues of a buddha.
Now, the veneration we accord the buddhas,
We deny beings. Why this difference?

To reach the state of the buddha, we must rely

simultaneously on ordinary beings and on enlightened beings. It is a very serious error to venerate to the buddhas while neglecting ordinary beings. For that matter, it is in the Buddha that we take refuge, and to him that we devote our faith. Now, the only things that interest this Buddha in whom we have faith are animate beings. Would it not be hypocritical to take refuge in the Buddha while neglecting those to whom the Buddha offers the refuge of his great love? If we truly love the Buddha, it is important that we not do anything that would go contrary to his heart. Is it not lamentable to believe in the Buddha and to mistreat, oppress, despise, and deceive the unfortunate ones that the Buddha only snatches to the "eyelets of his compassion"?

Were it an ordinary being, a really close friend, one would respect his or her sensitivity, one would seek to avoid what displeases that person, one would say to oneself that if one did this, he or she would be sad, that if one ignored that person, he or she would be pained. When one has a friend who is a vegetarian, it is unsuitable to eat meat in his or her presence—this would be to ignore that person. If we are ashamed to take no account of a friend, who is but an ordinary being, then it will be necessary to take a little account of the enlightened opinion of the buddhas and bodhisattvas. This way we have of acting always seems pitiful to me. When one has faith in the Buddha, it is pathetic to regard "ordinary" beings as beings to be crushed, or on whom to "take things out." Those who are Buddhists ought to consider this carefully.

There is no problem for others, if they think that they are at a lecture.

At the moment, I am going to speak as a Buddhist.

Having reflected in this way on the spirit of Awakening, Buddhists ought to practice in a spirit of having faith in the Buddha, and loving the Dharma, all the while respecting the enlightened thought of the Buddha.

Even when we are acting only for ourselves, it is in the measure of our altruism that what we do will bring temporary well-being and assistance in the long term. If, on the contrary, we neglect other animate beings through obsession with our own personal good, we fall into the partial vision of nirvana proper to the arhat of the Hearers, which also presents the fault of holding oneself in high esteem. This deficiency is the effect of a lack of esteem for others. Being practitioners, disciples of the Buddha, we shall exercise ourselves in the perfectly pure actions of the Buddha. Of all the Buddha's numerous actions, which counts the most? The spirit of Awakening, which consists of preferring others to oneself.

We shall stick to this direction, then, even if we have not yet attained the goal. The essential is to think that we shall persist even if we have not yet succeeded. As we read in *Journey Toward the Awakening:*

> What need of many explanations?
> Between the one who acts for himself
> And the Buddha who acts for others,
> Observe the difference!

Until the present we have, with consciousness and diligence, preferred ourselves to all others. Up until this day, we have done only this: cherish ourselves while disdaining others. And look at the result. Today, now that we have heard some of the defects attached to cherishing oneself, and some of the qualities attached to cherishing others, we ought to concentrate carefully, and to reduce our self-esteem as much as we can, while developing the esteem we have for others to the greatest degree possible. If we do so, the sun of happiness will rise, and the good of others as well as our own personal good will be accomplished. From this moment, we can hope for this. Then tell yourselves this: "I have taken the resolution to exercise myself in the way opened by the bodhisattvas, the children of the Conqueror, by following their perfect example."

What people have the power to accomplish their projects, and to consecrate themselves to the good of others all the way to the accomplishment of their ultimate good? To be capable of doing the good of others with sure foot, using our personal experience, it is indispensable that we have realized what is called the absolute body for oneself. It is necessary to realize the absolute body in order to accomplish the good of others by exchanging the absolute body for the formal body for others. So this is how one must think: "To easily accomplish the ultimate good of all animate beings, my elderly mothers in infinite numbers, I shall myself attain to buddhahood in two bodies."

Here, then, the cause is the aspiration to consecrate oneself to the good of others, and "spirit of Awakening" is the name for the spiritual strength accompanying the aspiration to consecrate oneself to omniscience. At the moment, this is only an artificial idea, and not the authentic spirit of Awakening. We cannot say that we are going to produce the spirit of Awakening today and that we shall instantly be bodhisattvas.

To engender and cultivate the spirit of Awakening,

we must meditate on it, meditate again, and always meditate, for a long time, shoring up our meditation with
the accumulation of merits and wisdom, and being
purified of the veils. If we meditate on this subject
without ceasing, then at the end of a great many lives we
shall arrive, perhaps. But it may also take kalpas. Nor is
it impossible for this to take but a few years.

Be this as it may, and whatever way we have chosen,
we shall have to begin by gradually forming a clear idea.
Only afterwards shall we move to the experience: at
first, experiences with effort, then without effort, and
finally without the least artifice, without even having to
think about it. Then naturally, spontaneously, the
aspiration to consecrate ourselves to the Awakening
will splice with the aspiration to consecrate ourselves to
the good of others, and, whether we are walking, lying,
or sitting, everything will remind us of the spirit of
Awakening. Then only shall we have experienced it
once and for all. This can only occur at the end of a
lengthy training.

from A Flash of Lightning in the Dark of Night:

A GUIDE TO THE BODHISATTVA'S WAY OF LIFE

by *the Dalai Lama*

Indian Buddhist master Shantideva's classic *Bodhicharyāvatara (The Way of the Bodhisattva)* is a guide for developing *bodhichitta*—a sense of loving compassion for others. Here the Dalai Lama talks about how to draw upon the wisdom of this text in our daily lives.

1. *Now that diligence has been developed,*
   I will set my mind to concentrate.
   For one whose mind is loose and wandering
   Lives between the fangs of the afflictions.

To strengthen our practice, it is necessary to develop one-pointed concentration of the mind. For this we first need to understand the disadvantages of being distracted. Lack of concentration prevents us from keeping our minds focused on the object of meditation. The mind follows any thoughts that arise, and it is then all too easy for negative emotions to grow. Any positive actions we do will not realize their full effect. Distraction is therefore a major defect, and it is very important to counteract it by developing mental calm (*shamatha*).

The practice of mental calm is not unique to Buddhism. Non-Buddhist traditions include methods for developing mental calm through which it is possible to attain the state of concentration of the formless celestial beings (*devas*) in the realm of *nothing at all*. In this state negative emotions are allayed but not entirely eliminated—they remain latent. Mental calm on its own, therefore, is not uniquely special. But this one-pointed concentration is very important in developing fully the power of positive actions, and it is crucial for our practice of clear insight (*vipashyanā*). The Mādhyamika view, which is common to both Sūtrayāna and Māntrayāna, is established through analytical reasoning until we obtain certainty in it. This is something very subtle, and unless our power of concentration is stable, there is a danger of losing this view of emptiness. The more stable our concentration is, the clearer will be our understanding of emptiness.

What do we mean by meditation? First, there is meditation through analysis, whereby we repeatedly examine an object until we gain a degree of certainty concerning its nature. When we cannot proceed any further with analysis, we let ourselves repose in the state of clarity and confidence that we have achieved. This is placement meditation. It is the latter type of meditation that is used in practices such as visualizing deities and training in mental calm, where one is developing the power of concentration.

One can also meditate on devotion, in order to understand and increase it; or on impermanence, where one contemplates an object and the way in which it is constantly changing; or on emptiness, realizing that the object has no true existence.

There are many ways to describe the perception of things. In meditation it is important to be able to distinguish between the perceived object, the object in itself, the object as it is considered to be, and the object of intention. We should also study the five defects to be avoided in mental calm meditation, mentioned in the *Treatise on the Center and Extremes*.

In brief, meditation is a way of training and transforming the mind, and this it certainly does. For our purposes, the main thing is to develop the one-pointed concentration of mental calm and to meditate on bodhichitta. For concentration to become clear, we need the right conditions, namely, freedom from outer distractions. The ideal is to meditate in a secluded place that is conducive to physical and mental serenity.

> 3. On account of loved ones and desire for gain,
>   Disgust with worldly life does not arise.
>   These are, then, the first things to renounce.
>   Such are the reflections of a prudent man.

> 4. The penetrating insight of a mind that calmly rests
>   Destroys completely all afflicted states.
>   Knowing this, one must begin by searching for tranquility,
>   Found by those who turn with joy their backs upon the
>   world.

> 7. If for other beings there is craving,
>   A veil is cast upon the perfect truth,
>   Wholesome disillusion melts away,
>   And finally there comes the sting of pain.

8. My thoughts are all for them,
  And by degrees my life is frittered by.
  My family and friends will fade and pass,
  And yet for them the changeless doctrine is forsaken.

As we are impermanent, is it really worth being so attached to others, who are also impermanent? Is it really worth getting angry with them? Let us reflect on this and stop the stream of clinging and aversion.

9. If I act like those who are like children,
  Sure it is that I shall fall to lower states.
  Why then keep the company of infants
  And be led by them in ways so far from virtue?

Ordinary beings dominated by gross attachment and hatred are like children. If we behave like them, we will not achieve anything for ourselves, and it will be impossible for us to benefit them. One minute they are our friends, the next they turn against us. However hard we try, it is difficult to please them. And when we do not listen to them, they become angry.

13. Associate with childish ones—what follows?
  Self-praise, putting others down, and
  Chattering about the pleasures of sam såra.
  Every kind of vice is sure to come.

14. This kind of link between myself and others
  Will be productive only of misfortune:
  They will bring no benefit to me;
  Neither shall I do them any good.

• • •

It is therefore better to keep our distance from such beings. In doing so, however, we should avoid offending them, and when we do meet them, we should be courteous and do what we can to make them happy, without becoming too familiar.

> 16. *Like bees that get their honey from the flowers,*
> *Take only what is consonant with Dharma.*
> *Treat them like first time acquaintances;*
> *Do not be familiar with them.*

Let us not be attached to ephemeral pleasures. It is only ignorant and confused people who spend their time amassing possessions. They end up with suffering a thousand times as great as the happiness they seek.

> 19. *This being so, the wise man does not crave,*
> *Because from craving fear is born.*
> *And fix this firmly in your understanding:*
> *All that may be wished for will fade naturally to nothing.*

> 20. *For though they get themselves a wealth of property,*
> *Enjoying reputation, sweet celebrity,*
> *Who can say where they have gone to now,*
> *With all the baggage of their affluence and fame?*

What point is there in hoping for people's approval and fearing their criticism? If a few people sing our praises, there is not much to be happy about, because there might be many more who are secretly criticizing us. We need not worry when a few criticize us, because there are others who have only praise for us. The wants and needs of others are so various that it is impossible for us ordinary beings to satisfy them all. Even the Buddhas themselves cannot do so. So it is better to distance ourselves from the childish and consider instead the advantages of living in solitude.

> 25. *In woodlands, haunt of stag and bird,*
>   *Among the trees where no sounds jar upon the ear,*
>   *Such would be my pleasant company.*
>   *When might I go and make my dwelling there?*

> 26. *When will I live and make my home*
>   *In cave or empty shrine or under spreading tree,*
>   *And have within my breast a free, unfettered heart,*
>   *Which never turns to cast a backward glance?*

In such secluded places we can give up attachment to our belongings and bodies and devote all our time to meditation.

> 28. *When might I be free of fear,*
>   *Without the need to hide from anyone,*
>   *With just a begging bowl and few belongings,*
>   *Dressed in garments coveted by nobody?*

> 33. *Like those who journey on the road,*
>   *Who halt and make a pause along the way,*
>   *Beings on the pathways of the world,*
>   *Halt and pause and take their birth.*

> 34. *Until the time comes round when*
>   *Four men carry me away,*
>   *Amid the tears and sighs of worldly folk—*
>   *Till then, I will away and go into the forest.*

35. *There, with no befriending or begrudging,*
    I will stay alone, in solitude,
    Considered from the outset as already dead,
    Thus, when I die, a source of pain to none.

In short, in lonely places one is able to meditate with one-pointed concentration, free from personal concerns and attachment. Thoughts of the Buddha and his teachings come naturally to mind.

Shāntideva continues by pointing out the mistake of being attached to sensual pleasures. As the *Bodhicharyā-vatara* was originally addressed to a community of monks, this section deals especially with the defects of the female body, but it should be understood that a woman practitioner can apply the same method of reflection to men's bodies.

40. *Sending messengers and go-betweens*
    With many invitations to the bride,
    Avoiding, in the quest, no sin
    Or deed that brings an evil name,

41. *Nor acts of frightful risk,*
    Nor loss and ruin of their goods and wealth.
    And all for pleasure and the perfect bliss,
    That utmost penetrating kiss

42. *Of what in truth is nothing but a heap of bones,*
    Devoid of self, without its own existence!
    If this is all the object of desire and lust,
    Why not pass beyond all pain and grief?

Think about it: the person to whom we are so

attracted, and for whom we have undergone so many ordeals, is only a mass of flesh and organs and rather unpleasant substances. What is it then that we are attached to—the person's body or mind? If we check carefully, we find that we cannot point at any real thing that is the source of our attachment.

54. *"But it is the skin and flesh I love*
    To touch and look upon."
    Why then do you not wish for flesh alone,
    Inanimate and in its natural state?

55. *The mind of the one you love so much*
    Eludes your touch; this mind you cannot see.
    Everything that sense perceives is not the mind,
    Therefore, why indulge in pointless copulation?

Let us examine the body. First of all, it originates from the procreative fluids of the parents. Once mature, it is made up of blood, flesh, organs, and bones. Were we to find any one of these things left on the ground, we would be utterly revolted. Why then are we not repelled by the body, which is wholly made up of disgusting elements?

63. *Thus the unclean nature of such things*
    Is manifest, and yet if even now I harbor doubts,
    Then I should go to charnel grounds
    And look upon the fetid carrion.

A large part of what we eat and drink to sustain this body ends up as an unending stream of urine and excrement, filling the sewers we find so offensive. But the very reason there are sewers is that our bodies are full of excrement. The body is no different from a sewer! As we have seen, it originates from filth, consists of filth, and churns out filth. Only when we think about the body from this point of view, says the *Garland of Jewels*, will our attachment to the body begin to diminish, if not entirely disappear.

Again, take someone with a very beautiful body. Suppose the skin were removed and the body opened up. Even in a living person, the internal organs are a gruesome sight. Our desire would soon give way to revulsion. Attachment to the body is illusion on top of illusion, and we should do our best to undo it.

> 70. *Did you see the heaps of human bones*
> *And feel revulsion in the charnel ground?*
> *Then why such pleasure in your cities of the dead,*
> *Filled with animated skeletons?*

We experience endless difficulties trying to find the ideal partner, and once we have done so, we do not always get on well together. We cannot have children, or we have too many, and bringing them up adds to our problems. Of course, in the beginning the novelty is enjoyable, but if we examine things closely, we find that suffering just follows on suffering. This is why the sūtras refer to "the malady of household life."

As for wealth, we go to great lengths to obtain it, and are even prepared to lose our lives for it. Once we have it, we are forever afraid of losing it. Because of wealth, brothers and sisters are set at odds, couples break up. When we do not have it we suffer; when we have it we also suffer!

79. *The suffering of guarding what we have, the pain of losing*
     all—
     We should see the endless troubles brought on us by
     wealth.
     Those distracted by their love of property
     Will never have a moment's freedom from the sorrows of
     existence.

80. *Those indeed possessed of many wants*
     Suffer many hardships, all for very little
     Mouthfuls of the hay the oxen get,
     Their fine reward for having pulled the cart!

For the smallest of pleasures, people waste their human lives that have cost them a disproportionately greater effort to obtain.

82. *All that we desire is sure to perish,*
     And then into infernal pain we fall.
     The constant little hardships and fatigue
     We undergo, and all for no great matter—

83. *With a millionth part of such vexation*
     Buddhahood itself can be attained!
     The pains the lustful take exceed by far the troubles
     Of the path of freedom and will give no freedom at the
     end.

So we should examine the things that excite our distracted thoughts. Gradually these thoughts will become less strong, and our minds will become more calm. Then we will be able to meditate one-pointedly on bodhichitta.

The main meditation on bodhichitta consists of considering oneself and others to be equal and then exchanging oneself with others. As Shāntideva says:

The mighty Buddhas, pondering for many kalpas,
Have seen that this and only this will save
The boundless multitudes of beings
And bring them easily to supreme joy! [chap. I, v. 7]

The masters of the Kadampa tradition left detailed teachings on different ways of practicing bodhichitta. By generating bodhichitta through such practices, we can purify all our obscurations and accumulate positive actions. It is said that we have to accumulate merit over three uncountable kalpas, but these terms are relative. With the attitude of bodhichitta such enormous amounts of merit are quickly and easily achieved. All the learned and accomplished masters, from the Buddha through Nāgārjuna and his disciples down to our own present teachers, took the practice of considering others more important than themselves as the foundation of their own practice. Through this they were able to benefit themselves and others on a vast scale.

Anyone who has good thoughts, who does a lot to help others, and who leaves behind good memories is respected by people all over the world, regardless of whether they are religious or not. On the other hand, the ignorance, arrogance, and obstinacy of certain individuals, whether their intentions were good or evil, have been at the root of all the tragedies of history. The mere names of these ruthless tyrants inspire fear and loathing. So the extent to which people will like us naturally depends on how much or how little we think of others' good.

Speaking of my own experience, I sometimes wonder why a lot of people like me. When I think about it, I cannot find in myself any specially good quality, except for one small thing. That is the positive mind, which I try to explain to others and which I do my best to develop myself. Of course, there are moments when I do get angry, but in the depth of my heart, I do not hold a grudge against anyone. I cannot pretend that I am really able to practice bodhichitta, but it does give me tremendous inspiration. Deep inside me, I realize how valuable and beneficial it is, that is all. And I try as much as possible to consider others to be more important than myself. I think that's why people take note of me and like me, because of my good heart.

When people say that I have worked a lot for peace, I feel embarrassed. I feel like laughing. I don't think I have done very much for world peace. It's just that my practice is the peaceful path of kindness, love, compassion, and not harming others. This has become part of me. It is not something for which I have specially volunteered. I am simply a follower of the Buddha, and the Buddha taught that patience is the supreme means for transcending suffering. He said, "If a monk harms others, he is not a monk." I am a Buddhist monk, so I try to practice accordingly. When people think this practice is something unique and special and call me a leader of world peace, I feel almost ashamed!

A good heart is the source of all happiness and joy, and we can all be good-hearted if we make an effort. But better still is to have bodhichitta, which is a good heart imbued with wisdom. It is the strong desire to attain enlightenment in order to deliver all beings from suffering and bring them to Buddhahood. This thought of helping others is rooted in compassion, which grows from a feeling of gratitude and love for beings, who are afflicted by suffering.

Traditionally there are two methods for developing this sort of care and gratitude. One is to reflect on the fact that all beings have at some time in the succession of their lives been our parents, or at least close friends, so that we naturally feel grateful to them and wish to take on their suffering in exchange for our happiness. The other method is to understand that others suffer in the same way as we do, to see that we are all equal, and to reflect on what is wrong with egotism and on the advantages of altruism. We can use whichever of these two methods suits us best or practice them both together.

In either case, it is necessary first to understand what we call suffering. It is easy enough for us to feel compassion for people who are starving, in pain, or in great distress and for animals who are maltreated. But when we think of human and celestial beings who are very happy, we tend to feel envious. This is because we have not really understood what suffering is and that all beings suffer. Apart from the more obvious torments of *suffering added to suffering* and *suffering of change*, there is *all-pervading suffering*. Because of the latter, as long as we are in samsāra, we can never have lasting happiness. Once we have reflected on and understood this for ourselves, we can apply this understanding to others. Then we start to feel compassion and think, I must free all these beings from suffering.

However, to actually do so, we have to change our approach to this life and to our future lives. First we must reflect on impermanence, on the certainty of our own death, and on the fact that we can never know how soon we might die. After death, we will not simply vanish: the positive and negative actions we have done will determine how we are reborn. Our negative actions might cause us to be reborn in the lower realms, for example as animals—exploited, maltreated, and butchered by humans or devoured by other animals.

So to free ourselves from the ocean of suffering, we should begin to study and practice the path of liberation. We might hope to see some result after a few years, but speaking realistically, we should plan on probably having to continue our practice over many lives to come. In each of these lives we are going to need a proper support for practice, namely, a human body, without which it will be impossible to make progress. The first stage on the path, therefore, is to ensure a good human rebirth. So although our final aim is to achieve enlightenment for all beings, we have to begin the path by following the discipline of avoiding the ten nonvirtuous actions and practicing the ten virtuous actions.

To summarize, we start by getting rid of our attachment to nonspiritual goals, first in this life and then in future lives. Having seen the suffering inherent in samsāra, we resolve to free ourselves, and as we extend this attitude to other beings, we develop compassion and generate bodhichitta. We have to go through these stages of training the mind in the right order, like going up some stairs or like building the foundation before we build a wall. If we follow the path gradually in this way, the result we have will be stable. But if we simply say, "For the sake of all beings . . ." however strong our wish to help beings might be at that moment, it will not be stable unless it is well founded on the correct practice of the earlier stages.

In the beginning we should have a clear, overall view of the path, so that we know what we are aiming at in our practice and can recognize the level we have reached. Then, as we practice regularly, we may experience profound changes in our minds, but these experiences only occur when we are concentrating in sessions of meditation. Later, after meditating for a long time, we find that these experiences occur spontaneously when we encounter particular circumstances, without our needing to concentrate in meditation.

Take the example of bodhichitta. After we have meditated on bodhichitta for a while, a change occurs in our minds, but only when we are actually thinking of bodhichitta. This is what is called a fabricated experience. It is not the bodhichitta of a real Bodhisattva. As we maintain progress, however, we reach a point where the mere sight of an animal or bird causes the thought to well up from the depth of our hearts, When will I ever attain enlightenment for this being? This is what we call a natural experience, and at this point true bodhichitta has taken root in us. We can genuinely call ourselves practitioners of the Mahāyāna and are then on the lesser path of accumulation.

Proceeding on the middle path of accumulation, we then begin the greater path of accumulation of merit, which lasts three uncountable kalpas. This is followed by the path of connection with its four stages of warmth, climax, endurance, and supreme realization. Then as we start on the path of seeing, we gain the wisdom of the first Bodhisattva level. In this way, we gradually traverse the five paths and ten levels and ultimately attain Buddhahood. These paths and levels are therefore related to our own inner transformation through the practice of bodhichitta.

> 90. *Strive at first to meditate*
> *Upon the sameness of yourself and others;*
> *In joy and sorrow all are equal.*
> *Be the guard of all, as of yourself.*

In what way are others equal to us? Just like us, they naturally want to be happy and to avoid suffering. Although on analysis we are unable to find an "I" that truly exists, we are still convinced that it does exist, and we therefore consider that we have a right to be happy and a right to escape unhappiness. But this is also the case for all other beings, so there is no particular reason why we should be any more important than them. Why should we accomplish only our own happiness and not be responsible for others' happiness? Why should we make an effort to avoid suffering for ourselves and not be responsible for doing the same for others?

When we try to protect our bodies, we also protect the parts of the body, such as our hands and feet. Similarly, since the happiness and suffering of others are all part of the same happiness and suffering that is ours, we must protect others from suffering just as much as we protect ourselves and strive for others' happiness just as we do for our own.

Our own sufferings, though not felt by others, are certainly hard for us to bear. So it is natural that we should try to protect ourselves from suffering. Similarly, others' pain, even if we do not feel it, is no less unbearable for them. But as we are related to all other beings, as we owe them our gratitude and they help us in our practice, let us try to dispel their suffering as well as ours. All beings equally want to be happy, so why should we be the only ones to get happiness? Why should we be protected from suffering and others not be?

> 94. *So I will dispel the pain of others,*
> *Since pain it is, just like my own.*
> *And others I will aid and benefit,*
> *For they are living beings, just like me.*

> 97. *—Since the pains of others do no harm to me,*
> *Why protect and make a guard against them?*
> *—But why to guard against "my" future pain, which*
> *Does no harm to this, my present "me"?*

One might think that one has to protect oneself from future suffering because the "I" that suffers now and the "I" that will suffer in the future are the same. This is wrong, because what we think of as "I" is a succession of instants in a continuum of consciousness, and the "I" of the moment that will suffer in future is different from the "I" of the present moment.

> 99. *It is surely for the sufferer himself*
> *To parry any injury that comes!*
> *The pain felt in my feet is not my hand's;*
> *Why then does my hand protect my foot?*

If one were to think that everyone should take care of his or her own suffering, one could argue that the hand should protect only itself and no other part of the body: there is no reason why the hand should protect the foot. Although we might find this argument convenient, it is not at all logical. Let us stop being stubborn and thinking only of ourselves.

> 101. *Labeled continuities and aggregates,*
> *Such as strings of beads and armies, are deceptive;*
> *Likewise, there is none who has the pain.*
> *Who is there to be oppressed by it?*

> 102. *But if there is no subject suffering,*
> *There can be no difference in the pain of self and other.*
> *Simply, then, since pain is pain, I will dispel it.*
> *What use is there in making such distinctions?*

When we talk about "I" and "beings," these are not independent entities. They are false labels applied to a continuum of impermanent elements, just as "necklace" is applied to a string of beads or "army" to a collection of soldiers. However, if beings have no real existence, who is in pain? Why try to dispel suffering? Although the "I" does not truly exist, in relative truth everyone wants to avoid suffering. This is sufficient reason for dispelling the sufferings of others as well as our own. What is the use in discriminating?

> 103. *Thus, the suffering of everyone*
> *Should be dispelled, and here there's no debate.*
> *To free myself from pain means freeing all;*
> *Contrariwise, I suffer with the pain of beings.*

We might think, If I meditate on compassion and

think of the suffering of others, it will only add to the intense pain I already have. We only think like this because we are narrow-minded. If we do not want to help beings, then their suffering will be endless. But if we can develop a little compassion and make an effort to dispel the suffering of others, then that suffering will have an end. Without our taking the responsibility to help others, there can be no limit to suffering. When we develop a broad mind and feel compassion for others, this is vastly beneficial. Any small difficulties we might experience are worthwhile.

> *105. If through such a single pain*
> *A multitude of sorrows can be remedied,*
> *Such pain as this all loving ones*
> *Should strive to foster in themselves and others.*

The great Bodhisattvas are prepared to do anything, even lose their lives, if it will eradicate the misery of numerous other beings.

> *107. Those whose minds are practiced in this way,*
> *Whose happiness it is to soothe the pain of others,*
> *Will venture in the hell of unremitting agony*
> *As swans sweep down upon a lotus lake.*

> *108. The oceanlike immensity of joy*
> *Arising when all beings are set free—*
> *Is this not enough? Does this not satisfy?*
> *The wish for my own freedom, what is it to me?*

For a Bodhisattva who wears the armor of determination, the joy he has from alleviating the pain of

infinite beings is sufficient on its own, even if he suffers a little himself. How could achieving liberation for
ourselves alone, while abandoning our promise to liberate others, be better than that?

> *109. The work of bringing benefit to beings*
> *Will not, then, make me proud and self-admiring.*
> *The happiness of others is itself my satisfaction;*
> *I will not expect some ripening reward.*

Let us never think, If I help others, I will accumulate
positive actions. I will be a virtuous person and in the
future I'll be happy. This is not the point. Let us do
positive actions with profound compassion to relieve
others' unhappiness, and let us dedicate these actions to
their well-being, from the depth of our hearts, without
the slightest notion of future personal reward.

We shall now discuss the exchange of self and others.
This practice consists of putting ourselves in the place
of others and putting others in our own place. If we
train in this, we come to consider others more important than ourselves, so that their happiness and suffering become more important than ours, and when
they are harmed, we feel it as acutely as when we ourselves are harmed. This is not difficult to do once we
have realized the disadvantages of thinking only of ourselves and the benefits of cherishing others. Our
exchange of self and others becomes so vivid and strong
that it is easy for us to give our lives for others. And by
others we mean all beings everywhere.

· · ·

114. Just as hands and other limbs
  Are thought of as the body's members,
  Shall I not consider other beings
  As the limbs and members of a living body?

We should not be deterred by the difficulty of such a practice. It is a question of getting used to it through training. For example, it is possible to become used to a person whose mere name once made one afraid. One can even reach the point where one cannot bear to be separated from that person.

120. Those who desire speedily to be
  A refuge for themselves and other beings,
  Should take the place of others, giving them their own,
  Undertaking thus a sacred mystery.

This sure method for protecting others, including oneself, is nevertheless difficult for those with a limited understanding of bodhichitta. This is why Shantideva refers to it as a "sacred mystery." As he points out, the principal obstacle is cherishing oneself:

121. Because of our attachment to our bodies,
  We are terrified by only little things.
  This body, then, the source of so much fear—
  Who would not revile it as the worst of enemies?

122. Wishing to relieve our bodies' wants,
  Our hungry mouths, the dryness of our throats,
  We lie in wait along the road
  And steal the lives of fishes, birds, and deer.

> *123. For their bodies' service and advantage*
> *There are those who even kill their fathers or their*
>   *mothers*
> *Or steal what has been offered to the Triple Gem,*
> *Because of which they will be burned in deepest hell.*

To sustain this body of ours, to which we are so attached, we kill other beings. To make it comfortable, we steal. To satisfy its ephemeral desires, we indulge in indiscriminate sexual activity. In short, because of the importance we attribute to our bodies, we accumulate a lot of negative actions. If we let our bodies do whatever they want, it can only be to our loss and detriment.

> *124. Where then is the prudent man*
> *Who wants to pamper and protect his body,*
> *Who does not disregard and treat with scorn*
> *What is for him a dangerous enemy?*

> *125. "If I give this, what is left for me?"*
> *Thinking of oneself—this is the path of evil ghosts.*
> *"If I keep this, what is left to give?"*
> *Concern for others is the way of gods.*

If we harm and impoverish others to further our own interests, we shall be reborn in lower realms, such as the hells. On the other hand, if we forget ourselves in order to benefit others, if we are prepared to give our own lives to save the lives of others, giving them whatever is necessary for their welfare, then we shall gain happiness and all perfection.

The result of wishing to be superior to others, to be famous, will be lower rebirth or rebirth as an idiot, in abject misery, with an ugly body. On the other hand, true humility, treating others as more important than ourselves, will lead to our being reborn in the higher realms, where we will be respected and influential. If we force others to work for us and serve us, inconsiderately abuse them, in future rebirths we shall end up as their servants or even their servants' servants. Whereas if it is we who spend our lives serving others, we shall be reborn as kings and leaders.

These, then, are the benefits to be gained from regarding others as more important than oneself and the disadvantages of giving oneself precedence.

> 129. *All the joy the world contains*
> *Came through wishing happiness for others;*
> *All the misery the world contains*
> *Came through wanting pleasure for oneself.*

> 130. *Is there need for lengthy explanation?*
> *Childish beings look out for themselves;*
> *Buddhas labor for the good of others.*
> *See the difference that divides them!*

> 131. *If I do not give away*
> *My happiness for others' pain,*
> *Buddhahood will never be attained,*
> *And even in samsāra, joy will fly from me.*

Our greatest enemy is to consider ourselves more important than others, which leads us and others to certain ruin. From this attachment to "I" arises all the harm, fear, and suffering in this world. What, asks Shāntideva, am I to do with this great demon?

135. *If there is no self-surrender,*
   Sorrow likewise cannot be avoided.
   A man will not escape from being burned
   If he does not keep away from fire.

136. *To free yourself from harm*
   And others from their sufferings,
   Give away yourself for others,
   Holding others dear as now you do yourself.

137. *"For I am now beneath the power of all,"*
   This, O mind, must be your certainty;
   Now no longer shall you entertain a thought
   But to contrive the benefit of beings.

138. *My sight and other senses, now the property of others—*
   To use them for myself would be illicit.
   How much more so is it disallowed to use
   My faculties against their rightful owners.

As we have taken the vow to devote ourselves solely to helping other beings and from the depths of our hearts have given everything to them, we should consider that our bodies are no longer ours but belong now to them. So we must never use any part of our bodies to do anything that does not help others. Whatever we can see in ourselves that is good, let us snatch it away from ourselves and use it to serve others.

• • •

We come now to a practice that is special to the
Bodhicharyāva-tara:

> 140. *Think of lesser beings as yourself,*
> *And identify yourself with others,*
> *Then, your mind relieved of scruples,*
> *Cultivate a sense of envy, pride, and rivalry.*

Here we begin by evaluating our own good and bad
qualities and, on this basis, comparing ourselves with
others, distinguishing between those who are equal
to us, those who are superior, and those who are inferior. To do this we make a distinction between our new,
good side—which has seen what is wrong with considering ourselves more important than others and the
benefits of regarding others as more important than
ourselves—and our old, bad side, the egotistic "I." The
new "I" now identifies itself with other beings and takes
their side. The old "I" has three aspects: superior,
equal, and inferior. And the new "I," which is now
identified with others, has these three aspects as well. We
shall use these two distinct "I's" to develop successively a
sense of jealousy, competition, and pride.

First, we look at the good qualities in which we surpass others. Identifying ourselves (our new "I") with
these inferior beings, we make ourselves jealous of the
superior qualities of the old, egotistic "I." It is not fair,
we cry, that he is respected while we are not!

> 141. *"He is the center of attention; I am nothing!*
> *I am poor without possessions, unlike him;*
> *Everyone looks up to him, despising me;*
> *All is well for him; for me there's only bitterness.*

> *142. "All I have is sweat and drudgery,*
> *While there he's sitting at his ease.*
> *He is great, respected in the world;*
> *I'm an underdog, a well-known nobody."*

If we find this comparison too humbling, we should not get discouraged at our lack of good qualities. Let us remember that all beings possess the potential for enlightenment and that we can attain Buddhahood if we make the effort. There is no reason, therefore, to be discouraged.

> *143. "What! A nobody without distinction?*
> *Not true! I do have some good qualities.*
> *He's not the best, he's lower down than some,*
> *While, compared to some, I'm excellent!"*

It is not our fault that we are inferior but the fault of the negative emotions. These notions of superiority and inferiority are entirely relative. We tell the old "I": You are only superior because I am inferior, so if you want to stay superior, you will have to put up with me while I strive for enlightenment. What use are your good qualities if they don't benefit me? In this way, when we see qualities in ourselves that make us better than others, we should exchange roles and destroy our feelings of superiority.

Next we take those who are our equals, and again siding with them, we develop a sense of competition with our old "I," thinking only of getting the better of him and making him miserable.

> *148. "I will noise abroad by every means*

My qualities to all the world,
Ensuring that whatever qualities he has
Remain unknown to anyone.

149. *"My faults I will conceal.*
   I, not he, will be the object of devotion;
   I, not he, will gain possessions and renown;
   I will be the center of attention.

150. *"I for long will look with satisfaction*
   On his humiliation and disgrace;
   I will render him despicable,
   The mock and laughingstock of all.

Finally, we think of those aspects in which we are
inferior to others, and then looking at our old "I"
through others' eyes, we develop a sense of pride.

151. *"The rumor is that this unhappy wretch*
   Is trying to compete with me!
   How could he be like me in intelligence,
   In learning, beauty, wealth, or pedigree?

152. *"Oh, the pleasure, sending shivers*
   Up my spine, I have and revel in
   To hear that everyone is talking
   Of how talented I am!

153. *"Well then, even if he does have something,*
   I'm the one he's working for!
   He can have enough to live on;
   I'm the boss, though, and the rest is mine!

• • •

154. "I will wear his happiness away;
    I will always hurt and injure him.
    He's the one who in samsāara
    Did me mischiefs by the thousand!"

Putting ourselves in the place of others is very helpful for seeing the faults of the egotistic "I," and we become deeply disgusted with it. When we practice like this, using jealousy as a tool, let us imagine that our old "I" is very good-looking, well-dressed, wealthy, powerful, and has everything he needs. Then we imagine ourselves as an impartial spectator in the midst of a crowd of paupers, dressed in rags, the lowest of the low. Now observe the old "I," who since time without beginning has thought only of himself and has never given a thought for others. To further his own interests, he has enslaved others and has not hesitated to kill, steal, lie, slander, and selfishly indulge in sex. He has been nothing but a burden on others' lives. When we look at the egotistic "I" in this way, true disgust will well up in our hearts. And as we identify ourselves with these other beings, in all their misery, we will feel closer to them, and the wish to help them will grow.

We should make our practice on competitiveness and pride equally vivid and real. Let us remind ourselves of all the negative actions the "I" has made us do, all the harm it has done us, making us suffer and causing endless suffering for others, too. This is our real enemy. Would it not be wonderful to make it suffer more than we do, or even make it disappear altogether? Should we not be genuinely proud if we could break it and render it powerless?

• • •

156. The truth, therefore, is this:
  You must wholly give yourself for others.
  The Buddha did not lie in what he said;
  The benefits therefrom are later sure to come.

Having examined all that is wrong with considering ourselves more important than others, and having seen all the harm such an attitude brings, we should revolt against its domination and never let the thought of our own importance influence us.

170. Every thought of working for myself
  Is now rejected, cast aside.
  "Now you have been sold to others,
  Stop your whining, be of service!"

171. For if, through being inattentive,
  I do not deliver you to others,
  You will hand me over, this is certain,
  To the guardians of hell.

173. It is thus: If I wish for happiness,
  I should never seek to please myself.
  So it is that if I wish to save myself
  I must always be the guardian of others.

Shāntideva stresses particularly the dangers of being attached to one's body.

174. As much as this my human form
  Is cosseted and guarded,
  Indeed to that extent
  It grows so sensitive and peevish.

175. And one who falls to such a state,
The earth in its entirety
Is powerless to satisfy.
Who can therefore give him all he craves?

Attachment to the body can only bring us suffering. If we cherish it because it is useful to us, then we should regard everyone else's bodies in the same way, because their bodies are useful to them.

184. Therefore, free from all attachment,
I will give this body for the benefit of beings;
Thus, though many blemishes afflict it,
I shall take it as my necessary tool.

Until now, we have let ourselves be dominated by our clinging to "I." It is high time we put a stop to this childish behavior by following in the footsteps of the Bodhisattvas, recalling the instructions on carefulness, and warding off dullness and sleep. Like those compassionate Heirs of the Conquerors, we should patiently practice day and night. If we can do that, it is certain our suffering will one day come to an end.

187. Thus, to banish all obscuring veils,
I shall turn my mind from the mistaken path,
And constantly upon the perfect object
I shall rest my mind in even meditation.

from My Land and My People

by *the Dalai Lama*

Pressure to submit to the Chinese government increased in Lhasa in 1959, and the city became a violent place. In this selection from his 1962 book the Dalai Lama describes the events that caused him to leave Tibet.

O n the first of March, 1959, I was in the Jokhang, the main temple of Lhasa, for the celebrations of the Monlam Festival. It was during that festival that I took my final examination as Master of Metaphysics. Of course, through all our political misfortunes, my religious education had been continuing. It was still my greatest interest. All my own inclination would have been to pursue religious studies in peace, if that had been possible. The examination by dialectical debate before a vast audience of monks and lamas, which I have described already, was a tremendously important occasion for me, and indeed for the whole of Tibet, and I was entirely preoccupied at that moment with religious questions.

In the middle of all the ceremonies and preparations for my final test, I was told that two Chinese officers wanted to see me. They were shown in—two junior officers who said they had been sent by General Tan Kuan-sen. They wanted me to tell the general a date on which I could attend a theatrical show he had decided to stage in the Chinese army camp. I had already heard of this plan and had promised to go, but I really could not concentrate on anything else just then, so I told the officers I would arrange a date as soon as the ceremonies were finished in ten days' time. They would not be satisfied with that, but kept on pressing me to decide on a date at once. I repeated that I could only fix the date when the ceremonies were over, and finally they agreed to take that reply to the general.

This visit was curious. Normally, unless the general called on me himself, messages from him were sent through whichever of my officials were most concerned. Invitations to social functions were normally sent through Donyerchemo Phala, my Senior Chamberlain, or Chikyab Khempo, the Chief Official Abbot, and my representative in the Cabinet.

So the unusual procedure of sending junior officers to see me personally, and of sending them to the temple, immediately aroused suspicion among all my people who came to know of it. Apart from the resentment it understandably created among my officials, everyone felt the general was once again trying to lower the Dalai Lama in the eyes of his people.

It had been our painful experience under the Chinese regime that I did not have the option even to decline a social invitation if it did not suit me, except at the risk of incurring the displeasure of the Chinese and causing unpleasant repercussions. Their annoyance in such a case always found vent in some other direction, and so we thought it wiser, in the interest of the country, to suffer such minor humiliations in silence, rather than risk a further stiffening of the general Chinese policy of relegating me and my government to a position of subordination.

Nothing more was heard of this strange invitation before I left the temple for the Norbulingka on the fifth of March. My procession to the Norbulingka had always been a great occasion, and in previous years the Chinese had taken part in it, but this year everybody noticed that no Chinese attended.

It was two days later, on the seventh of March, that I had another message from the general. His interpreter, whose name was Li, telephoned to the Chief Official Abbot and asked for a definite date when I could attend the performance in the Chinese camp. The Abbot consulted me, and at my instance he told Li that the tenth of March would be convenient.

The arrangements to be made for my visit were not discussed until the ninth of March, the day before it was due. Then, at eight o'clock in the morning, two Chinese officers came to the house of the Commander of my Bodyguard, Kusung Depon, and told him they had been sent to take him to the Chinese headquarters to see Brigadier Fu, whose title was Military Advisor. Kusung Depon had not had his breakfast, and told them he would come at ten o'clock. They went away, but came back an hour later to tell him he must come at once, as the brigadier was waiting impatiently.

Later that morning, Kusung Depon came back to the Norbulingka in a state of distress. He spoke to my Chief Official Abbot and Senior Chamberlain, and they brought him to see me, and he gave me a verbatim account of what had happened.

The brigadier was looking angry, he told me, when he arrived at his office. "The Dalai Lama is coming here tomorrow," he said abruptly, "to see a dramatic show. There are some things to settle. That is why I have sent for you."

"Has the date been fixed?" Kusung Depon asked him.

"Don't you know?" snapped the brigadier. "The Dalai Lama has accepted the general's invitation and he is coming on the tenth. Now I want to make this clear to you: There will be none of the ceremony you usually have. None of your armed men are to come with him, as they do when he goes to the Preparatory Committee. No Tibetan soldier is to come beyond the Stone Bridge. If you insist, you may have two or three Tibetan bodyguards, but it is definitely decided that they must not be armed."

These unusual orders were a most unpleasant shock to my commander. The Stone Bridge was the limit of the vast army camp which contained the Chinese head-quarters. The existence of this camp within two miles of the Norbulingka had always been an eyesore to every patriotic Tibetan. As long as the Chinese kept it to themselves, the people of Lhasa had tolerated it. But the very idea of the Dalai Lama going into it for any purpose was extraordinary, and Kusung Depon knew that the people would dislike it. If I had to go without a bodyguard, it was more extraordinary still. By custom, an escort of twenty-five armed guards accompanied the

Dalai Lama wherever he went, and armed troops were always posted along the route. Kusung Depon knew that if this custom were to be suddenly stopped, an explanation would have to be given to the public. So he asked the brigadier for a reason. It was an innocent inquiry, but it further annoyed the brigadier.

"Will you be responsible if somebody pulls the trigger?" he shouted. "We don't want trouble. We shall have our own troops unarmed when the Dalai Lama comes. You can post your men on the road as far as the Stone Bridge if you like, but none of them are to come beyond it under any circumstances. And the whole thing is to be kept strictly secret."

There was much discussion among my officials when Kusung Depon returned and told us of these orders. There seemed to be no alternative but to comply with them, and plans for my visit were made accordingly.

But no one could help feeling that the whole of the Chinese invitation was suspicious, and their wish to keep the visit secret made the suspicion worse. It would have been quite impossible to keep any journey I made outside the Norbulingka a secret, unless a total curfew had been enforced throughout the town. The moment I prepared to go out, the word always went round and the whole of Lhasa turned up and lined the route to see me. And at that time, there were many extra people in the city who would also be certain to come. Most of the monks who had been at the Monlam Festival had left, but a few thousand still remained, and there were also several thousand refugees. At a rough estimate, there may have been a hundred thousand people in Lhasa just then, and perhaps that was the highest population the city had ever had.

So to keep order along the route on the following day, my officials decided to post the usual Tibetan guards as far as the Stone Bridge which led into the Chinese area, and they also made plans to ensure that the crowd would not overflow beyond the bridge. On the afternoon of March ninth, they told the Tibetan police on duty along the road to warn people that on the next day there would be special traffic restrictions and nobody would be allowed beyond the bridge.

They took this precaution in all good faith, because crossing the bridge was not normally forbidden, and they thought there might be tragic consequences if people innocently crossed it to see me pass and the Chinese soldiers tried to force them back. But the result was the reverse of what they intended. A rumor spread at once throughout the city that the Chinese had made a plan to kidnap me. During the evening and night of the ninth of March excitement and agitation grew, and by the morning most of the people of Lhasa had decided spontaneously to prevent my visit to the Chinese camp at any cost.

There was another fact which made people all the more certain that a trap had been laid to abduct me. A meeting of the Chinese National Assembly was due to be held in Peking in the following month, and the Chinese had been pressing me to go. Knowing the mood of the people, I had been trying to avoid accepting the invitation, and had not given the Chinese government any definite answer. But in spite of that, just over a week before, they had announced in Peking that I was coming. That announcement without my consent had already made people in Lhasa very angry, and naturally they concluded that the strange new invitation was simply a ruse to fly me out against my will to China.

There was also an even more somber suspicion in the people's minds. It was widely known in Tibet that in four different places in the eastern provinces, high lamas had been invited to parties by the Chinese army commanders and had never been seen again: three had been killed, and one imprisoned. It seemed that this method of luring people away from anyone who might try to protect them was a Chinese custom.

The suspicion of the ordinary people of Lhasa also spread among the officials of my government, through yet another unusual act by the Chinese authorities. Normally, when the Chinese invited me to any social function, they also invited all the highest Tibetan officials. But on this occasion, until the evening of the ninth of March, no officials except my own personal staff had been invited. Late that night, two Chinese officers came to the Norbulingka with invitation cards, but only for the six members of my Cabinet; and verbally they made the unusual request that the Cabinet members should not bring more than one servant with them. By custom, my Senior Chamberlain always accompanied me wherever I went, as the Chinese knew very well, but neither he nor any other officials were included in the invitation.

In spite of their suspicion, my officials did not try to persuade me not to go; but my Cabinet decided to accompany me, instead of going separately, which was the normal practice, because they felt that if anything unpleasant happened, they would at least have the satisfaction of not having left me alone.

The following day was destined to be the most

momentous Lhasa had ever seen. At noon I was supposed to take the unprecedented step of entering the
Chinese camp without an escort. But when I woke up
that morning, I had no idea of what the day was really
going to bring. I had slept badly because I had been
worrying about it. At five I got up, and went as usual to
my prayer room. Everything was perfectly orderly, and
perfectly peaceful and familiar. The butter lamps were
burning before the altars, and the small golden and
silver bowls had been replenished with sweet-smelling
saffron water, like liquid gold, and the fragrance of
incense permeated the air. I offered prayers and meditated, and then I went downstairs and out to the
garden, where I always liked to walk in the early
morning.

At first I was preoccupied with my worries, but I soon
forgot them in the beauty of the spring morning. The
sky was cloudless. The rays of the sun were just touching
the peak of the mountain behind the distant monastery
of Drepung, and beginning to shine on the palace and
chapels which stood in my Jewel Park. Everything was
fresh and gay with spring: the spears of the new green
grass, the delicate buds on the poplar and willow trees,
the lotus leaves in the lake thrusting up to the surface
and unfolding to the sun—all was green. And since I was
born in the Wood Hog Year, and wood is green,
astrologers would have said that green was my lucky
color. Indeed, for that reason my personal prayer flags
were green, and they were flying from the roof of my
house and beginning to stir in a gentle morning breeze.

That was the last brief moment of peace of mind I
was to know. It was broken by shouts, sudden and dis-
cordant, from beyond the wall of the park. I listened,

but I could not distinguish the words. I hurried indoors, found some of my officials, and sent them to find out what was happening. They soon came back to tell me that the people of Lhasa seemed to be streaming out of the city and surrounding the Norbulingka, and that they were shouting that they had come to protect me, and to stop the Chinese taking me to the camp.

Soon all the palaces were astir with anxious people. Messengers kept coming to me with further news. The crowd was countless—some said there were 30,000 people. They were in a state of turbulent excitement, and the shouts were furious anger against the Chinese. Hour by hour the turmoil grew. I myself went to pray in a small chapel which had been built by the Seventh Dalai Lama and dedicated to Mahakala, the militant aspect of Chenresi, endowed with the power of protection against evil. Eight monks had already been there for several days, offering continuous prayer.

Two members of my Cabinet, Liushar and Shasur, drove up to the palace about nine o'clock in Chinese army jeeps with Chinese drivers, which was their usual practice. The people grew even more excited when they saw the Chinese drivers, but the ministers did not have much difficulty in getting through the crowd and into the palace.

But a little later, another minister, Samdup Phodrang, drove up in his own car escorted by a Chinese officer. Then for a moment the crowd got out of control. Samdup Phodrang had only recently been appointed to the Cabinet, and only a few people in Lhasa knew him by sight. He was wearing a Tibetan robe of yellow silk, and he would probably have been able to come in through the gates without any trouble if he had been alone, but the crowd thought the car was Chinese and jumped to the conclusion that the Chinese officer had come to take me away. Somebody threw a stone at him—the panic reaction spread, and the car was bombarded with stones. One of them hit Samdup Phodrang on the temple and knocked him unconscious. Even when he was lying unconscious, the people did not recognize him; but thinking they had mistakenly injured one of my officials, some of them picked him up and carried him to the hospital of the Indian Consulate.

A little later still, another member of the Cabinet, Surkhang, approached the palace in his jeep, but he could not drive up to the gate because by then the crowd had completely blocked the road. He got out of the jeep some distance away and walked through the crowd and entered the gate with the help of a Tibetan official who was stationed there.

These three ministers, having been in the crowd themselves, all realized that something must be done very quickly to avert a crisis—they thought the crowd might try to attack the Chinese headquarters. They waited some time for Ngabo, who was also a member of the Cabinet, but he did not come. Later we learned that he had gone to the Chinese camp, apparently in the belief that I would be there, and then thought it would be unsafe for him to come out again—as indeed it might have been, for the Chinese would have sent an escort with him and they would have been stoned like Samdup Phodrang's escort.

But finally they decided they could not wait any longer, and the three of them held a meeting together with Chikyab Khempo, the Chief Official Abbot, who also had ministerial rank. Then they came to see me. They told me the people had decided I must not be taken to the Chinese camp for fear that I would be abducted and taken away to China. The crowd had already elected a kind of committee of sixty or seventy leaders, and taken an oath that if the Chinese insisted I should go, they would barricade the palace and make it impossible for me to be taken out of it. And the Cabinet told me the crowd was so alarmed and resolute that it really would not be safe for me to go.

By the time the Cabinet members came to see me, I could hear what the people were shouting: "The Chinese must go; leave Tibet to the Tibetans"—all their slogans demanded an end of the Chinese occupation and of Chinese interference with the Dalai Lama's rule. Hearing the shouts, I could feel the tension of these people. I had been born one of them, and I understood what they were feeling and knew that in their present state of mind they were uncontrollable. And that knowledge was confirmed, later in the morning, when I heard with great pain and sorrow that a monastic official called Phakpala Khenchung had been manhandled and finally stoned to death by the angry mob. This man had become notorious in Lhasa because of his close association with the Chinese occupation forces. Earlier that morning he had attended a daily congregation of monastic officials called the Trungcha Ceremony, and for some unknown reason, about eleven o'clock, he rode towards the Norbulingka on a bicycle, wearing a semi-Chinese dress, dark glasses and a motorcyclist's dust mask, and carrying a pistol unconcealed in his belt. Some of the crowd took him for a Chinese in disguise; others thought he was bringing a message from the Chinese headquarters. Their anger and resentment against everything Chinese suddenly burst into fury, and murder was the tragic result.

This outbreak of violence gave me great distress. I told my Cabinet to tell the Chinese general that I could not attend the performance, and also that it would be unwise for anyone from his headquarters to come to the Norbulingka at present, because that might anger the crowd still further. My Senior Chamberlain telephoned to the general's interpreter and gave him this message, with my apologies and regret. The interpreter agreed that my decision was correct, and said he would give the message to the general.

At the same time I also told the Cabinet to tell the people who had surrounded the palace that if they did not wish me to go to the Chinese camp, I would not go. Minister Surkhang got in touch with the leaders whom the people had chosen and told them I had canceled my visit, and about noon a loudspeaker was used to make a similar announcement to the crowd. It was greeted with jubilant cheers from outside the gates.

The mental stress of that morning was something I had not experienced before during the brief period of my leadership of the people of Tibet. I felt as if I were standing between two volcanoes, each likely to erupt at any moment. On one side, there was the vehement, unequivocal, unanimous protest of my people against the Chinese regime; on the other, there was the armed might of a powerful and aggressive occupation force. If there was a clash between the two, the result was a foregone conclusion. The Lhasan people would be ruthlessly massacred in thousands, and Lhasa and the rest of Tibet would see a full-scale military rule with all its persecution and tyranny. The immediate cause of the explosive situation was the question whether I should go to the Chinese camp or not. But at the same time, I was the only possible peacemaker, and I knew that at all costs, for the sake of my own people, I must try to calm the anger of the people and pacify the Chinese who would certainly be even angrier.

I had hoped that the announcement that I was not going would end the demonstration, and that the people would go home in peace. But it was not enough. Their leaders said they would not go unless I assured them I had not only canceled the visit for that day, but had also decided not to accept any invitation in the future to go to the Chinese camp. Nothing seemed too high a price to pay to avert a disaster, so I gave the assurance they wanted. Then most of these chosen leaders left; but most of the rest of the people still stayed outside the palace and would not go away.

At about one o'clock I told my three ministers to go to see General Tan Kuan-sen and explain the whole situation to him personally. There was still a vast multitude outside the gates determined to prevent anyone leaving, and the appearance of the ministers at the gates made the people suspect that I might be following them. The ministers explained to the crowd, with some difficulty, that I had instructed them to go to the Chinese headquarters and tell the general that I could not come to his theatrical performance. On this assurance the crowd insisted on searching the ministers' cars to make sure that I had not been hidden in one of them, but when they had satisfied themselves about that, they let the ministers go. During that discussion at the gate, the spokesmen of the crowd said they had decided to choose a bodyguard from amongst themselves and post it all around the palace to prevent the Chinese getting in to take me away. The ministers tried to persuade them not to do that, but they would not accept their advice.

When the ministers came back that afternoon, they told me what had happened at the Chinese headquarters. General Tan Kuan-sen was not there when they arrived, but ten other officers were waiting for them, apparently engaged in a serious conversation; and with them was Ngabo, my other Cabinet minister, dressed in Tibetan clothes instead of the Chinese general's uniform which he had recently had to wear when he was in attendance at the Chinese offices. Ngabo was sitting with the officers, but he did not seem to be taking part in their discussion. He did not leave his seat to join the ministers when they entered.

For some time, not a word was spoken by either side about the events of the day. The Chinese officers seemed to be unconcerned, and they inquired politely about the ministers' health. But the atmosphere suddenly changed when General Tan Kuan-sen came in and took charge of the proceedings.

The ministers told me the general seemed very angry when he came into the room. His appearance was intimidating, and the ministers rose nervously from their seats to show him respect. For a few minutes, he seemed to be speechless with rage, and he did not greet the ministers. Surkhang opened the conversation by telling him that I had sent them to explain what had happened to prevent me from attending the dramatic performance. He said I had had every intention of coming, but the people's wishes were so strongly against it that I had had to give up the idea. The other two ministers also added their explanations. By the time the interpreter had finished, the general was visibly red in the face. He rose from his seat and started pacing up and down the room, apparently beside himself with anger. After a great appearance of effort, he managed to control himself and sat down again. Then with studied deliberation and slowness of speech, he began a harangue against the ministers and "Tibetan reactionaries." Although he seemed to be trying to control his temper, his voice often rose sharply and his simmering anger burst out in rude and abusive language. He was using Chinese words which are never spoken in any polite Chinese society. The general point of the harangue was that the government of Tibet had been secretly organizing agitation by the people against the Chinese authorities and helping the Khampas in their rebellion. Tibetan officials had defied the orders of the Chinese and refused to disarm the Khampas in Lhasa—and now, drastic measures would be taken to crush the opposition to Chinese rule.

Two other generals made similar tirades. One of them declared the time had come to "destroy all these reactionaries. . . . Our government has been tolerant so far," he said, "but this is rebellion. This is the breaking point. We shall act now, so be prepared!"

My bewildered ministers took these harangues as an ultimatum of military action if the popular agitation did not cease at once. They were convinced the prospect was dangerous and involved the safety of the person of the Dalai Lama; and they felt that if anything happened to me, there would be nothing left of Tibet. They tried to counsel patience. Shasur told the general that the Chinese should try to understand the ordinary Tibetan people and be patient and tolerant. They should not make a serious situation worse by retaliation. And he assured him that the Cabinet would do all that was possible to prevent an outbreak of lawlessness among the Khampas or any other Tibetans who might be foolhardy enough to try to provoke a clash of arms with the Chinese occupation forces. But the Chinese generals would not accept this assurance or listen to this advice.

Deeply perturbed, the ministers came back to the Norbulingka about five in the evening. By then a part of the crowd had dispersed, though there was still a large number of people surrounding the main gate. Those who had left, we learned later, had gone into the city to hold public meetings and stage mass demonstrations against the Chinese. At the meetings they denounced the Seventeen-Point Agreement on the ground that the Chinese had broken it, and they demanded once more that the Chinese should withdraw. At six the same evening, about seventy members of the government, mostly junior officials, together with the leaders chosen by the crowd and members of the Kusung Regiment (the Dalai Lama's bodyguard) held a meeting inside the Norbulingka grounds and endorsed the declaration which had been made at the meetings in the city. They also made a declaration that Tibet no longer recognized Chinese authority; and soon afterwards, the Kusung Regiment declared that they would no longer take orders from Chinese officers, and they discarded the Chinese uniforms which they had been made to wear and appeared again in their Tibetan dress.

As soon as I heard of these decisions, I sent instructions to the leaders stating that their duty was to reduce the existing tension and not aggravate it—to be patient and meet all events with calm and forbearance. But by then the resentment of the people was so bitter, and their suspicion of the Chinese so great, that my advice seemed to have no effect on them at all.

Late in the evening of the same day, a letter from General Tan Kuan-sen was delivered to me. It was the first of three letters he sent me within the next few days, and I replied to all of them.

These letters were published by the Chinese, after all the events in Lhasa were over, to support their own propaganda. They used them to try to prove that I wanted to seek shelter in the Chinese headquarters, but was kept under duress in the Norbulingka by what they called a "reactionary clique," and finally abducted out of the country to India against my will. This story was repeated in some of the foreign press which was favorably inclined towards Communist China, and I was shocked to hear over a year later that it had been quoted by a member of the British peerage in the House of Lords. As it is the very opposite of the truth, I want to describe the circumstances in which these letters were written, and my reasons for writing them, and to say once and for all that when I left Lhasa I went of my own free will. The decision was mine alone, made under the stress of a desperate situation. I was not abducted by my entourage; I was not under any pressure to go from anybody, except in so far as every Tibetan in Lhasa could see by then that the Chinese were preparing to shell my palace and that my life would be in danger if I stayed there.

The general's letters to me were written in friendly terms which would have seemed more sincere if I had not already been told of his rage by my ministers. He said he was concerned for my safety and invited me to take refuge in his camp.

I replied to all his letters to gain time—time for anger to cool on both sides, and time for me to urge moderation of the Lhasan people. And to this end I thought it would be foolish to argue with the general, or to point out that Chinese protection from my own people was the very last thing I needed. On the contrary, I decided to reply in a way which I hoped would calm him down. And this I could only do by seeming to accept his sympathy and welcome his advice. In my first letter I told him how embarrassed I had been at my people's action in preventing me from coming to his entertainment. In the second letter, I told him I had given orders that the people surrounding the Norbulingka should disperse, and I concurred with his point of view that these people, under the pretext of protecting me, were only working to undermine the relations between the Chinese and our government. And in the third letter, I also added that I must separate the people who supported new ideas and those who opposed them before I could visit his headquarters.

Even if I had thought at the time that these letters would be quoted against me later, I would still have written them, because my most urgent moral duty at that moment was to prevent a totally disastrous clash between my unarmed people and the Chinese army.

And perhaps I may repeat once more that I could not approve of violence, and so I could not approve of the violent attitude the people of Lhasa were showing. I could and do appreciate the affection for me, as the symbol of Tibet, an attitude which was the immediate cause of the anger they were showing against the Chinese on that fateful day. I could not blame them for their anxiety for my safety, because the Dalai Lama represented most of what they lived and worked for. But I was certain that what they were doing could only lead to disaster if they continued, and as Head of State I had to try by every means to curb their feelings and stop them bringing about their own destruction under the weight of the Chinese army. So the advice I gave them was given in the fullest sincerity, and although my letters to the Chinese general were written to disguise my true intentions, I felt and still feel that they were justified.

But by the following day, the eleventh of March, it was clear that the Lhasan people were becoming even more difficult to control. On that day they posted six guards near the Cabinet office inside the Norbulingka and warned the ministers that they would not be allowed to leave. Presumably they suspected that the Cabinet might make some kind of compromise with the Chinese and so defeat the popular demand that the Chinese should leave Tibet. The Cabinet convened an emergency meeting. Only four of the six ministers were present, because Samdup Phodrang was still too ill from his injury to be able to come, and Ngabo refused to come out of the Chinese camp. But these four decided to make another effort to persuade the people to call off their demonstration, and they sent for the leaders of the crowd.

At that meeting, the leaders seemed to be more

amenable and they told the Cabinet they would tell the people to disperse. They also said they were sorry Samdup Phodrang had been hurt, and asked the Cabinet to deliver some presents from them to him by way of apology.

In that somewhat more conciliatory mood, the people probably would have dispersed before long, and the efforts which I and the Cabinet had been making to bring the demonstration to a peaceful end would probably have succeeded; but then two more letters arrived from the general, one to me and one to the Cabinet. The letter to the Cabinet completely defeated our efforts. It said that the "rebels" had put up barricades on the north side of Lhasa, on the road towards China, and told the Cabinet to order them to be removed at once. It warned the Cabinet that if this was not done, "serious consequences would follow, for which the responsibility would rest with Surkhang, Liushar, Shasur, and Donyerchemo."

The Cabinet sent for the leaders of the people again and advised them to remove the barricades, so that the Chinese could not find an excuse in them for more repression. But that advice had exactly the wrong effect. The leaders absolutely refused to demolish the barricades. They said they had put them there to protect the Norbulingka by keeping Chinese reinforcements out of the city, and if the Chinese wanted them removed, the obvious conclusion was that they did mean to attack the Palace and capture the Dalai Lama. They also said that the Chinese themselves had put up barricades in front of the temple and taken similar precautions to protect their Tibetan supporters, such as Ngabo. If the Chinese could use barricades to protect Ngabo, they asked, why should they object to the people of Lhasa protecting the Palace? This was unfortunate logic, but the leaders could not be persuaded to see the Chinese orders in any other way; and the unhappy result was that they became more apprehensive about my safety and refused to disperse the crowd. The people became more uncompromising, appointed six commanders from among themselves to strengthen the defense of the Palace, and announced that they would not leave the Palace unguarded whatever happened.

This development distressed me very much. I felt it was one step more toward disaster. So I decided to speak to the people's leaders myself. I sent for them, and all seventy of them came, and in the presence of the Cabinet and other senior officials I did my best to dissuade them from their actions. I told them the Chinese general had not compelled me to accept his invitation; I had been consulted and given my consent before the invitation was issued. I said I was not in any fear of personal danger from the Chinese, and they must not create a situation which could have such serious consequences for the people. I knew this would offend their feelings, but I had to tell them what I felt in the sincerest hope that the normal peace of Lhasa might be restored to some extent.

The leaders did not question my advice or contradict me. They quietly left the meeting and held a conference among themselves by the outer gate of the Palace. They agreed that it was impossible for them to disobey my orders, but there was a long argument about what would happen to me if their protection was withdrawn. In the end, they carried out my wishes to the extent of holding no more meetings within the

Norbulingka. Instead of that, they met at the village of Shol, at the foot of the Potala, and sent reports of their decisions to me and the Cabinet after each meeting. These reports amounted to a repetition of their earlier declarations: they would continue to protect me, and the Chinese must leave Lhasa and Tibet and allow the Tibetans to manage their own affairs.

So the next two days dragged by. The situation seemed to be static and the problems to be insoluble, but obviously things could not go on as they were. Something must happen soon, for better or worse.

General Tan Kuan-sen's third and last letter to me arrived on the morning of the sixteenth of March, and I replied to it on the same day. Afterwards, the Chinese published both these letters. But they did not say that in the same envelope with the general's letter there was another sent to me by Ngabo. He had not attended any Cabinet meetings since the crisis started. Now he wrote to warn me that he did not think there was much chance of peace. He suggested that I should try to "destroy the hostile designs of the reactionaries," and cut all my connections with the people's leaders. He said he gathered the people had an "evil plan" to remove me from the Norbulingka. If that was true, it would be very dangerous for me, because the Chinese had taken the strictest measures to prevent my escape. And even if I did escape, he said, in the present international situation I would never be able to return to Lhasa. And then he said: "If Your Holiness with a few trusted officers of the bodyguard can stay within the inner wall, and hold a position there, and inform General Tan Kuan-sen exactly which building you will occupy, they certainly intend that this building will not be damaged."

So Ngabo knew what we had only guessed: that the Chinese did intend to destroy the Palace and the crowd, but still wanted to do it, if they could, without also killing me.

He wrote to the Cabinet too, more or less repeating what he had written to me, and urging them to get the people away from the Palace, or at least to see that they stayed outside the walls. He said he understood the difficulties, and if they could not make the people go, they should try to take me out of the Palace and into the Chinese camp for my own safety. Meanwhile, they should send a sketch map of the Palace showing the position of the building I was occupying.

I replied to the general's letter in much the same way that I had written to him before. It still seemed to me that the only chance of persuading him not to attack the crowd and the Palace was to seem to fall in with his wishes. I did not tell him which building I was in. I felt that so long as the Chinese did not know exactly where I was, there was still some chance they would not use artillery; if we told them, it seemed certain that the rest of the Norbulingka would be laid in ruins. I told him again that I would come to his camp as soon as possible. I had no intention of going, but I hoped this promise would persuade him to delay his order to attack and enable us to get the people away in time. That was the last of the letters I wrote to him.

The whole atmosphere round the Palace by then was extremely tense. Outside its inner wall was a vast multitude of excited angry people. Most of them had armed themselves with sticks, spades or knives, or whatever other weapons they could muster. Among them were some soldiers and Khampas with rifles, a few machine guns, and even fourteen or fifteen mortars. Hand to hand, with fists or swords, one Tibetan would have been worth a dozen Chinese—recent experiences in the eastern provinces had confirmed this old belief. But it was obvious that their strength was useless against the heavy equipment which the Chinese could bring to wipe them out. Practically, they had nothing to fight with except their own determination to protect me.

But within the inner wall, in the immediate precincts of the Palace, everything had the appearance of calm and peace. There were no signs of anything untoward. The garden was quiet as usual. The peacocks strutted about with their plumes held high, unconcerned about the human turmoil; singing birds were flying from tree to tree, mixing their music with that of the fountains near the rock garden; the tame deer, the fish, and the brahmini ducks and white cranes were as placid as ever. A contingent of my bodyguard, out of uniform, was even watering the lawns and flower beds. The atmosphere was still typical of Tibet, where for centuries people have sought for peace of mind and devoted themselves through their religion to finding the path towards freedom from sorrow and suffering.

On the sixteenth of March news began to come in of the Chinese preparations for destroying this peaceful place. People reported to the Cabinet, and thence to me, that all the artillery in the district was being brought in to sites within range of the city, and of the Norbu-lingka in particular. A man who worked on a hydro-electric plant which was being built about eight miles east of Lhasa reported that four mountain guns and twenty-eight heavy machine guns, which were usually kept there, had been secretly taken to Lhasa during the night of the fourteenth, escorted by several truck loads of Chinese soldiers. A district official from Bomtue, fifteen miles east of Lhasa, told us of twenty heavy guns which had been sent toward the city. On the evening of the thirteenth, and again on the fifteenth, two giant Chinese military vehicles with three soldiers in each were found near the northern gate of the Palace with mechanical instruments, apparently taking measurements. When they saw that the people were watching them they hurriedly drove away, and the people's guards who saw them jumped to the conclusion that they were taking the measurements for ranging heavy guns on the Palace. In the night a hundred new Chinese trucks were seen moving slowly toward the Potala, and from there to the Chinese camp. On the following morning, fifteen or twenty Chinese in civilian clothes were seen perched on telegraph poles, apparently mending the wires, but the people concluded they were taking more readings for range finding. Our people did not know much about artillery and they may have been wrong, but that was what they believed.

Besides all these observations, there were rumors of fresh troops arriving from China by air. By the night of the sixteenth, the people were certain that the Chinese were about to shell the Palace, and that danger might come without warning at any moment. Their feelings rose to a state of panic, but they still would not leave the Palace and abandon it and me. Everyone in authority tried to pacify them, but their fury against the Chinese was uncontrollable. For the crowd and for my ministers and myself, that was a very disturbed night, and nobody could sleep.

When morning came, rumors were still springing up

and spreading, and destruction still seemed imminent. It seemed to me and my Cabinet that the situation was completely desperate. We held a meeting. There was only one question to discuss: how could we prevent the destruction of the Palace and the massacre of the thousands of people round it? We could only decide to make another appeal to the Chinese general not to use force to disperse the crowd, but to wait till the Cabinet had tried again to persuade them to leave in peace. So the Cabinet hurriedly wrote a letter to Ngabo to this effect. They said the people were acting foolishly and under the stress of emotion, but there was still hope that they could be persuaded to leave the Palace in the end. And they also suggested that Ngabo should help them to take me to the Chinese camp. They pointed out that this would be very difficult, because the whole area round the Palace was controlled by the people, but they said they would do their best. They sent a special code with that letter and asked Ngabo to use it in his reply, because the popular guards round the Palace had started to censor any letters which came into their hands. The sole purpose of that letter, of course, was to conciliate the Chinese general. In fact, it would have been quite impossible for me to have gone to the Chinese camp. I would indeed have been willing to go there and throw myself on the mercy of the Chinese if that would have prevented the massacre of my people; but the people would never have let me do it.

It was very difficult to send that letter, because the popular guards were on the alert and would not allow officials to leave the Palace. But one of Minister Shasur's attendants succeeded in slipping out, pretending he was going shopping in the city, and he managed to deliver the letter to Ngabo and come back with his reply. This was a brief polite acknowledgment. He said he was pleased at the Cabinet's proposal that I should be moved to the Chinese camp and promised to send a detailed answer later; but that answer did not come until after all was over.

About four o'clock that afternoon, while I was discussing Ngabo's answer with the ministers, we heard the boom of two heavy mortar shells fired from a nearby Chinese camp. And we also heard the splash of the shells in a marsh outside the northern gate.

At those two isolated shots, consternation and anger reached a final climax in the crowd. No explanation has ever been given of why they were fired, but those who heard them could only think the attack had begun and the Palace was the target. Within the Palace everyone felt the end had come and that something drastic had to be done without any more delay, but nobody could decide what to do.

It was I who had to find the answer and make the decision; but with my inexperience in the affairs of the world it was not easy. I have no fear of death. I was not afraid of being one of the victims of the Chinese attack. I honestly believe that my strict religious training has given me enough strength to face the prospect of leaving my present body without any apprehension. I felt then, as I always feel, that I am only a mortal being and an instrument of the never dying spirit of my Master, and that the end of one mortal frame is not of any great consequence. But I knew my people and the officials of my government could not share my feelings. To them the person of the Dalai Lama was supremely precious. They believed the Dalai Lama represented Tibet and the Tibetan way of life, something dearer to them than anything else. They were convinced that if my body perished at the hands of the Chinese, the life of Tibet would also come to an end.

So when the Chinese guns sounded that warning of death, the first thought in the mind of every official within the Palace, and every humble member of the vast concourse around it, was that my life must be saved and I must leave the Palace and leave the city at once. The decision was not a small matter; the stakes were high; the whole future of Tibet depended on it. There was no certainty that escape was physically possible at all—Ngabo had assured us it was not. If I did escape from Lhasa, where was I to go, and how could I reach asylum? Above all, would the Chinese destroy our holy city and massacre our people if I went—or would the people scatter from the Palace when they heard that I had gone, and so perhaps would some lives be saved? Our minds were overwhelmed by such unanswerable questions. Everything was uncertain, except the compelling anxiety of all my people to get me away before the orgy of Chinese destruction and massacre began. This was the only positive worldly guide I had in making my decision. If I decided to stay, I would add even more to the distress of my people and of my closest friends. I decided to go. I need hardly say I prayed for guidance and received it.

from Violence and Compassion

by *the Dalai Lama and Jean-Claude Carrière*

This discussion between the Dalai Lama and screen-writer Jean-Claude Carrière (born 1931) considers exiled Tibetans' perspectives on the Chinese.

JEAN-CLAUDE CARRIÈRE: *It seems to me that the twentieth century has been the century of exile. It's often been characterized differently, by the total wars, by the holocausts, by the technological progress that we have discussed. But people frequently forget about the exile, voluntary or forced, of tens of millions of individuals, having to pass inspection on Ellis Island before being admitted to the United States, colonial soldiers drafted against their will, immigrant workers demanded by Europe, which today rejects them, displaced populations like the Vietnamese boat people, and others too numerous to mention. Never did any one century tear up so many roots.*

THE DALAI LAMA: I hadn't thought of it, but it's undoubtedly true.

JEAN-CLAUDE CARRIÈRE: *Yet we know that there is a profound link between a people and its land, and that this tie is the origin of a thousand customs, behaviors, and even beliefs.*

THE DALAI LAMA: Yes, that's certain.

JEAN-CLAUDE CARRIÈRE: *Still here and there we have undertaken to cut that link. You yourself have been living in exile for thirty-five years. The Chinese invaded Tibet in 1950, when you were fifteen. For nine years, you tried to resist, to negotiate. You met Mao Ze-dong and Jou En-lai. You made appeals to other powers, but it was all in vain. China wouldn't stop laying on Tibet the burden of increasingly harsh oppression, from massacres to colonization. Then you reached the decision to leave your country and your people to continue your struggle abroad, according to your methods.*

THE DALAI LAMA: That's right.

JEAN-CLAUDE CARRIÈRE: *Has exile helped you? Have you found strength in it?*

THE DALAI LAMA: Oh yes! Without a doubt. I can try to tell you why. When, at some point in our lives, we meet a real tragedy—which could happen to any one of us—we can react in two ways. Obviously we can lose hope, let ourselves slip into discouragement, into alcohol, drugs, unending sadness. Or else we can wake ourselves up, discover in ourselves a energy that was hidden there, and act with more clarity, more force.

JEAN-CLAUDE CARRIÈRE: *You chose the second way?*

THE DALAI LAMA: I hope so. I discovered at the age of

fifteen the brutal power of politics. I discovered pitiless imperialism, the cruel desire for conquest, the so-called law of arms. In my youth communism had a certain seductive appeal for me. It even seemed to me that a synthesis between Buddhism and communism was possible. Then I ran up against the incomprehensible contradictions of Chinese policy—the frenzy of slogans, the intoxication of millions of brains. I got to know all that in my adolescence, in my youth. After which came the disappointments, and finally the certainty, that Mao was none other than the "destroyer of the Dharma."

JEAN-CLAUDE CARRIÈRE: *You were only nineteen years old, in 1954, when you learned that India had signed an accord with China with which they abstained from challenging the military occupation of Tibet.*

THE DALAI LAMA: Yes, another disappointment. That one was diplomatic. Around the same time I became aware of the first attacks launched by the Chinese against the Tibetan religion, which they accused of being archaic and barbarous. Some of those attacks were treacherously indirect, such as the extermination campaigns against insects and rats, whereas Buddhism forbids us to kill even an animal.

JEAN-CLAUDE CARRIÈRE: *And the brutality too, the political executions?*

THE DALAI LAMA: Yes, the oppressive measures, and the atrocities of every kind, making collaboration impossible. Monasteries destroyed, works of art plundered, crucifixions, vivisections, dismemberments, entrails and tongues ripped out. We experienced all those horrors, and on our soil. In 1959, amid all the confusion, I finally followed the advice of an oracle that had several times advised me to leave; I decided to go into exile.

JEAN-CLAUDE CARRIÈRE: *Thirty-five years later that exile continues.*

THE DALAI LAMA: One positive aspect of the exile situation is that you look at your country differently. Thus, apropos of Tibet, all the ritual that surrounded my youth has lost its importance. From the first day of the year till the last, it was nothing but a long round of ceremonies, perfectly ordered, and which everyone took very seriously. This formalism regulated every last detail of our everyday life. You had to observe it even while talking, even while walking.

JEAN-CLAUDE CARRIÈRE: *Exile has erased the prestige of ritual?*

THE DALAI LAMA: To be sure. The solemn aspect touches me much less. It's inevitable. The flight and all that followed it, our patient struggle to get ourselves recognized by other nations, all my journeys, all my public addresses have brought me closer to reality. It also has to be said that exile has allowed me to discover the rest of the world, to meet other peoples, to become acquainted with other traditions. Nothing could be more useful. India has welcomed us. Our being installed in a free country has facilitated these meetings, which in the 1950s remained difficult in Tibet.

JEAN-CLAUDE CARRIÈRE: *Isn't India a sacred land for Buddhists?*

THE DALAI LAMA: Yes, it's *Aryabhûmi*, the land where the Buddha Sakyamuni was born for the last time, the land where he experienced illumination, where he preached. We have many centers in India, and every year I'm very moved when I return to Buddh Gaya, to the very spot where he found the awakening.

JEAN-CLAUDE CARRIÈRE: *Has this exile of thirty-five years created a new feeling among the Tibetans?*

THE DALAI LAMA: Yes, undoubtedly. A real "Tibethood." It was born from that difficult passage in the long history of Tibet. Centuries and centuries of rootedness can make you forget that feeling. The bonds with the earth seem secure, untouchable. Then something unexpected happens that calls those bonds into question. You discover a cynical brutality, the crushing use of force, your own weakness. Finally you leave, you never see your country except from far away. It gets ravaged, occupied, and still you realize that it hasn't disappeared, that it subsists in you, that you still feel Tibetan. Then you begin to wonder, What does being Tibetan mean?

JEAN-CLAUDE CARRIÈRE: *That no doubt explains all those efforts to open schools, to maintain the Tibetan language, music, song, dance?*

THE DALAI LAMA: We have created a system where all the instruction is given in Tibetan, even in the scientific disciplines.

JEAN-CLAUDE CARRIÈRE: *And that developed the language?*

THE DALAI LAMA: Inevitably, and strengthened our union. We have something to defend. Among our efforts have been literary publications, such as *Jang Chon* ("Young Shoots") and *Tibetan Art and Literature.* After 1959, the Chinese police in Tibet hunted down the creators of that young literature, which they labeled reactionary. Every work had to be authorized for publication by the party cell, and such permits were very hard to get. The pioneer of this literature, the novelist Thondup Gyal, committed suicide in 1985. He was one of those who bitterly criticized the traditions and beliefs of Tibet, which he felt were responsible for the present-day enslavement.

JEAN-CLAUDE CARRIÈRE: *Apropos of Tibet, haven't you spoken in several of your books about a collective karma?*

THE DALAI LAMA: That's an intimate part of our classical teaching. What is true for an individual—who will feel in one of his or her existences the effects, favorable or not, of his or her *karma*—is true for groups, for a family, say, and also for a nation, for a people.

JEAN-CLAUDE CARRIÈRE: *So Tibet had something to "pay"? This chain of events was inevitable?*

THE DALAI LAMA: One might wonder. For a very long time Tibet cut itself off from the world. It refused all change, all outside influences. It wanted to believe that it alone possessed the truth, that it could live in isolation.

JEAN-CLAUDE CARRIÈRE: *But the world reminded Tibet that it was there.*

THE DALAI LAMA: Very harshly. And we wonder in fact if our collective *karma* didn't lead us to that confrontation, which ended in disaster.

JEAN-CLAUDE CARRIÈRE: *That would be a subtle form of collective responsibility.*

THE DALAI LAMA: Perhaps.

JEAN-CLAUDE CARRIÈRE: *Do you still believe in it today?*

THE DALAI LAMA. As always in Buddhism, you have to distinguish causes from conditions. The principal causes of aggression, of so many misfortunes and sufferings, have to be looked for in the former lives, and not necessarily among the Tibetans.

JEAN-CLAUDE CARRIÈRE: *Among other peoples?*

THE DALAI LAMA: Perhaps even on other stars, in other galaxies. Everything is connected to everything else. No event can be considered isolated, unrelated to the others. We have already spoken about that. Other sensitive and responsible beings, by their behavior, have managed to create a negative *karma*, whose effect is felt at that particular moment. This boundless chain of causes and consequences is almost impossible to untangle, but it exists. All our acts have a weight. That weight will make itself felt, one day or another, here or there, individually or collectively. This is a major reason why we should respect the way of the Dharma.*

JEAN-CLAUDE CARRIÈRE: *And the conditions?*

THE DALAI LAMA: For the conditions, the Tibetans themselves are certainly responsible.

JEAN-CLAUDE CARRIÈRE: *Out of blindness?*

THE DALAI LAMA: No doubt. Out of ignorance of the rest of the world, of China, India, the political tensions, the upheavals brought on by World War II. Many Tibetans thought that our country was an extraordinary territory transcending the common laws and even the passage of time.

JEAN-CLAUDE CARRIÈRE: *Because of Buddhism?*

THE DALAI LAMA: Yes, in part, because of the Buddha

---

* This notion of Dharma is no doubt one of the radical points separating East and West. The position of the individual, of his or her status and rights, and hence the existence of his or her ego—such individualism already exists in Christian tradition. But destinies, even eternal salvation is an individual affair. The idea of a whole nation being condemned to Gehenna or called to Paradise is quite alien to Christianity. The individual always has the possibility of encountering the truth and "winning salvation" or choosing Hell. The laws of modern republics have only confirmed our capacity to choose.

Here at Dharamsala, an immense effort is demanded of the individual to penetrate into the self, and to seek the inner calm. Despite this practice, no one forgets that he or she is nothing but an unstable substance, continuously made and unmade, with no independent individual existence. For that very reason each sees him or herself related to all the rest of the world.

Dharma. A whole people following the just law and faithfully accomplishing its rituals, necessarily had to guarantee protection for that same people.

JEAN-CLAUDE CARRIÈRE: *Did all the inhabitants of Tibet share that feeling?*

THE DALAI LAMA: Not all of them. A large number, yes. And among them certain high dignitaries, responsible for the defense of the country, who believed in invisible protectors.

JEAN-CLAUDE CARRIÈRE: *Against the perfectly visible aggressors.*

THE DALAI LAMA: This was an aberration, complete blindness in the face of destiny. During the Chinese invasion in 1950, when the young Communist army was crossing our borders, these high dignitaries entrusted our defense to our deities. One official, now deceased, assured me that we had no cause for concern: our gods would protect us from the Chinese.

JEAN-CLAUDE CARRIÈRE: *You were fifteen years old.*

THE DALAI LAMA: And everything disposed me to believe what I was told: my childhood, the way I had been chosen, my meticulous education, my life at Potala, the incense that accompanied my walks. But my eyes were opened very quickly, as you can imagine. In the middle of the twentieth century prayers matched with cannons?

The government put its confidence in the divinities, but on the other hand it ignored the prophecies and the oracles.

JEAN-CLAUDE CARRIÈRE: *The people in charge didn't want to hear them?*

THE DALAI LAMA: The ones responsible weren't responsible.*

Not all Tibetans, however, were living in the same illusion. My predecessor, Thupten Gyatso, the thirteenth Dalai Lama, when he died in 1933, clearly pointed out in his testament that one day communism would pose a terrible danger. He already understood that we could never physically resist our great neighbors, China and India, that we had to use an adroit diplomacy; and so he turned to our small neighbors, Nepal and Bhutan.

---

* This discussion certainly did not make the Dalai Lama smile. Oracles, prophecies, and premonitory dreams play an important role in Tibetan tradition even to this day. These oracles are monks, mediums who have received special training. Divinities can become incarnate in their body, transforming their face and voice in a trance, and speaking through their mouth. In this state their face reddens, their eyes become bloodshot, and their tongue gets thick and pendulous. The broken words they utter are received and interpreted by other monks. The most celebrated is the oracle of Nechung, the incarnation of the god Pehar. The Tibetan government employs him in what might be called an official capacity.

The Dalai Lama doesn't seem to doubt the truth of this tradition. He writes that after the death of the grand lamas, their bones melt, and then one can see images in them or read in them letters that indicate which deity is protecting the deceased. Thus we see what can be called "a supernatural dimension" slipping into a body of thought that aims to be rigorous, and that strives to maintain nothing unless it comes from experience.

It's impossible (and absurd) to pick and choose here. From the most profound analysis to the most naive belief, all this belongs to the same structure; and at the same time every fiber of the teaching sheds light on all the others.

JEAN-CLAUDE CARRIÈRE: *What did he propose to them?*

THE DALAI LAMA: A sort of common defense: raise an army, train it as best as possible.

Just between us, this isn't strictly practicing non-violence.

JEAN-CLAUDE CARRIÈRE: *How did Nepal and Bhutan react?*

THE DALAI LAMA: They didn't react. They quite simply ignored the offer. Now I can see the whole range of my predecessor's vision. For example, he wanted to bring to Lhasa some boys from the region of Kam in the east—it's a harsh territory, thinly populated, close to China—and give them the rank of real Tibetans, with a complete military education. Politically, that was very farsighted. He was already advancing the idea that the defense of a land has to be assured by the people who occupy it.

JEAN CLAUDE CARRIÈRE: *Then they have to be given arms?*

THE DALAI LAMA: That's what he said. The man felt very keenly the movement of the world around him. He wanted to go with the changes, not leave his country behind, or by the wayside.

JEAN-CLAUDE CARRIÈRE: *If that vision had materialized, would Tibet have been able to resist twenty years later?*

THE DALAI LAMA: I'm convinced it would have. But he wasn't listened to. The dignitaries didn't follow his orders. That's what we call the conditions, one could also say the circumstances, of collective *karma*. In the Buddhist conception of action, no event can be isolated, nor produced without a chain of causes, conditions, and consequences. And so we stubbornly seek for the conditions, which are easier to detect than the causes, which are often far removed from the event.

As far back as 1961, the Dalai Lama, who had become what he calls a "politician despite himself," proposed a constitution, which was accepted. Since then he has never ceased presenting and defending, on every occasion, the cause of his country, of his people.

First of all, he passes on information. Thus we have learned about the extermination of more than a million Tibetans (one out of six), repressive measures of all kinds, population transfers, expropriations, internment in concentration camps, brutal application of birth control policy, and forced sterilization of women. Then there is the deforestation, the use of Tibetan territory as a nuclear waste dump, and above all, a systematic Chinese colonization. Nowadays their techniques are being refined: while young Chinese, after three years of military service, must return to their home province, those stationed in Tibet are obliged to stay there. Estimates put the current Chinese population in Tibet at around 9 million, so the Tibetans are now a minority in their own homeland. The Tibetan "race" is in danger of disappearing.

In the 1960s, the United Nations voted a number of resolutions on Tibet that have remained a dead letter. But little by little the world began to wake up. In 1985, ninety-one members of the U.S. Congress signed a letter of support, addressed to the President of the People's Assembly in Beijing. In 1987, the Dalai Lama himself was invited to Washington to speak before the Committee on Human Rights. Aware of how unrealistic it would be to demand immediate independence, pure and simple, for Tibet, he proposed a "five point peace plan."

The plan foresees the transformation of Tibet into a zone of peace, China's abandoning its policy of colonization, respect for democratic freedoms, fundamental human rights for the Tibetan people, the restoration and protection of the environment (to begin with, by stopping all nuclear activity), and, finally, the opening of serious negotiations on the future status of Tibet.

In 1988, before the European Parliament in Strasbourg, he developed and explained these five points. He proposed, in particular, to turn Tibet into a vast demilitarized zone and a sort of natural park, the largest in the world, where environmental restoration would be exemplary. All the international organizations working to defend human rights would have their place in that territory of *ahimsa*, or nonviolence. Separated by a vast neutral region, India and China could withdraw the troops that they continue to maintain, at great expense, in the Himalayan regions.

In 1989, the awarding of the Nobel Prize for peace seemed to reinforce his proposals.

JEAN-CLAUDE CARRIÈRE: *When you received the Nobel Prize many people discovered the problem of Tibet. They picked up maps in order to simply find out where Tibet was located, and furthermore became* *interested in what was happening between Tibet and China. It must also have helped with the heads of state around the world.*

THE DALAI LAMA: Naturally. Some received me officially, others privately. Always these diplomatic reasons. In any case, it got easier for me to meet the people in charge and talk to them.

JEAN-CLAUDE CARRIÈRE: *Even the Chinese leaders?*

THE DALAI LAMA: Yes, even with the Chinese, the Nobel Prize played a positive role there too.

JEAN-CLAUDE CARRIÈRE: *Yet when you put forth your proposals, when you set up a ministry, gathered deputies and opened offices in various foreign capitals, the Chinese refused to see anything in all that but reactionary moves and an attempt at "secession." The Chinese continue to imprison any Tibetans who show loyalty to you or their traditions. At the same time, those who support China are rewarded by the occupiers. The exile continues, but from time to time Lhasa is shaken by demonstrations which are immediately repressed. It is said the situation is worse today than ever.**

THE DALAI LAMA: Tibet has been independent for centuries; it isn't anymore. We have to look things in the eye. We are asking for autonomy, we don't dream of independence anymore. But we don't want to negotiate except on the basis of mutual respect. Conditions

---

* The Dalai Lama's assistants suggest that the only chance for an accord would be a severe crisis in China itself. But there is no reason to anticipate one. President Clinton personally intervened in 1993, apparently to no avail. In February 1994, a French newspaper spoke of a project of "federation," but the Dalai Lama denies the report.

today are not those of the past, and we are ready to take our inspiration from the words of Deng Ziaoping: "One country, two systems." But the minds of the Chinese aren't going in that direction, not at this moment, anyhow.

JEAN-CLAUDE CARRIÈRE: *I've heard the Chinese are demolishing the old quarters of Lhasa.*

THE DALAI LAMA: Yes, under the pretext that they're unhealthy. The situation is bad.

JEAN-CLAUDE CARRIÈRE: *What can one do? Can international pressure play a role?*

THE DALAI LAMA: It's essential. Above all it must not ease up, because the Chinese sometimes show that they're sensitive to it. Every time I make a public statement, wherever in the world it might be, there are Chinese in the hall. Sometimes I even speak to them, and they know how to behave very agreeably. This attitude does indicate that they're following my activities, that they're interested in what I say, even if in their newspapers they accuse me of all sorts of things. Sometimes they accuse me of personal ambition, of counterrevolutionary thinking, of wanting to restore a theocracy. The classic charges.

JEAN-CLAUDE CARRIÈRE: *Are you optimistic?*

THE DALAI LAMA: Yes. Because Tibet's cause is just. I'm sure of it. And also because China won't be able to remain aloof from freedom forever.

. . .

On the one hand the Dalai Lama promotes a vigilant realism, a renewed effort to adapt to this changing world—an effort all the more meritorious because in ancient Tibet, a kingdom of impermanence, things used to seem forever immutable.

On the other hand, the dream persists of a sort of ideal land, beyond the ranges of the Himalayas, like the Shangri-La of *Lost Horizon*, a miraculously protected land, where peace-minded people could meet. A land that would be an example to the world, where Buddhism, free of its ancient formalism, would find its true function of lookout and explorer.

Utopia? It's never certain. The difficult dreams are part of us, too. They draw us and they help us, assuming they don't lead us to a paradise regained. They can bring us to slip a little of Tibet inside each one of us.

JEAN-CLAUDE CARRIÈRE: *Can politics be reconciled with* ahimsa?

THE DALAI LAMA: Yes, that ought to be possible. Why not? Look at our century. It thought up, or worked out, a whole gamut of things to make violence the rule in human relations, from world war, with the destruction of entire cities, to genocide, to institutional torture, to terrorism as a form of action. All these methods have failed, and always will.

JEAN-CLAUDE CARRIÈRE: *Why?*

THE DALAI LAMA: Because they're superficial. They crash against the powerful ground of our nature, which is made of goodness and generosity. Let's take the example of the Israelis, who have gone through forty years of hatred. Even if the extremist groups on both sides continue to chant—and to practice—that vain and bloody hatred, some day or other they'll have to make peace. The promotion of hatred leads to nothing but hatred. Violence is the worst of arbitrators. Mutual respect is inevitable.

JEAN-CLAUDE CARRIÈRE: *At the end of the* Mahābhārata, *King Yudhisthira finally ascends the throne. He is the very son of Dharma, and consequently called "Dharmâraj." For once Dharma itself is king. And under his leadership the world will come to know thirty-six years of peace and prosperity.*

But that perfect direction does not suppose any relaxation of the king's vigilance. If Yudhisthira appears with the Dharma in his right hand, he always holds a rod in his left. And he is ready to use it. That's what the king is there for.

THE DALAI LAMA: Naturally, but in the world of today, authority must be exercised in the name of the law, under the control of the constitution. And that authority must above all else be benevolent. It must not punish for punishment's sake.

JEAN-CLAUDE CARRIÈRE: *You are opposed to the death penalty?*

THE DALAI LAMA: Absolutely opposed to it. My predecessor abolished it in Tibet. Today I find it unbelievable that it persists in large countries like China and India. In the name of justice they are still killing people in the country of Mahatma Gandhi! In the very land where the Buddha taught! The death penalty is pure violence, a barbaric and useless violence. Dangerous even, because it can only lead to other acts of violence. As all violence does.

JEAN-CLAUDE CARRIÈRE: *So punishment has to be limited to imprisonment?*

THE DALAI LAMA: The supreme punishment ought to be a life sentence, as with you. And without any brutality.

I've noticed that even today in films they never really kill the animals. They tranquilize them with injections, so that they'll look dead. Except in the Chinese movies: there they really do kill them, right out in the open. I've also seen in Chinese scientific films rats with their skulls open. Horrible. And they show that on television.*

Also, the faithful who go on pilgrimage to Mecca have to sacrifice an animal, but at least the sacrifice isn't shown.

I strive as best I can to bring about harmony everywhere. Millions of acts of violence every instant are destroying that harmony. Why add more to the list? Why practice and show violence when it's not inevitable? The slaughter of an animal is an injury to universal harmony. I really have a horror of that.

---

* I was tempted to tell him that real death, on the screen, is not the exclusive property of Chinese film directors. In Western films we kill pigs and chickens on the screen. A live ox is cut into pieces in *Apocalypse Now*, and rabbits and partridges are slaughtered en masse in *The Rules of the Game*. There are numerous examples in many other films. If we look close, death, real death, is constantly there.

At this very moment, in Tibet, I'm told that thousands of animals are killed by the Chinese, for simple amusement. Dogs, for example. They cut off a paw, or some other part of the body, or else they strip off the skin, and they let them go around that way till they die. Look at the mentality that's developing there.

JEAN-CLAUDE CARRIÈRE: *Which has to be fought against?*

THE DALAI LAMA: Of course. As you were saying apropos of Dharmâraj, you always have to hold the rod in one hand and make use of it if necessary. Yes, one way or another, there has to be a system of discipline.

JEAN-CLAUDE CARRIÈRE: *Despite the goodness of our nature?*

THE DALAI LAMA: That natural goodness has a lot of trouble manifesting itself.

JEAN-CLAUDE CARRIÈRE: *It's simpler to be cruel.*

THE DALAI LAMA: Simpler for some people, certainly. To be cruel is to stop along the way. It's to give up, for one reason or another, the task of penetrating our own depths. It's remaining attached to our irritated or exasperated surface.

JEAN-CLAUDE CARRIÈRE: *It's pitching the battle on bad terrain.*

THE DALAI LAMA: Precisely. That's why I believe that from infancy onward you have to give the highest place to education. I keep coming back to that. Along with that education there has to be a practice of the mind, in the form of meditation, and if possible the soothing influence of a united family, of a happy marriage.

JEAN-CLAUDE CARRIÈRE: *It's a beautiful dream.*

THE DALAI LAMA: I know that. Still, such harmony exists. We can feel it strongly, sometimes. It's inscribed in the deepest part of us. It's our first tendency. There are, and there always will be evildoers, I know that, too.

JEAN-CLAUDE CARRIÈRE: *And hence the need for the rod?*

THE DALAI LAMA: To be used with as little brutality as possible.

from In Exile from the Land of Snows

by *John F. Avedon*

Journalist John F. Avedon became interested in Tibet when he met a Tibetan guerrilla on a Himalayan trek in the 1970s. Here he follows the Dalai Lama on a journey across India that includes stops at several Buddhist holy places.

*B*enares station, the Tito Gate, January 19, 6:10 a.m. The Dalai Lama's saloon, disconnected from the Gaya train, slides into a private siding beyond the terminal. After breakfast Tenzin Gyatso walks down the narrow corridor to wash in the bathroom at the rear of the car. His fellow travelers are busy unpacking clothes to store in the saloon before commencing the next stage of pilgrimage.

Outside, three Ambassadors, their drivers polishing the hoods, wait beside the track. Samdong Rinpoché, the erudite principal of the Institute of Higher Buddhist Studies in nearby Sarnath, waits, *kata* in hand, to welcome the Dalai Lama. Around him stand the usual rifle-toting police, heads wrapped in scarves against the early-morning chill. Beyond, the pale yellow domes of the Benares station, one of the more dramatic legacies of the British Raj, rise in the gray light, the halls beneath filled at this hour with files of sleeping travelers, wrapped in blankets, against the walls. Between them meander white, slack-jawed, sloe-eyed Brahmin cows. Benares is the Holy City, and the sacred animals, better fed than people, wander about freely, defecating in sloppy wet piles on the marble floor. The acrid stench of their urine wreathes the station. Beside the Dalai Lama's car, a lone beggar scans the track picking half-consumed refuse cast from trains. The shrill whistle of an approaching steam engine stabs the silence.

The Dalai Lama exits the saloon. Greeting Samdong Rinpoché, he strides across the platform to the lead Ambassador, a squat dark gray sedan, its windows tinted brown, the rear one draped by pink curtains. Dawa Bhotia, chief of security, joins the driver. Comfortably adjusted, he is rammed to the middle of the seat by the abrupt entrance of a Tibetan bodyguard—an ex-trooper of the Special Frontier Force. Mr. Dhawan, Delhi's liaison officer, joins the Dalai Lama in the back. The two other Ambassadors, both cream-colored, fill quickly. A jeep full of police, rifles bristling from its open sides, pulls behind the Dalai Lama's car as the column heads for the station's gate.

The drive goes due north from Benares. Here, in the Gangetic plain, lies the very cradle of classical Indian civilization. Forests of banyan, coconut, ebony, date palm and acacia once canopied the land. Six rivers, flowing down from the Himalayas to join the Ganges, produced a zone of unmatched fertility, giving rise, in turn, to India's ancient city-states. As centers of commerce, arts, politics and philosophy, their urban milieus were the prime setting for the Buddha's teaching. Following his first discourse, delivered in the Deer Park at Sarnath, five miles outside of Benares, he engendered a revolution in thought. Crippling the Brahminical system of worship and prevailing over the theistic and non-theistic philosophical sects alike, he won the adherence of virtually all the region's chief powers to his new science of mind, crowning India's golden age. What remains in present-day Uttar Pradesh can hardly resemble its glorious antecedents.

Trees tell the whole story. Almost none are left. Not just on the flat, expressionless land, but even by the roadside. Here, as across all India, whitewashed tree trunks mark the highway. Yet, an hour out of the city, the law against harming them is flagrantly broken. Hacked, mutilated stumps appear to either side, fitfully attacked, swatches of their bark randomly stripped off, branches shredded and torn, chopped halfway down their length. Throughout, armies of road workers are camped in low, smoke-blackened tents. Every five miles a new colony appears, the road beside it ripped into long rocky stretches. In its midst sit women and children, breaking large pink and gray stones into smaller stones, and these into gravel, their piles often stretching four feet high up to a quarter of a mile in length. The men dig and carry dirt, creating a new roadbed. This is the same work that the Tibetans have done, though in the case of Indian laborers, born to a lifetime of such toil, it seems a far bleaker fate. Driving through the road work is tortuous. The cars proceed at no more than thirty miles an hour, swerving between boulders and ditches. Despite their tightly shut windows, a choking skein of dust coats the inside. Allergic to dust, the Dalai Lama holds his outer robe across his face for the entire journey. After two hours he suggests a rest stop for the drivers in a small village. All save himself get out to stretch, relieve themselves—as everyone in India does, by the side of the road—and order a quick cup of sweet tea from a ramshackle mud-and-straw stall. At a second stop an hour later, the Dalai Lama asks Mr. Dhawan to buy oranges and apples for the party. The column continues on, joined by a new police jeep, the escort changing at each district border. A dead cow is passed; a dog has been run over, its intestines spilled onto the road. By the bank of a stagnant river, a group of villagers sit silently before a rectangular pyre bearing a white-shrouded corpse being consumed in bright flames, a tall plume of smoke rising skyward. The marshy field behind them is strewn with a dozen more corpses, bound in muslin, waiting their turn.

After four hours the cars pass quickly through a nondescript town, take a right turn off the main road and drive past a large grove of tall, leafless trees, standing like burnt-out candles around a gentle knoll topped by a faded building; a sad, disheartening sight: the second stop on the pilgrimage, Kushinagar, scene of the Buddha's *parinirvana* or death.

A bright blue and orange Ashoka Travelers Lodge, its giant heart-shaped doorway looking like the entrance to a "tunnel of love," faces the grounds. Surprisingly clean and modern, it is surrounded by a neatly mani-cured lawn, dotted by palm trees. Beneath the entrance wait the manager and his aides, ties and jackets yanked tight, twitching with nerves. A platoon of red-turbaned police, bayonets fixed on their rifles, shuffle anxiously about. A bulbous officer, holster jauntily angled at his side, peaked cap glinting in the midday sun, swagger stick tapping the palm of his hand, barks out a com-mand. As the Dalai Lama emerges from his car, rifles are jammed into the right shoulder, heels clicked, backs and eyes frozen. Led by the manager past the salute, the Dalai Lama is taken around the outside of the building, where, unprepared for an inspection, the rest of the shambling platoon seem to blush, gulp and shrivel inwards. Their fellows, freed from attention, do their best not to buckle, the rush of released tension visibly loosening their knees. The Dalai Lama is shown into the last room in a line opening on a shared veranda, and suddenly the excitement is over. It's just noon. For the first time since the pilgrimage began more than a week before, there is a free moment. A lone policeman is posted at permanent salute before the veranda; one of the Tibetan bodyguards pulls up a chair beneath the Dalai Lama's pastel-blue window frame. The entourage moves into adjacent quarters to unpack. The remaining police, their officer and a group of dis-trict officials who have arrived too late for the greeting, stand with the hotel staff, gawking at the Dalai Lama's door and the rather stern face of the bodyguard, plainly expressing that the show is over. But nothing, obvi-ously, has happened in Kushinagar in a long while, and even if the honored guest is hidden from view, his very presence, merely yards away, is ample reason to stay and stare—everyone does—for almost an hour more.

With the afternoon open ahead of them, Ngari Rinpoché, Dawa Bhotia and Mr. Dhawan pull up chairs in the warm sunlight before the porch. Towels and undershirts are placed close by to dry, following a quick washing. Newspapers are brought from the hotel lounge, among them a traveler's magazine, its cover featuring an article on Tibet. The photo depicts one of the handful of new white Toyota minibuses the Chinese have shipped to the country in their attempt, begun the previous year, to stimulate a tourist trade. This one, though, is stuck in the mud. Twenty-five ragged, poverty-stricken Tibetans, plainly recruited out of an adjacent field, are pushing it—a picture evidently not meant to be taken, much less used for a magazine cover. Ngari Rinpoché can't help but chuckle over the contradictions of the image, so symbolic, he feels, of his nation's fate. Silently he scans the article, the usual account of a Chinese show tour, conducted through a handful of recently refurbished monasteries in Lhasa. When he finishes reading he sits contemplatively and stares a hundred yards across the lawn and road to the grove of trees and the Parinirvana Temple in their midst.

The afternoon passes and, as the sun starts to set, a mist rises. It seeps from the moist earth, smudging the juncture of sky and land. Kushinagar, it seems, is grieving still. A burnt scent, conveyed in the smoke from nearby cooking fires, cloaks the grove where the Buddha died. The urgent, ascending wail of a lone bird contorts the silence. A waxing moon rises slowly over the temple and hangs there, its pallid light evanescent and mournful.

Three months prior to dying, the Buddha informed his disciples that his life's work was complete. At the close of the rainy-season retreat, he led them to Kushinagar, a small wattle-and-daub town in the jungle. There, lying on a couch between twin sal trees, he urged the order to ask any questions they yet had concerning his teaching. When none was forthcoming, he entered meditation and opened his eyes again in the third watch of the night only to deliver his final words: "I exhort you, brethren," he is reported to have said. "Decay is inherent in all component things. Work out your own salvation with diligence." Wrapped in new-spun cloth, the Buddha's corpse was cremated in an iron vessel on a pyre of fragrant wood decked with offerings by the people of Kushinagar. His remains were then divided among a group of eight kingdoms, republics and other claimants, each building, along with one for the vessel and another for the fire's embers, a commemorative stupa or cairn in their region.

The following morning the Dalai Lama wakes at five to meditate. After making offerings and prostrating to the image of the Buddha on the makeshift altar in his room, he sits on a cushion and assumes the prescribed position: legs crossed, eyes half-closed, tongue lightly resting behind the inside upper row of teeth. With one palm placed over the other in his lap, the tips of either thumb gently touching, he sets the Mahayana motive to obtain Buddhahood in order to benefit all beings. Like every Buddhist practitioner, he then contemplates the cardinal themes of his religion: the precious nature of a human life, impermanence, the inevitable unfolding of cause and effect, and voidness. As a tantric lama, however, his efforts soon turn to the advanced techniques that afford Tibetan Buddhism its reputation for possessing the world's most complex spiritual practices. By various procedures he endeavors to strip away the outer, more coarse levels of consciousness to expose the fundamental essence of mind: Clear Light. Once it is manifest, he focuses this most refined state of mind on emptiness, thereby beginning to eliminate the innate misconceptions of concrete existence, as well as their latencies or underlying traces, which together obscure omniscience. At the same time the Dalai Lama uses the energy of the Clear Light to generate a subtle body, capable of passing through matter unobstructed and multiplying itself infinitely to bring about benefit to beings throughout the cosmos. In this way he practices to attain both the mind and body of Buddha together, remaining absorbed in meditation for an hour and a half. Once finished, he dedicates the merit gained to the welfare of all sentient beings, prostrates once more and shortly, upon hearing a soft knock on the door, admits Lobsang Gawa, who bears his breakfast on a covered tray.

At nine o'clock the Dalai Lama visits the Parinirvana Temple. As he steps from his room, a squad of police present arms. This time Tenzin Gyatso slows his pace, gives the men a piercing look, walks in formal review down their length and at the end of the line actually salutes them. Entering his Ambassador, he is whisked across the street to where 200 Tibetans—also on pilgrimage—are lined up, *katas* in hand. Around them lie a maze of ruins: the ruddy brick walls of ancient monasteries and temples. Ahead, on the highest ground, stands the temple, a pale yellow oval building newly built for the 2,500th celebration of the Buddha's birth in 1956. At its door, the Dalai Lama takes off his shoes, dons his formal robe and, entering, prostrates three times on a red and gold cloth placed by an attendant on the marble floor. Six feet away, running the length of the room, lies a fifth-century statue depicting the Buddha at the moment of his death, reclining on his right side, head supported by the palm of one hand. It is believed to lie over the exact spot where he died. The Dalai Lama approaches and helps to drape a splendid fifteen-foot silk scarf in offering across the statue's upper shoulder and back. Circumambulating once, he returns to the front of the narrow room, touches his forehead in homage to the base of the statue and then, joined by the monks accompanying him, sits to recite the Heart Sutra and seven-limb *puja*, the two short but, for Tibetans, most popular Mahayana Buddhist prayers. The brief commemoration done, he leaves.

Outside, explosions rend the air, crows cawing frantically after each. A celebration is in progress and the thunderous noise comes from fireworks. Three thousand Indian Buddhists have convened to unveil a statue of a Burmese monk who lived and recently died in Kushinagar. After a brief stop at the small Tibetan monastery staffed by a lone monk, south of the temple, the Dalai Lama is driven over to address them.

From its start, the gathering has been in a semi-delirious state. Far into the previous night the celebrants blasted Indian film music over a public address system erected under a billowing red tent, suspended by a forest of old bamboo poles. The bodyguards turned uneasily in bed, their shoulder holsters creaking. There was a good deal of rustling in the other rooms until finally, incredulous, Ngari Rinpoché strode through the "tunnel of love" and across the street to request silence. The organizers insisted they had only meant to express their joy at the Dalai Lama's presence, but early the next morning, irrepressibly, the commotion picked up again, with cherry bombs booming across the countryside and a flushed skinny man zealously exhorting the crowd, in the style of Indian political rallies, to cheer for the Dalai Lama. Thus, along with breakfast, "*Dalai Lama Khi Jai!*" and "*Buddha Bhagavan!*" ("Long live the Dalai Lama!" and "The Buddha is Victorious!") are pelted over the P.A. In crescendoing waves, continuing right through to the Dalai Lama's arrival hours later, the haranguer still at his fearsome task, now hoarsely leading the frenzy while jumping about onstage, gesticulating wildly, his microphone jammed every few moments into an armpit to permit him the requisite round of applause topping each cheer. Like most Indian Buddhists, the people are members of the "scheduled classes" or "untouchables," millions of whom converted to Buddhism in the mid-fifties without any knowledge of the religion, simply to escape their caste designation.

As the Dalai Lama begins his speech, a troop of Indian monks dressed in a motley array of yellow, orange, tangerine and maroon robes, all wearing sunglasses, doze in the heat at the back of the stage. "Yellow Robbers—none of them study, they just live off the people," observed a disgruntled Western pilgrim earlier in the day. "Did you see those sleeping idiots?" he offers later, still disgusted by the often less than spiritual incentives for a religious vocation in India.

"Not one of them knew the words to the prayer. Don't they even know monks look terrible in sunglasses?" he adds, flabbergasted. Meanwhile, during the Dalai Lama's speech, large portions of the crowd, like overexcited children at a party, boisterously exit the tent, their declaimer madly policing the aisles to force them back to their seats. When the Dalai Lama departs, the man hurtles to the stage to set off more cheers, which, however, never come. The crowd has found better sport. With the honored guest in their midst, they mob his party, not so much for blessings, as to be compressed with the object of their passions in the ultimate climax to their festival. After a great deal of trampling and commotion, the Dalai Lama finally arrives at his car and drives away, the mob scene behind oddly unchanged from the squabbling over the Buddha's remains reported to have occurred after his demise two and a half millennia before.

An hour and a half later, Tenzin Gyatso enters a large auditorium. A thousand professors and graduate students, members of the Nagarjuna Buddhist Society (one of the foremost Indian academic groups researching original Buddhist texts), convened at the University of Gorakhpur, give him a standing ovation. Speaking extemporaneously, the Dalai Lama reflects on the relation of scholarship to Buddhism, noting that despite India's fervid desire to import scientific knowledge from the West, it must not forfeit its ancient learning. It is not a religious seminary. It is a large university, yet virtually all of the introductory speeches refer to the Dalai Lama as the living manifestation of the Buddha, unselfconsciously joining intellect and faith. When the talk is over, the Dalai Lama receives a long line of well-wishers in an adjacent room; hundreds, though, ignore him completely. Compelled by a greater force, apparently, than reverence, they descend on the long tables of chipped teacups and plates adorned with free cakes and sandwiches. The professors, in fact, act as though they are half starved. After ten minutes of unabated gulping and chewing, the food and drink has vanished. Conditions in Gorakhpur—the city of almost 300,000 in which the next two nights will be spent—illustrate why.

Though no one is dying in the streets, clearly, very little food is available. The best restaurant in town caters to the Dalai Lama's entourage. On both days the menu is identical: cauliflower, rice, a bony meat dish and, for dessert, rice pudding, invariably coated with insecticide. The diet for those unable to eat such relatively resplendent fare is a lifelong pinwheel of rice, bread and *dhal* broken only by an occasional egg or fish caught from the flat soupy waters of a nearby river. Here is India's major problem, not the burgeoning famine of Bihar, but chronic malnutrition affecting hundreds of millions, shortening lives and abetting disease. Gorakhpur is not a happy place. In particular, it evinces the ever-increasing implosion of people that is consuming all India's cities. And with a spiraling population pollution is legion. A thirty-foot-thick canopy of pungent smoke, spewed from tens of thousands of cooking and coal fires, wraps the town, so dense that at night headlights penetrate no more than a dozen yards through the gloom. A continual citywide conflagration seems to be in progress. At its very center, not far from the train station, the party is boarded in two government guest houses. Their staff is bemused and venal both; alternately in awe of the guests and vicious to one another when work must be done. It is clear in the murderous grimace of the manager and the craven, half-fed slouch of his assistants what price a life of deprivation extracts from the human character; the impulse to put self before others is a constant prerequisite for survival. Their antagonistic inertia, too, is a form of endurance, so much so that, with the first guest house filled, Mr. Dhawan himself has to organize relocation for half the party to a second.

"Raghh! Damn bugs!" rips the night. A door bangs open and out of the second guest house, clad in his underwear and waving a pistol in the air, leaps Ngari Rinpoché. "Damn bugs! Eat all of me, you buggers!" he yells. Then, his small automatic jammed back into its holster, he runs into the building and reappears dragging a mattress. Throwing it on the dew-drenched lawn, he tears off his watch and scowls at the time: 4:00 a.m. There hasn't been a moment of sleep since going to bed at midnight. The sea of smog smothering Gorakhpur holds billions of mosquitoes, many malarial, but inside this guest house so many have collected, feeding on generations of Indian officials, that the air can barely be breathed. They swarm in clouds the size of basketballs, their buzzing irradiating the room. "Enjoy the concert tonight," said Dawa Bhotia, bidding Ngari Rinpoché good evening earlier, while carrying over his shoulder the mosquito net he had not forgotten to bring along. Without one, sleep is impossible. Now, out on the lawn, silhouetted by the limp moonlight trickling down like saliva onto the black earth, Ngari Rinpoché earns only ten minutes of peace before, having located a new prey, the outdoor hordes converge. Sleep then is entirely forsaken.

Over Tea with the Dalai Lama

by *Pico Iyer*

Journalist and travel writer Pico Iyer (born 1957) has
been interested in the Dalai Lama since meeting him in
the 1970s. In this exchange they discuss the Dalai
Lama's thoughts on change and the current state of
Tibetan affairs.

I was lucky enough to visit the Fourteenth Dalai
Lama at his modest, colorful cottage in
Dharamsala for the first time in 1974, when I
was still a teenager. Since then, I've tried to
return to the northern Indian town as often as I can,
partly to witness the Tibetan struggle, and partly to
enjoy the presence and wisdom of the Dalai Lama.
Like more and more people these days, I've also been
fortunate enough to see and hear him in Los Angeles,
in Malibu, in New York and New Jersey, at Harvard
and in San Francisco, but there's always something

special about listening to him at his home, the snow-caps in the distance, and the hopes of Tibetans palpably, poignantly, in the air.

One recent autumn, I went to conduct a series of interviews with His Holiness during a rare respite in his schedule when he was officially on retreat. Dharamsala is radiant in the fall, the days dawning sharp and cloudless and the nights so full of stars that the real world can feel very far away. I wanted to know how Tibetan Buddhism was changing as its exile deepened, as its practices and teachers got sent around the world, in person and in the movies, and how, in a new global age, with more pressures and possibilities than ever before, the Dalai Lama could keep up his uniquely difficult balancing act of serving as political leader and spiritual teacher at once.

Every day we met in his room at 2 p.m., and over tea talked for as long as I had questions and he had time. Whenever my cup of tea was empty, His Holiness noticed it before I did.

PICO IYER: *I think the last time I was in this room was eight years ago. How have things changed since then?*

HIS HOLINESS THE DALAI LAMA: Less hair, I think. Both of us!

I think at a global level there is perhaps more hope, in spite of these very tragic things, like Yugoslavia and Rwanda. Regarding Tibet, I think on the positive side there is much more awareness, and as a result, concern and support are growing. Even some governments—publicly, as well as behind the scenes—are making an effort to do something for Tibet. On the other hand, inside Tibet the Chinese policies are very hard, very destructive.

So overall, I am very optimistic regarding Tibet. For the near future, no hope. But in the long run, definitely. It's only a matter of time—things will change.

PICO IYER: *And in your own life, things must have changed a lot in the last eight years.*

HIS HOLINESS THE DALAI LAMA: Not much. My general physical health is very good. My spiritual practice— not much opportunity. But as usual, I carry on. So I'm still the same person. You also are the same person. I am very happy to have a reunion with an old friend I've known since your father's time.

PICO IYER: *Yes, in fact, my father came to visit you just after you came to India.*

HIS HOLINESS THE DALAI LAMA: Yes. Very early.

PICO IYER: *Your Holiness is officially on retreat at the moment. It must be difficult to find the time for your spiritual practice because of all the things you have to do out in the world.*

HIS HOLINESS THE DALAI LAMA: Yes. Also, each time I receive some new teaching, that adds something to my daily practice. So nowadays, my daily recitation, compulsory, normally takes about four hours.

PICO IYER: *Every day?*

HIS HOLINESS THE DALAI LAMA: Usually I wake up at

3:30 in the morning. Then immediately I do some meditation, some exercise—prostrations—then bathe. Then a little walking outside. All this time I am reciting some mantra or doing some meditation. Then at 5:15, I breakfast and at 5:30 listen to the Voice of America Tibetan language broadcast. The BBC East Asia broadcast often mentions something about Tibet or China, so I usually listen to that.

After breakfast, I do some more meditation and then usually study some Tibetan philosophy or important texts. If there's some urgent business I come here to my office, and sometimes before lunch I read newspapers and magazines—*Newsweek*, *Time*, *Far Eastern Economic Review*, some Indian newspapers.

Oh, yes. At 7:30 I always listen to the BBC world news. Always. I am addicted. When I visit some foreign country and I can't listen to it because of the time change, or not having enough time, I really feel something is missing that day. I feel I don't know what's happened in the world. The BBC is always very good, and, I really feel, unbiased.

After my lunch I come here to my office until about 5:30. Then at 6:00 I have my evening tea—as a Buddhist monk, no dinner, sometimes just a few biscuits or some bread. At that time I always watch BBC television. Then evening meditation for about one hour and at 8:30, sleep. Most important meditation! Sleep is the common meditation for everyone—even for birds. The most important meditation. Not for nirvana, but for survival!

PICO IYER: *Nowadays, it must be almost impossible for Your Holiness to pursue some of your previous hobbies, like photography.*

HIS HOLINESS THE DALAI LAMA: No longer any interest. Until early 1960, I had some interest in photography, but not since then. Of course, I still love different flowers. And occasionally I do some manual work, some repair work, of watches and small instruments.

PICO IYER: *No previous Dalai Lama has faced your situation of being responsible for a diverse, worldwide community. There are those still in Tibet, who are cut off from you in some ways; there are exiled Tibetans scattered all around the world, and there are all the new Tibetan Buddhists in the West. It must be difficult to keep in touch with all of these groups and make sure things are going in the right way.*

HIS HOLINESS THE DALAI LAMA: More and more people are showing interest about Buddhism, and there's an increase in the number of Buddhist centers. But unlike the Catholic system, these are more or less autonomous. I have no responsibility. Of course, if occasionally people come here and ask me something, I give some suggestions. Otherwise, there's no central authority. They're all quite independent.

PICO IYER: *But if perhaps they're practicing in an unorthodox way, or doing things that you think are not in the true spirit of Buddhism, that must be difficult for you, even if you're not responsible for them.*

HIS HOLINESS THE DALAI LAMA: Generally, no. Of course, there were some scandals—money scandals, sexual scandals—and at that time, some Westerners told me they were seriously concerned that because of these accusations all Buddhism may suffer. I told them, "Buddhism is not new. It is more than 2,500 years old, and during that time such scandals have happened. But basic Buddhist teaching is truthful. It has its own weight, its own reasons, its own beauties, its own values. If individuals, even lamas, are doing wrong things here and there, it will not affect the whole of Buddhism."

But it's also important to have discipline, especially those people who carry responsibility. When you are teaching others, when you are supposed to improve the quality of others' lives and their mental states, first you should improve yourself. Otherwise, how can you help other people? And perhaps because of these scandals, it seems there's more discipline, more self-restraint.

PICO IYER: *It must be a great worry of yours that Tibetans will lose their connection with their culture—both those inside Tibet, and in a different way, the ones outside Tibet. It must be hard to keep the continuity.*

HIS HOLINESS THE DALAI LAMA: Inside Tibet, yes. There are clear signs of the degeneration of the Tibetan traditions, and of moral principles. In recent years, there have been a number of murder cases in the Tibetan community in India. All of them took place among people newly arrived from Tibet. This shows the degeneration of the spirit of tolerance and self-discipline. And then in Tibet itself, there is gambling and also prostitution. I was told there are many Chinese prostitutes, as well as some Tibetans. And also drugs—the refugee community has some, and it seems there are some drugs in Lhasa and the bigger towns in Tibet.

My main worry is the preservation of Tibetan culture. Tibetan political status is of course important,

but to keep alive the Tibetan spirit, the Tibetan cultural heritage, that's my main concern. This not only
benefits the six million Tibetan people, but also is of
interest for the larger community—particularly, in the
long run, to the Chinese. There are millions of young
Chinese who are sometimes called the "Lost Genera-
tion." I feel that particularly in the field of human
values, they're completely lost. In that vacuum, Tibetan
Buddhist culture can make a contribution.

PICO IYER: *Do you think that Tibetan Buddhism is going to have to
change as it's practiced by more and more non-Tibetans?*

HIS HOLINESS THE DALAI LAMA: No, I don't think so.
Some Westerners—even some Tibetans have told me
that they feel it needs some kind of modification. But
I feel there's no need of such things, as far as the basic
Buddhist teaching is concerned. Buddhism deals with
basic human problems—old age, illness, suffering.
These things, whether in today's world or a thousand
years ago, whether in India or China or America,
they're always the same.

PICO IYER: *Though Buddhism is now being practiced in countries
with very different cultures and histories.*

HIS HOLINESS THE DALAI LAMA: In any religious tradition, there should be two aspects: one is the cultural
aspect, the other is the teaching or religious aspect. The
cultural aspect, that can change. When Buddhism
reached other countries from India, the cultural aspect
adapted according to new circumstances. So we refer
today to Japanese Buddhism, Chinese Buddhism, Tibe-

tan Buddhism. Similarly, we will eventually have Western Buddhism. That, naturally, will come.

But where the basic teaching is concerned, I think it should be the same. For example, all authentic Tibetan scholars, whenever some important matter comes up, always rely on quotations of an earlier Indian scholar. Without that, we do not believe it's authentic. So you see, the teaching has been the same for 2,500 years. That's why I feel it's not correct to call Tibetan Buddhism "lamaism." With this incarnation, the Dalai Lama has been called, especially by the Chinese, "living Buddha." Now that is totally wrong. The Chinese word for "lama" means "living Buddha." But in Tibetan, the word "lama" is a direct translation of "guru." So "guru" and "lama" have the same meaning—someone who should be respected because of his wisdom, or because of the indebtedness one owes to him. So the rough meaning is "someone worthy of respect." No implication of "living Buddha." Some Western books also sometimes say "living Buddha" when they describe me, or "god." Totally wrong!

PICO IYER: *I remember you once said that among the Buddhist virtues, humility was perhaps more easily practiced in Tibet than in the West. I was wondering whether there are other values that are more difficult to practice in this new context?*

HIS HOLINESS THE DALAI LAMA: In a Western society, it might be difficult to undertake a good meditation practice because of the fast pace of life there. But then you see, the solitude of some Christian monks and nuns is more remarkable than in Tibet. These monks and nuns live in their monasteries or nunneries all the rest of their lives, with no contact with the outside world. One monastery in the south of France has no radio, no newspaper. Completely cut out! And meals also are quite poor. And no proper shoes, only sandals. So most of them, for the rest of their lives, remain there almost like a prisoner. Wonderful!

So eventually Buddhist monasteries in the West can establish a similar pattern to some of these Christian monasteries. Then I don't think there will be any difficulties. They can spend all day on meditation.

PICO IYER: *These days you probably spend more of your time talking to non-Buddhists than to Buddhists, because you travel so much and you're speaking to so many different audiences.*

HIS HOLINESS THE DALAI LAMA: Perhaps yes, perhaps yes. Whenever I have the opportunity to talk or speak outside the Tibetan community, my basic concern is with secular ethics. I make a distinction between spirituality with faith and spirituality without faith—simply to be a good human being, a warm-hearted person, a person with a sense of responsibility. Usually I emphasize the secular ethics, and it seems this is beneficial. I explain the basic human values, or human good qualities, such as compassion, and why these are important. I explain that whether one is a believer or a nonbeliever is up to the individual, but even without a religion, one can be a good human being.

I notice the majority of the audience appreciates this—with or without faith, just being a good human being. They're more receptive. That is important. The majority of people in the world are non-believers, and we can't argue with them and tell them they should be believers. No! Impossible! Realistically speaking, the majority of humanity will remain non-believers, and it doesn't matter. No problem! The problem is that the majority have lost or ignore the deeper human values, such as compassion and a sense of responsibility. Then we really are faced with a problem. That is our big concern. Wherever there is a society or community or family without these good human qualities, then even one single family cannot be a happy family. That's perfectly clear.

Certain emotions, such as hatred, create such a clear demarcation of "we" and "they." Immediately, there is a sense of enemy. There is so much competition, so much negative feeling towards your neighbor, and on your neighbor's side, also a negative attitude towards you. Then what happens? You are surrounded by enemy, but the enemy is your own creation!

Recently I am emphasizing that due to the modern economy, and also due to information and education, the world is now heavily interdependent, interconnected. Under such circumstances, the concept of "we" and "they" is gone: harming your neighbor is actually harming yourself. If you do negative things towards your neighbor, that is actually creating your own suffering. And helping them, showing concern about others' welfare—actually these are the major factors of your own happiness. If you want a community full of joy, full of friendship, you should create that possibility. If you remain negative, and meantime want more smiles and friendship from your neighbors, that's illogical. If you want a more friendly neighbor, you must create the atmosphere. Then they will respond.

PICO IYER: *So we need to be reminded of our most basic, most fundamental, responsibilities.*

HIS HOLINESS THE DALAI LAMA: That's my main emphasis. I really feel the important thing is the promotion of secular moral ethics. That's what we really need. Those emotions or actions which ultimately bring happiness or satisfaction, they are positive. Because we want happiness. Those emotions and actions which ultimately bring suffering, we should consider negative. Because we do not want suffering. These are basic human values—no connection to Creator, no connection to Buddha.

PICO IYER: *Do you worry that in the Tibetan community, so much responsibility falls on you personally that even if you try to spread the responsibility among more and more people, they're reluctant to take it because they hold you in such high regard? It's hard to change those age-old beliefs.*

HIS HOLINESS THE DALAI LAMA: Yes, that's true. I often tell people "You should carry on your work as if I didn't exist." Sooner or later, that day will come, definitely.

PICO IYER: *You must be concerned about what happens when you are not around anymore—the likelihood of the Chinese just choosing their own Dalai Lama.*

HIS HOLINESS THE DALAI LAMA: No, there isn't much problem! In the long run, yes, the Chinese want to control the future selection of the Dalai Lama. There is also the possibility there will no longer be any Dalai

Lama—according to some information, the Chinese are thinking like that. Okay. Whatever they like, they can do. Nobody can stop them. But that won't affect the Tibetan mind. So it doesn't matter.

PICO IYER: *There's nothing you can do to protect your incarnation from the Chinese?*

HIS HOLINESS THE DALAI LAMA: The Chinese certainly may recognize one Dalai Lama, but to the Tibetan people, that won't be the Dalai Lama. They will not accept him. So I am not much concerned. And the very institution of the Dalai Lama—whether it should continue or not—that's up to the Tibetan people. At a certain stage, the Dalai Lama institution will cease. That does not mean the Tibetan Buddhist culture will cease. The Tibetan Buddhist culture will remain, and should remain, I think, as long as Tibetan people remain. But institutions come and go, come and go.

PICO IYER: *Nowadays, so many people want to talk to you and they may have a whole variety of different motives. Is that a difficult thing?*

HIS HOLINESS THE DALAI LAMA: For me there is no difference. Of course, sometimes they have different motivations, that's possible, but for me that's no problem. I treat every human being the same, whether high officials or beggars—no differences, no distinctions.

PICO IYER: *Along similar lines, you always stress that it's important to put everything to the test of reason, and not accept things automatically. I wonder if more and more people are inclined to take you as a teacher, and just to accept everything that you say.*

HIS HOLINESS THE DALAI LAMA: Yes. A kind of blind faith! Yes, that also is happening. But I never feel that I'm a teacher. I never accept anyone as my disciple, including Tibetans. I usually consider them as my dharma friend. In a few exceptional cases, if we've known each other many years—if there's some kind of genuine trust on the basis of awareness—then sometimes I accept to be their guru, and they consider themselves as my disciple. But usually I consider them as my spiritual friend. So many foreigners ask me to accept them as my disciple. And I say, no need for that kind of acceptance. Just to be a dharma friend is much healthier, much better, and I also feel much more comfortable. Usually that is my response when someone requests me to accept them as a disciple.

PICO IYER: *One of the English poets once said, "A little knowledge is a dangerous thing." I wonder if Tibetan culture and Tibetan Buddhism are more subject to distortions, because lots of people in the world now know just a little bit about them.*

HIS HOLINESS THE DALAI LAMA: Yes. There are some new opportunities to exploit this location. In the field of Tibetan medicine, in some Tibetan arts, and in Buddhism also, some people are making claims for themselves without having the proper knowledge. Some Tibetans lived in India or Nepal with no record of any teaching, but after a few years in the West, they became very great lamas. I think some foreigners are a little bit surprised. They consider their lama very great, but when they reach India or Nepal, they inquire of some Tibetan, "Such and such a lama, where is he?" The Tibetan doesn't know, and sometimes says, "That's not a lama, not a great teacher." It happens, but okay, no problem. So long as it benefits someone, that's good.

PICO IYER: *There are lots of movie stars who are interested in Buddhism, and, as Your Holiness knows, there are even Tibetan monks represented in advertisements and fashion magazines. I wonder if, as Tibet has become better known, that has become a difficulty because people associate Tibet with rich and famous people?*

HIS HOLINESS THE DALAI LAMA: If there are people who use Tibetans or the Tibetan situation for their own benefit, there's very little that we can do. The important thing is for us not to be involved or associate with these people for our own interest.

Some reporters are curious about actors who are showing a keen interest about Buddhism. In fact, they imply that I'm becoming almost a celebrity myself. But my feeling is that I don't care about people's background, so long as they have sincere motivation, honest, clean desire. Then, of course, I will give them an opportunity, and I will treat them as a friend. I do not pay importance to what their background is.

The important thing is that on our side, our motivation should be very clear, should be very honest. Personally, I am a Buddhist monk. I am a follower of Buddha. From that viewpoint, meeting one simple, innocent, sincere, spiritual seeker is more important than meeting a politician or a prime minister. These reporters usually consider politics as something most important, so meeting with a politician becomes something very significant for them. But for me, meeting with ordinary people, making some contribution to peace of mind, to deeper awareness about the value of human life—that, I feel, is very important. When I see some result, then I feel, "Today I made some small contribution."

PICO IYER: *Your Holiness has such a complicated life, because there are so many different roles you have to play. What do you find most difficult?*

HIS HOLINESS THE DALAI LAMA: Meeting with politicians is one experience I feel is rather difficult. I have to meet these people and appeal to them, but there's nothing concrete that I can tell them about Tibet because the situation is so complicated. The problem is so big that even if these leaders sincerely want to help, they can't do anything! But if I don't meet with them, that also is wrong. It's better to meet. The worst thing is that occasionally some formality is also involved. That, I don't care for. Once, at Salzburg, they invited me to speak at a festival, and I told them some of my usual thoughts, about the difficulties, the gap between rich and poor, and these sorts of things. Afterwards, the Austrian chancellor said that I broke all the taboos. It was a festival, so I suppose some praise, some nice words, were expected.

PICO IYER: *It's a good thing, to broach some serious topics.*

HIS HOLINESS THE DALAI LAMA: I felt, here everything is very nice, very beautiful, but at the same time, human beings in some other part of the world are still facing starvation. So this is the gap—rich and poor, south and north—that I talked about. It seems my informality—my radical informality—sometimes helps people. Some of these problems are in their minds also, but they do not find it easy to speak out about it. Perhaps.

PICO IYER: *Are you disappointed by what the governments of the world have managed to do for Tibet?*

HIS HOLINESS THE DALAI LAMA: Of course, I do feel they could do more, but at the same time, I see clearly their difficulties. China is a big nation, a very important nation, so you cannot ignore China. You have to deal with China.

To isolate China is totally wrong. China must be brought into the mainstream of the world community. In the economic field, the Chinese themselves want to join, but we in the world community also have the moral responsibility to bring China into the mainstream of world democracy, which the Chinese people themselves also want. When we deal with China, we need to create genuine, mutual trust, and within that, we should make these wrong things clear. Certain matters of principle should be very firm, within the friendly atmosphere.

I feel the greatest obstacle is Chinese suspicion, over-suspicion. So long as this suspicion remains, you can't solve this problem. So first remove suspicion, then close relations, close contact. Not confrontation, but rather persuasion and interaction.

So you see, relations with China for these Western nations are very delicate, very complicated. Under such circumstances, I feel the amount of support we receive is very, very encouraging. We have no money, we have no oil, we have nothing to offer. Tibet is a small nation, we are bullied by the Chinese, and we have suffered lots of human rights violations and destruction. The world's concern comes not from economic or geopolitical interest, but purely from human feeling and concern for justice. I think that is very encouraging. It is genuine support that comes from the heart. I think it is a great thing.

I tell audiences a few reasons why they should support Tibet. One is ecology. Because of Tibet's high altitude and dry climate, once the ecology is damaged, it takes a longer time to recover. The Chinese are very eager to exploit Tibet and the possibility of damage is great. Because no many important rivers have their source in Tibet, this would eventually affect large areas in this part of the world.

Second, Tibetan culture, Buddhist culture, creates a certain way of life, based on peaceful relations with fellow human beings, peaceful relations with nature, peaceful relations with animals. I think that kind of culture is necessary, useful, for the world at large. Such a cultural heritage, which can help millions of people, is now facing extinction.

Finally, if we believe in peaceful solutions through non-violence, then we should support the success of the Tibetan struggle, which has been a non-violent approach right from the beginning. If it fails, then it's a setback on a global level for a new pattern of freedom struggle through non-violence. The only way to solve conflict is through dialogue, through non-violent principles. Once the Tibetan non-violent struggle eventually succeeds, it can be an example of that.

PICO IYER: *Do you think Your Holiness will see Tibet again?*

HIS HOLINESS THE DALAI LAMA: Oh yes, certainly! Certainly. If I don't die tonight, or in the next few years. Oh, definitely. Another five years, ten years, I think things will change. I think there's real hope.

PICO IYER: *The challenges that you have had to face over the last 30 or 40 years—would those be part of the Dalai Lama's karma?*

HIS HOLINESS THE DALAI LAMA: Yes, of course. And also, I think, common karma.

PICO IYER: *So does that mean there's a kind of purpose or a reason for the difficulties being faced?*

HIS HOLINESS THE DALAI LAMA: Purpose, I don't know. That's very, very mysterious, very difficult to say. These karmic consequences—in some cases, they have some meaning, some significance.

But it is useful to look at tragedy from a different angle, so that your mental frustration can decrease. For example, our tragedy—becoming refugees, a lot of destruction in our country—this also brings new opportunity. If still we were in Tibet, Tibetan Buddhism would not be known in the outside world like it is. From that viewpoint, the more exposure, the better.

PICO IYER: *For the world, it has been a great gain, because before we didn't have access to Tibet.*

HIS HOLINESS THE DALAI LAMA: The knowledge about Tibet and Tibetan Buddhism now existing in the world is because of the tragedy that happened to Tibet. So there is one positive result of that.

PICO IYER: *And that inevitably means that some people with sincere hearts can learn a lot, but there will also be distortions.*

HIS HOLINESS THE DALAI LAMA: Truth has its own strength. So as time goes by, something truthful starts to grow, becomes stronger and stronger. Like the Tibetan cause, or also my position regarding Tibetan Buddhism, or some of our activities in India. At the beginning, perhaps it wasn't very popular, but as time goes on, it becomes well accepted. When something is truthful, its truthfulness becomes clearer and clearer.

PICO IYER: *My last question: Your Holiness has always been so good at finding a blessing or a teaching in anything that happens, even in suffering. I was wondering what is the saddest thing that's happened to you in your life?*

HIS HOLINESS THE DALAI LAMA: I think when I left the Norbulingka for exile that late night, and I left behind some of my close friends, and one dog. Then another was the final farewell when I was passing over the border into India. Saying farewell to my bodyguards, who were determined to return to Tibet—which meant facing death, or something like that. So these two occasions were of course very sad. But also, some occasions now when newly arrived Tibetans explain about their life stories, and tortures, and there are a lot of tears. Sometimes, I also cry. But usually, my tears come on a different occasion—that's when I talk about compassion, altruism, and about Buddha. I quite often become so emotional that tears come.

But I think sadness is comparatively manageable. From a wider Buddhist perspective, the whole of existence is by nature suffering. So, suffering is some symptom of samsara. That, also, is quite useful. That's why I sustain peace of mind!

PICO IYER: *Thank you so much.*

HIS HOLINESS THE DALAI LAMA: Thank you.

from Ethics for the New Millennium

by *the Dalai Lama*

The notion of our universal responsibility to other beings is central to the Buddhist idea of interdependence. Here the Dalai Lama stresses the need to do "as much as we can."

*T*hrough developing an attitude of responsibility toward others, we can begin to create the kinder, more compassionate world we all dream of. The reader may or may not agree with my advocacy of universal responsibility. But if it is correct that, given the broadly interdependent nature of reality, our habitual distinction between self and other is in some sense an exaggeration, and if on the basis of this I am right in suggesting that our aim should be to extend our compassion toward all others, we cannot avoid the conclusion that compassion—which entails ethical conduct—belongs at the heart of all our actions, both individual and social. Furthermore, although of course the details are open to debate, I am convinced that universal responsibility means that compassion belongs in the political arena too. It tells us something important about how we are to conduct our daily lives if we desire to be happy in the way I have characterized happiness. Saying this, I trust it is clear that I am not calling on everyone to renounce their present way of life and adopt some new rule or way of thinking. Rather, my intention is to suggest that the individual, keeping his or her daily way of life, can change, can become a better, more compassionate, and happier human being. And through being better, more compassionate individuals, we can begin to implement our spiritual revolution.

The work of a person laboring in some humble occupation is no less relevant to the well-being of society than that of, for example, a doctor, a teacher, a monk, or a nun. All human endeavor is potentially great and noble. So long as we carry out our work with good motivation, thinking, "My work is for others," it will be of benefit to the wider community. But when concern for others' feelings and welfare is missing, our activities tend to become spoiled. Through lack of basic human feeling, religion, politics, economics, and so on can be rendered dirty. Instead of serving humanity, they become agents of its destruction.

Therefore, in addition to developing a sense of universal responsibility, we need actually to be responsible people. Until we put our principles into practice, they remain just that. So, for example, it is appropriate for a politician who is genuinely responsible to conduct himself or herself with honesty and integrity. It is appropriate for a businessman or woman to consider the needs of others in every enterprise they undertake. It is appropriate for a lawyer to use their expertise to fight for justice.

Of course it is difficult to articulate precisely how our behavior would be shaped by a commitment to the principle of universal responsibility. For this reason, I do not have any particular standard in mind. All that I hope is that if what is written here makes sense to you, the reader, you will strive to be compassionate in your daily life, and that out of a sense of responsibility toward all others you will do what you can to help them. When you walk past a dripping tap, you will turn it off. If you see a light burning unnecessarily, you will do the same. If you are a religious practitioner and tomorrow you meet someone of another religious tradition, you will show them the same respect as you would hope them to show you. Or if you are a scientist and you see that the research you are engaged in may cause harm to others, out of a sense of responsibility you will desist from it. According to your own resources, and recognizing the limitations of your circumstances, you will do what you can. Apart from this, I am not calling for any commitment as such. And if on some days your actions are more compassionate than on others—well, that is normal. Likewise, if what I say does not seem helpful, then no matter. The important thing is that whatever we do for others, whatever sacrifices we make, it should be voluntary and arise from understanding the benefit of such actions.

On a recent visit to New York, a friend told me that the number of billionaires in America had increased from seventeen just a few years ago to several hundred today. Yet at the same time, the poor remain poor and in some cases are becoming poorer. This I consider to be completely immoral. It is also a potential source of problems. While millions do not even have the basic necessities of life—adequate food, shelter, education, and medical facilities—the inequity of wealth distribution is a scandal. If it were the case that everyone had a sufficiency for their needs and more, then perhaps a luxurious lifestyle would be tenable. If that was what the individual really wanted, it would be difficult to argue that they need refrain from exercising their right to live as they see fit. Yet things are not like that. In this one world of ours, there are areas where people throw surplus food away while others close by—our fellow humans, innocent children among them—are reduced to scavenging among rubbish, and many starve. Thus although I cannot say that the life of luxury led by the rich is wrong of itself, assuming they are using their own money and have not acquired it dishonestly, I do say that it is unworthy, that it is spoiling.

Moreover, it strikes me that the lifestyles of the rich are often absurdly complicated. One friend of mine who stayed with an extremely wealthy family told me that every time they went swimming, they were handed a robe to wear after. This would then be changed for a fresh one each time they used the pool, even if they did so several times in one day. Extraordinary! Ridiculous, even. I do not see how living like this adds anything to one's comfort. As human beings we have only one stomach. There is a limit to the amount we can eat. Similarly, we have only eight fingers and two thumbs, so we cannot wear a hundred rings. Whatever argument there may be concerning choice, the extra we have is of no purpose in the moment when we are actually wearing a ring. The rest lie useless in their boxes. The appropriate use of wealth, as I explained to the members of one hugely prosperous Indian family, is found in philanthropic giving. In this particular case, I suggested—since they asked—that perhaps spending their money on education would be the best thing they could do. The future of the world is in our children's hands. Therefore, if we wish to bring about a more compassionate—and therefore fairer society—it is essential that we educate our children to be responsible, caring human beings. When a person is born rich, or acquires wealth by some other means, they have a tremendous opportunity to benefit others. What a waste when that opportunity is squandered on self-indulgence.

I feel strongly that luxurious living is inappropriate, so much so that I must admit that whenever I stay in a comfortable hotel and see others eating and drinking expensively while outside there are people who do not even have anywhere to spend the night, I feel greatly disturbed. It reinforces my feeling that I am no different from either the rich or the poor. We are the same in wanting happiness and not to suffer. And we have an equal right to that happiness. As a result, I feel that if I were to see a workers' demonstration going by I would certainly join in. And yet, of course, the person who is saying these things is one of those enjoying the comforts of the hotel. Indeed, I must go further. It is also true that I possess several valuable wristwatches. And while I feel that if I were to sell them I could perhaps build some huts for the poor, so far I have not. In the same way I do feel that if I were to observe a strictly vegetarian diet not only would I be setting a better example, but I would also be helping to save innocent animals' lives. So far I have not and therefore must admit a discrepancy between my principles and my practice in certain areas. At the same time, I do not believe everyone can or should be like Mahatma Gandhi and live the life of a poor peasant. Such dedication is wonderful and greatly to be admired. But the watchword is "As much as we can"— without going to extremes.

A Biographical Sketch of the Fourteen Dalai Lamas

by *Glenn H. Mullin*

Glenn H. Mullin (born 1949) has written or translated many books on Tibetan Buddhism. This piece describes the history of the Dalai Lama's incarnations.

*T*he office of the Dalai Lamas of Tibet is one of the most unique institutions the world has produced. Shortly after a Dalai Lama dies, a committee is formed to find his reincarnation. Most Dalai Lamas have left mystical "clues" as to where they shall take rebirth, and these are always used as the basis of the search. In addition, oracles, famous lamas, clairvoyants and all the elements of Tibet's unusual society work together to locate and reinstate the young incarnation. Search parties are formed, likely candidates identified and then extensive tests are made. Each of the young candidates is shown items that belonged to the deceased Dalai Lama, such as rosaries, ritual implements, articles of clothing and so forth. These are mixed in with replicas, and the true incarnation is expected to choose correctly those articles that belonged to his predecessor.

The successful candidate is officially recognized and is enthroned with great regalia. He is then given to the best tutors in Tibet, and for the twenty or thirty years to follow is submitted to an intensive spiritual education in the Buddhist arts, sciences and humanities. At the conclusion of his studies he is expected to face examination by debating with dozens of Tibet's highest scholars before an assembly of some 20,000 monks and nuns from Tibet's greatest monastic universities. Only then is he invested with the powers of spiritual authority over the country. The present Dalai Lama is the fourteenth to hold this extraordinary office.

The name "Dalai" is in fact a Mongolian word, although the Dalai Lama lineage is older than the title. The first to be known as a Dalai was So-nam Gya-tso, who converted the Mongolian king Altan Khan and his nation to Buddhism in 1578. Rather than call the lama by his Tibetan name, Altan Khan translated the second part of it, or *Gya-tso*, which simply means "Ocean," into Mongolian. The result was the "Dalai Lama," or "Teacher [like the] Ocean." Dalai also is a term implying supremacy or greatness; consequently, an alternative translation would be "Supreme Teacher" or "Greatest Master." Thus the Mongolians were the first to use the title Dalai Lama. From them it spread through China and the Far East, and then to Europe and the Americas. It was never used by the Tibetans themselves, however, who preferred to call their spiritual leader by Tibetan epithets such as Kun-dun (the All-Purposeful One), Yi-shin Nor-bu (the Wish-fulfilling Gem) and Gyal-wa Rin-po-che (the Precious Adept). Because So-nam Gya-tso was considered to be a reincarnation of Gen-dun Gya-tso, and he in turn a reincarnation of Gen-dun Drub, Altan Khan's guru became known as the Third Dalai Lama. The two predecessors only posthumously came to be called the First and Second Dalai Lamas.

Although the Dalai Lamas are technically thought of as reincarnations of the same being, nonetheless each has manifested greatness in a unique way and has chosen his individual sphere of activity and attention.

The Dalai Lama I, Gyal-wa Gen-dun Drub, was born in Gur-ma of Zhab to in 1391 as the son of nomadic peasants. At the age of seven, he was placed by his mother in Nar-tang Monastery (of the Ka-dam Sect) for education. He was to become the greatest scholar/saint to be produced by this monastery, and his fame spread like a victory banner over all of Tibet. In 1447 he established Ta-shi Lhun-po Monastery at Shi-ga-tse, which was destined to become Southern Tibet's greatest monastic university. In writing he focused on the Ka-dam-pa practice traditions and also the Five Themes of Buddha's Teachings (*pramana, abhi-dharma, prajnaparamita, madhyamaka* and *vinaya*), which had been popularized in Tibet by the Sa-kya Sect. He was particularly famous for combining study and practice, and spent more than twenty years in meditational retreat. He passed away while sitting in meditation in 1474.

The Dalai Lama II, Gyal-wa Gen-dun Gya-tso, was born in 1475 in Yol-kar Dor-je-den. The son of a renowned yogi of the Nying-ma Sect, he was recognized at the age of four as Gen-dun Drub's reincarnation. He studied and wrote extensively on practices from various of the Tibetan sects, but is particularly renowned for his writings on the lineages of the Nying-ma, Shang-pa Ka-gyu and Ge-luk Nyen-gyu traditions. His principal focus was the tantric tradition. He is particularly noted for "discovering" and consecrating the La-tso "Lake of Visions" and establishing Cho-khor-gyal Monastery beside it. He is also noted for constructing Gan-den Po-drang house in Dre-pung Monastery. He passed away in 1542 while sitting in meditation.

The Dalai Lama III, Gyal-wa So-nam Gya-tso, was born in 1543 in Khang-sar of To-lung. Recognized at an early age as Gen-dun Gya-tso's reincarnation, he was placed in Dre-pung for education. He rapidly became known for his wisdom and accomplishment, and was appointed as the Dre-pung Abbot. His name spread throughout Asia, and Altan Khan of the Tumed Mongols became his disciple. He traveled to Mongolia in 1578, where the Tumeds formally adopted Buddhism under him. Here he established Tek-chen Cho-khor Monastery. Later he traveled widely throughout Eastern Tibet and Western China, where he taught extensively and established many monasteries, the most important being Li-tang and Kum-bum. He was noted for combining the Nying-ma and Ge-luk lineages in his practice, and for bringing civilization to the wild borderlands of Central Asia. He passed away in 1588 while still teaching in the northeast.

The Dalai Lama IV, Gyal-wa Yon-ten Gya-tso, is the only Dalai Lama to have been born outside of Tibet. He took birth in 1589 in Mongolia. A direct descendant of

Altan Khan, he fulfilled So-nam Gya-tso's promise to the Mongolians to return to them in his future life. Because he was born outside of Tibet, his official recognition and enthronement took longer than usual, and he was not brought to Tibet until he was twelve years old. Both he and his predecessor, the Third Dalai Lama, received opulent gifts from the Emperor of China and numerous invitations to visit the Manchu court; but both declined. The Fourth Dalai Lama did not write any significant works, but instead dedicated his time and energy to study, practice and teaching. He passed away in early 1617.

The Dalai Lama V, Gyal-wa Nga-wang Lob-zang Gya-tso, popularly known as "The Great Fifth," was born in Chong-gye in the Fire Snake Year, less than a year after the passing of Gyal-wa Yon-ten Gya-tso. This was to be the most dynamic of the early Dalai Lamas. He wrote as much as all other Dalai Lamas combined, traveled and taught extensively, and reshaped the politics of Central Asia. During his lifetime the three provinces of Tibet (Central, South and East) that had been divided into separate kingdoms since the demise of King Lang Dar-ma in the mid-ninth century, once again joined together to form a united Tibet, with the Great Fifth arising as the spiritual and secular ruler in 1642. He was invited to the Chinese court by the Ching Emperor to restructure the Buddhist monasteries. He visited Peking in 1652. He wrote on a wide variety of subjects, but is especially noted for his works on history and classical Indian poetry, and his biographies of eminent personalities of his era. His last great deed was to initiate the construction of the magnificent Potala Palace at Lhasa, which was not completed until after his death. He passed away in 1682 while engaged in a three year retreat. To ensure the completion of the Potala, he ordered that his death and the location of his reincarnation should be kept secret until after the main part of the building had been secured. The Great Fifth is also remembered for establishing a national system of medical care in Tibet, and initiating a program of national education.

The Dalai Lama VI, Gyal-wa Tsang-yang Gya-tso, was the only Dalai Lama not to maintain the monastic disciplines. Born in the Chi-me Ling-pa family in Southern Tibet on the Indian border (today the birthplace lies within Indian territory), he was located two years later and in 1688 placed in Nang-kha-tse for education. This was all kept secret at the time, and not revealed until the Potala Palace was completed in 1695. The Second Pan-chen Lama was sent to ordain and educate him, and he was enthroned in 1697. But he preferred sports and social life to the monasteries, and when he turned twenty years of age he gave back his robes and moved out of the official residence in the Potala into a small apartment that he had had built at the foot of the hill. He is remembered and loved for his romantic poems, his merry lifestyle and his disregard for authority. However, tragedy was to overtake him. Some Mongolians were displeased with his lack of external discipline and they invaded Lhasa and seized him in 1705. He died in 1706 while being transported to Mongolia. Tibetans nonetheless regard him as a true incarnation of the Great Fifth and interpret his unusual behavior as tantric wisdom manifested as a means of delivering a paranormal teaching to his people.

The Dalai Lama VII, Gyal-wa Kal-zang Gya-tso, was

born in 1708 in Li-tang, East Tibet. He was located soon thereafter, but due to troubles with Mongolia could not be officially recognized. Eventually in 1720 he was brought to Central Tibet and enthroned, but not until persistent rebellion had managed to oust the Dzungar Mongolians from Lhasa. Unfortunately this was accomplished with the aid of the Manchus, who regarded Mongolia as their principal enemy and saw the conflict as an opportunity to further their interests in Central Asia. This alliance was to lead to later political complications. The Seventh Dalai Lama was to prove very important to Tibetan religious history, however, and his simple and pure life as a monk won the hearts of his people. He wrote extensively, particularly on what are known as "the popular Tantras"; Guhyasamaja, Heruka Chakrasamvara, Vajrabhairava and Kalachakra. He is particularly renowned for his informal spiritual poetry and the many prayers and hymns he composed. He died in 1757.

The Dalai Lama VIII, Gyal-wa Jam-pal Gya-tso, was born in Tob-gyal of Tsang Province the following year. He was recognized and brought to Lhasa in 1762. It is this Dalai Lama who built the legendary Nor-bu Ling-ka in 1783 in the park to the west of Lhasa. Educated by the Third Pan-chen Lama, he exhibited wonderful spiritual qualities mixed with a distaste for political intrigue. During his lifetime, Tibet became, for the first time, very much aware of British colonial interests in Asia. It was due to this that she formed a defensive isolationist policy in 1802. Jam-pal Gya-tso passed away in 1804.

Each of the four Dalai Lamas to follow were to live short lives. There is speculation as to whether this was due to intrigue, increased disease due to an increased contact with the outside world, or simply lack of good karma on the part of the Tibetan people (the good karma of disciples being regarded by Tibetans as the primary cause for the long life of a high lama).

Be this as it may, the Dalai Lama IX, Gyal-wa Lung-tok Gya-tso, who was born in 1805, died in the spring of 1815. It was prophesied that this Dalai Lama would have obstacles to his lifespan, but that should he live to old age would perform the greatest deeds of all the Dalai Lamas. When he passed away, all of Tibet mourned the loss.

The Dalai Lama X, Gyal-wa Tsul-trim Gya-tso, born in 1816, was recognized and enthroned in 1822. He was in constant poor health and died in 1837 at the age of twenty-one.

The Dalai Lama XI, Gyal-wa Khe-drub Gya-tso, was born the following year in Gar-tar, Eastern Tibet. He was enthroned in 1855, but died eleven months later.

The Dalai Lama XII, Gyal-wa Trin-le Gya-tso, born a year later, was the only Dalai Lama whose selection was made on the basis of the "Golden Urn Lottery" decreed by the Chinese Emperor. Due to the fact that there had been no strong Dalai Lama for some time, Tibet's internal politics were becoming increasingly unstable. This Dalai Lama also died young, in the year 1875.

The Dalai Lama XIII, Gyal-wa Tub-ten Gya-tso, was born in 1876 in Southeast Tibet at Tak-po Lang-dun of peasant stock. Recognized in 1878 and enthroned a year later, he was to provide the strong spiritual and political leadership necessary to revive a Tibet that had become confused and entangled by the colonial age with its intrigues, conflicts and power struggles. Placed in power in 1895, he saw Tibet through the Anglo-Russian conflicts of the late nineteenth century, the British invasion of 1904 and then the Chinese invasion of 1909. The Tibetans managed to supress this latter attack after three years of effort, and in 1912 all Chinese soldiers in Tibet surrendered and were deported. Unfortunately he was unable to get Tibet admitted to the League of Nations. England, afraid that an independent Tibet would be an easy prey to expansionist Russia, insisted on Tibet legally being regarded internationally as being under the suzerainity (though not under the sovereignty) of China. Nonetheless, the Thirteenth banned all Chinese from Tibet, and this remained de facto throughout his life. This was the first Dalai Lama to have extensive contact with the West, and he was deeply loved by those who met him. Sir Charles Bell's Portrait of the Dalai Lama (Collins, London, 1946) testifies to the respect the British held for him. He completed his studies at an early age, and then in 1914 entered the three year meditational retreat. During the later years of his life he attempted to modernize Tibet, although his efforts met with considerable resistance from the powers that be. In 1932 he prophesied the future invasion of Tibet by China and urged his people to prepare themselves. He wrote extensively, although the demands of his era required him to dedicate much of his time to reviving and restoring his nation and the spirit of his people. He traveled to Mongolia, China and India, and spent many years on the road in his efforts to keep his tiny country from being crushed by the ploys of the superpowers—England, Russia and China. He passed away in 1933.

The Dalai Lama XIV, Gyal-wa Ten-zin Gya-tso, was

born on July 6, 1935, in Tak-tser, East Tibet. Located
and recognized two years later, he was brought to Central Tibet in 1939 and enthroned. This is the Dalai
Lama whom we in the West have come to know and
love. The Chinese invasion of Tibet in the 1950's and
the mass exodus of the Tibetan refugees that followed,
although a terrible human tragedy, has had the effect
of making the Dalai Lama and the high Tibetan Lamas
accessible to the Western world for the first time. The
Fourteenth Dalai Lama has now made numerous
teaching tours of the West. The depth of his learning,
wisdom and profound insight into the nature of
human existence have won him hundreds of thousands
of friends around the world. His humor, warmth and
compassionate energy stand as living evidence of the
strength and efficacy of Tibetan Buddhism, and of its
value to human society.

The concept of the *tul-ku*, or Incarnate Lama, was an
integral aspect of Tibetan culture. The Dalai Lama was
but one of the approximately one thousand such *tul-ku*
incarnates; but he was somehow special amongst them,
a king of *tul-kus*, above and beyond the perimeters of
this or that sect of Tibetan Buddhism. The temporal
ruler over all of Tibet, he was in addition the spiritual
leader not only of Tibet but of all those lands where
Tibetan Buddhism predominates, such as Mongolia,
Western China, Northern India, and so forth. His
devotees were not limited to the six million Tibetans,
but to the tens of millions of Buddhists who inhabit
these vast lands, a territory larger than the entirety of
Europe. Now that Tibet no longer exists as an independent nation, his secular position has diminished
somewhat; but his spiritual influence has only grown.

Moreover, the respect of the international community for the Tibetan Lamas and Tibetan Buddhism has tremedously increased.

The destruction of Tibet and its future resurrection were prophesied by the eighth-century Indian sage Padma Sambhava, who also prophesied, "When the iron bird flies and horses run on wheels, the Dharma will be carried to the land of the Red Man." Perhaps the suffering of Tibet and the amazing dignity of the Tibetans in the face of it was the necessary catalyst to bring the wealth of Tibetan culture to the world's attention.

When asked about the above prophecy, His Holiness the Dalai Lama XIV answered, "Prophecy or no prophecy, the Western world is showing strong interest in Buddhism. More and more universities are offering Buddhist studies, and hundreds of Buddhist meditation centers have appeared around the world. I myself firmly believe that Buddhism is the property of mankind, not of any particular people or nation, It has a lot to offer to mankind in terms of understanding and developing the mind. Through understanding the mind and increasing its creative qualities we increase human peace and happiness. If we Tibetans can contribute to this in any way, we are most pleased to be able to do so. . . . There are many elements in Buddhism that could benefit the world, many methods for cultivating higher love, compassion and wisdom. Everyone benefits by increasing these qualities. . . . People do not have to become Buddhists in the formal sense in order to use the Buddhist techniques. The purpose of the teachings is only to benefit living beings. . . . The world is deeply in need of peace, love and understanding. If Buddhism can make a contribution to this end, we would be happy to do so. We are all on this planet together. We are all brothers and sisters with the same physical and mental faculties, the same problems and the same needs. We must all contribute to the fulfillment of the human potential and the improvement of the quality of life as much as we are able. . . . Mankind is crying out for help. Ours is a desperate time. Those who have something to offer should come forward. Now is the time. . . ."

Acknowledgments

Many people made this anthology.

At Marlowe & Company and Avalon Publishing Group:
Thanks to Ghadah Alrawi, Will Balliett, Linda Kosarin, Matthew Lore, Shona McCarthy, Sue McCloskey, Dan O'Connor, Neil Ortenberg, Paul Paddock, Susan Reich, David Riedy, Simon Sullivan, and Mike Walters for their support, dedication and hard work.

At The Writing Company
Nathaniel May did most of the research for the book. Nate Hardcastle provided valuable help. Taylor Smith, Mark Klimek and March Truedsson took up slack on other projects.

At the Portland Public Library in Portland, Maine:
Thanks to the librarians for their assistance in finding and borrowing books and other publications from around the country.

Thanks to Maria Fernandez for overseeing production and Shawneric Hachey for his work obtaining rights to use various material.

Finally, I am grateful to the Dalai Lama and to the other writers whose work appears in this book.

Excerpt from *Freedom in Exile: the Autobiography of the Dalai Lama* by the Dalai Lama. Copyright © 1990 by Tenzin Gyatso, His Holiness, The Fourteenth Dalai Lama of Tibet. Reprinted by permission of HarperCollins Publishers, Inc. ✤ "Inside Out: The Dalai Lama Interviewed by Spalding Gray" by Spalding Gray. Copyright © 1991 by *Tricycle: The Buddhist Review*. Reprinted by permission of *Tricycle: The Buddhist Review*. www.tricycle.com ✤ Excerpt from *Kindness, Clarity, and Insight* by the Dalai Lama. Copyright © 1985 by Snow Lion Publications, Inc. Reprinted with permission of Snow Lion Publications, Inc., Ithaca, NY, 14851. ✤ Excerpt from *Awakening the Mind, Lightening the Heart* by the Dalai Lama. Copyright © 1995 by the Library of Tibet. Reprinted by permission of The Wylie Agency, Inc. ✤ "Meditations on the Ways of Impermanence" from *Selected works of the Dalai Lama VII: Songs of Spiritual Change* by the Seventh Dalai Lama, translated by Glenn H Mullin. Copyright © 1985 by Snow Lion Publications, Inc. Reprinted with permission of Snow Lion Publications, Inc., Ithaca, NY, 14851. ✤ Excerpt from *Stages of Meditation* by the Dalai Lama. Copyright © 2001 by Snow Lion Publications, Inc. Reprinted with permission of Snow Lion Publications, Inc., Ithaca, NY, 14851. ✤ Excerpt from *The Joy of Living and Dying in Peace* by the Dalai Lama. Copyright © 1997 by the Library of Tibet. Reprinted by permission of The Wylie Agency, Inc. ✤ Excerpt from *Four Essential Buddhist Commentaries* by the Dalai Lama. Copyright © 1982 by the Library of Tibet. Reprinted by permission of The Wylie Agency, Inc. ✤ Excerpts from *My Land and My People* by the Dalai Lama. Copyright © 1962 by the Dalai Lama. Reprinted by permission of the Office of His Holiness the Dalai Lama. ✤ Excerpt from *Seven Years in Tibet* by Heinrich Harrer. Copyright © 1954. Reprinted by permission of the author. ✤ Excerpt from *Buddha Heart, Buddha Mind: Living the Four Noble Truths* by the Dalai Lama. Copyright © 2000 by Tenzin Gyatso, His Holiness, The Fourteenth Dalai Lama of Tibet. Reprinted by permission of The Crossroad Publishing Company. ✤ Excerpt from *A Flash of Lightning in the Dark of Night: A Guide to the Bodhisattva's Way of Life* by the Dalai Lama. Copyright © 1994 by Association Bouddhiste des Centres de Dordogne. Reprinted by arrangement with

Bibliography

The selections used in this anthology were taken from the editions listed below. In some cases, other editions may be easier to find. Hard-to-find or out-of-print titles often are available through inter-library loan services or through Internet booksellers.

Avedon, John F. *In Exile from the Land of Snows*. New York: Knopf, 1979.

Bskal-bzań-rgya-mtsho (translated by Glenn H. Mullin), *Selected Works of the Dalai Lama VII: Songs of Spiritual Change*. Ithaca, NY: Snow Lion Publications, Inc., 1985.

Bsod-nams-rgya-mtsho (translated by Glenn H. Mullin), *Selected Works of the Dalai Lama III: Essence of Refined Gold*. Ithaca, NY: Snow Lion Publications, Inc., 1985. (For "A Biographical Sketch of the Fourteen Dalai Lamas" by Glenn H. Mullin.)

Bstan-'dzin-rgya-mtsho. *Ethics for the New Millennium*. New York: Riverhead Books, 1999.

Bstan-'dzin-rgya-mtsho. (Translated and edited by Jeffrey Hopkins.) *Kindness, Clarity, and Insight*. Ithaca, NY: Snow Lion Publications, Inc., 1984.

Bstan-'dzin-rgya-mtsho. *A Flash of Lightning in the Dark of Night: A Guide to the Bodhisattva's Way of Life*. Boston: Shambhala, 1994.

Bstan-'dzin-rgya-mtsho. *Awakening the Mind, Lightening the Heart*. New York: HarperCollins Publishers, 1995.

Bstan-'dzin-rgya-mtsho. *Buddha Heart, Buddha Mind: Living the Four Noble Truths*. New York: Crossroads Publishing Company, 2000.

Bstan-'dzin-rgya-mtsho. *Four Essential Buddhist Commentaries*. Dharamsala, India : Library of Tibetan Works & Archives, 1982.

Bstan-'dzin-rgya-mtsho. *Freedom in Exile: The Autobiography of the Dalai Lama*. New York: HarperCollins Publishers, 1990.

Bstan-'dzin-rgya-mtsho. *My Land and My People*. New York: McGraw-Hill, 1962.

Bstan-'dzin-rgya-mtsho. *Stages of Meditation*. Ithaca, NY: Snow Lion Publications, Inc., 2001.

Bstan-'dzin-rgya-mtsho. *The Joy of Living and Dying in Peace*. San Francisco: HarperSanFrancisco, 1997.

Bstan-'dzin-rgya-mtsho with Jean-Claude Carrière. *Violence and Compassion: Conversation with the Dalai Lama*. New York: Doubleday, 1996.

Gray, Spalding. "Inside Out: The Dalai Lama Interviewed by Spalding Gray". First appeared in *Tricycle: The Buddhist Review*, 1991.

Harrer, Heinrich. *Seven Years in Tibet*. New York: EP Dutton, 1954.

Iyer, Pico. "Over Tea with the Dalai Lama". First appeared in *Shambhala Sun*, November 2001.

About the Editor

CLINT WILLIS is the editor of *Why Meditate?* and *Son of Man: The Best Writing About Jesus.* He also is series editor of Adrenaline Books. His anthologies for that series include *Epic: Stories of Survival from the World's Highest Peaks, Mob: Stories of Death and Betrayal from Organized Crime,* and *Fire Fighters: Stories from the Front Lines of Fire Fighting.* He lives in Maine with his wife and family.